The Entertainment Machine

The Entertainment Machine

American Show Business in the Twentieth Century

Robert C. Toll

OXFORD UNIVERSITY PRESS

Oxford   New York   Toronto   Melbourne

1982

P
92
·U5
T65
1982

Oxford University Press

OXFORD   LONDON   GLASGOW
NEW YORK   TORONTO   MELBOURNE   AUCKLAND
DELHI   BOMBAY   CALCUTTA   MADRAS   KARACHI
KUALA LUMPUR   SINGAPORE   HONG KONG   TOKYO
NAIROBI   DAR ES SALAAM   CAPE TOWN

and associate companies in
BEIRUT   BERLIN   IBADAN   MEXICO CITY   NICOSIA

First published by Oxford University Press, New York, 1982
First issued as an Oxford University Press paperback, 1982

Library of Congress Cataloging in Publication Data

Toll, Robert C.
  The entertainment machine

  Bibliography: p.
  Includes index.
    1. Mass media—United States.   2. Performing arts—
United States.   3. United States—Popular culture.
  1. Title.
  P92.U5T65   30.2'3   81-16930
  ISBN 0-19-503081-8   AACR2
  ISBN 0-19-503232-2 (pbk.)

Printing (last digit): 9 8 7 6 5 4 3 2 1

Printed in the United States of America

For Judy
Who Makes It All Worthwhile

Preface

If popular performers from the early 1880s were somehow transported to the early 1980s, they undoubtedly would be shocked at the explicit sex and violence in contemporary show business. But they might not be too surprised at the popularity of *Raiders of the Lost Ark,* Willie Nelson, *42nd Street, Search for Tomorrow,* or *Laverne and Shirley.* In the 1880s as in the 1980s the public loved action-adventure, popular music, musicals, romantic sensuality, and comedy. But while the performers from the past would be generally familiar with today's popular entertainment genres, they would be completely baffled and bewildered by modern entertainment media. In the 1880s people either went out to watch a live performance, or they stayed home and entertained themselves. In the early 1980s relatively few people ever go to a live performance. But they tune in network television day and night, follow the latest news on car radios, go to see current films, listen to pop music on tape cassette players and portable radios, watch "X" rated movies on home video machines, play record albums on elaborate stereo sound systems, and unconsciously hum along with "Muzak" in supermarkets and department stores. Wherever they go and whatever they do, the American people enjoy an incredible entertainment bonanza provided by an astonishing array of entertainment machines. Modern show business cannot be understood without a thorough knowledge of these technological entertainment media. Many people condemn the new media; others praise them. But few contemporary

Americans understand them any better than those mythical performers from the 1880s would.

The purpose of this book is to explain the entertainment revolution that occurred when modern technology was applied to popular entertainment. The first section of the book focuses on the creation and impact of the new show business media—silent film, sound motion pictures, phonographs and recordings, radio, and television. It examines each medium's development, popularization, distinctive qualities, special features, and relationships with other media. Every show business medium has its own strengths and weaknesses, which, quite apart from current trends and tastes, shape the form and content of its entertainment. The media serve as filters or lenses through which the popular genres flow and are modified on the way to the public. The second and longer section of the book examines these media filters at work as they entertained America. Separate chapters on westerns, popular music, musicals, crime, sexuality, and comedy compare the media's differing treatments of the same genre throughout the twentieth century, as the form and content of show business evolved in response to changes in popular media and in popular tastes.

Though the book ranges over nearly a century, stepping back to get perspective, to identify underlying patterns, and to see the big picture, it is neither an abstract, theoretical treatise nor a broad survey skimming over the surface. Rather, it is a highly selective examination of modern American show business media in operation. To make this a concise and engaging discussion, the chapters focus on a limited number of people, innovations, trends, and productions that *represent* the most important and influential developments in the twentieth-century entertainment revolution.

Because of the limited number of examples that can be included, it seems especially important to explain how they were chosen. Since the book is about popular entertainment, it concentrates on examples with the widest influence and largest audiences. At times this means that a popularizer is discussed rather than an innovator who never reached a broad audience. But wherever possible the book focuses on the work of artists who were creative, influential, and popular, especially those who fully understood and mastered a particular medium. Of the many radio comedians, for instance, only Jack Benny is discussed at length because he pioneered a *radio* comedy style and format that many others adopted. The nation's creative sub-cultures—Afro-American, Latin American, and Country and Western—are included only when they strongly influence the entertainment that reached the general public. Similarly, modern technology is explained in layman's terms where necessary, but the book concentrates on the broad effects and significance of the new hardware. One of the most difficult parts of writing this book has been the continual need to delete outstanding examples in every category to maintain the focus, to allow depth of discussion, and to limit the length. The ultimate judgment about the wisdom of the selections should depend on how well they have contributed to the book fulfilling its goal of explaining the effects of modern technology on American show business, one of the nation's most democratic and most influential institutions.

Oakland   R. C. T.
March 1982

Acknowledgments

I owe thanks to many people for assisting with the manuscript. My friends Richard and Merren Carlson read early versions of every chapter and helped greatly with the complex job of organizing this wide-ranging book. Filmmaker-historian Geoffrey Bell critiqued several chapters and gave me the benefit of his knowledge of film, his good taste, and his keen eye for the visual. My editor, Sheldon Meyer, executive vice president of Oxford University Press, worked closely with me throughout the long, difficult process of refining the book's concepts, structure, and organization. After working with him on three books, I am still amazed by Sheldon's knowledge, perception, and judgment.

I also owe thanks to a number of people for assisting me with the illustrations, especially: Mary Corliss, the stills archivist of the Museum of Modern Art's department of film: Val Almendarez of the national film information service of the Margaret Herrick Library at the Academy of Motion Picture Arts and Sciences; Curator Dorothy L. Swerdlove and her staff at the Billy Rose Theatre Collection of the New York Public Library's Performing Arts Research Center; curator Jeanne.T. Newlin and assistant curator Martha R. Mahard of the Harvard Theatre Collection; Cynthia A. Hoover, curator of the division of musical instruments of the Smithsonian Institution's National Museum of American History; Rick Giacalone, vice president for visual communications of the American Broadcasting Company; Joe Riccuiti of the National Broadcasting Company's photo files; and James J. Sirmans, associate director of press information for CBS Entertainment.

My greatest debts are to my wife, Judy, who is a superb researcher, a perceptive critic, a patient listener, and a loving partner.

R. C. T.

Contents

Illustrations follow page 74 and page 156

The Entertainment Machine

Introduction

America's Amusement: The Stage as an Entertainment Medium

Stunned by Al Jolson's breathtaking performance in the stage musical *Sinbad*, critic Gilbert Seldes, who had just spent eighteen months in Europe during World War I, rhapsodized about Jolson's impact: "One had forgotten that there still existed in the world a force so boundless, an exaltation so high, and that anyone could still storm heaven with laughter and cheers." The only comparable experience Seldes could think of in 1918 was the exhilarating sight of the awe-inspiring Manhattan skyline. But you did not have to be fresh from war to feel Jolson's explosive energy and electrifying magnetism. Even jaded Broadway audiences interrupted his performances by screaming "Jolie, Jolie," leaping out of their seats, and rushing forward to try to touch him, as they had done on the opening night of *Sinbad* when he rocked them to their feet with "Rockabye Your Rockabye Baby to a Dixie Melody." "He does more than make 'em laugh," Seldes observed of Jolson's effect on audiences, "he gives them what I am convinced is a genuine emotional effect ranging from the thrill to the shock." Other critics, using powerful new machine age metaphors, described Jolson as an "electrical personality," a "human dynamo," with "explosive power," "galvanic animation," and "violent energy." His prancing, ad-libbing, head-bobbing, finger-snapping performances even jolted other great entertainers. Eddie Cantor, one of the biggest stars in the golden age of live show business, recalled that when he went to a matinee to see Jolson, "something happened that afternoon. For five weeks I just

3

couldn't work properly again. I couldn't compete with Jolson."[1] No one could. There was only one Jolson.

Other live performers who may not have been the equals of Jolson, but who still could work a little bit of his unforgettable magic—the magic of the live performer playing to the live audience—entertained the American public in the heyday of live show business. Between approximately 1850 and the 1920s people all over the country left their homes and crowded into ornate big city theaters and into modest country tents to watch live performances by accomplished professionals and by inexperienced amateurs. Though the productions were of every conceivable size, type, and quality, they shared the common characteristics of the live stage, America's first major entertainment medium.

American show business was born in the rapidly growing cities of the Northeast in the 1840s when P. T. Barnum and other promoters discovered that they could make a great deal of money producing inexpensive, crowd-pleasing entertainment that average city people could enjoy, understand, and afford. As common people flocked to see the new, popular shows, theater capacities jumped from a few hundred seats to thousands, and ticket prices plummeted from several dollars to twenty-five cents or less. The uninhibited working-class audiences left no doubt about their feelings. With lusty cheers and hissing catcalls, the new theater audiences got the entertainment they wanted. In 1833 in the 4000-seat Bowery Theatre in New York City, for instance, when patrons disliked a symphonic overture, they hollered for "Yankee Doodle," forced the orchestra to change its tune, and "evinced their satisfaction by a gentle roar." "It is the American people who support the theatre," a popular reviewer argued, "and this being the case, the people have an undoubted right to see and applaud who they please and we trust their right will never be relinquished. No never!"[2] Performers quickly learned to please the boisterous crowds or to be run off the stage and replaced by entertainers who would. From its inception American show business was shaped by its intimate relationship with its broad, vocal audiences. That relationship endured as long as live entertainment provided most of America's amusement.

Before the Civil War producers learned they could fill their huge theaters if they staged a wide range of popular fare. Average Americans loved plays with democratic themes and common people as heroes and heroines, foot-tapping music and dance, what passed for

Afro-American culture, exciting daredevils, handsome men and shapely women, and all kinds of comedy. If the public could get all these in one show, all the better—and in the early days it could. Whether the featured play of an evening at the theater was *The Original, Aboriginal, Erratic, Operatic, Semi Civilized and Demi-Savage Extravaganza of Pocahontas* or the Shakespearean tragedy *King Lear,* ticket buyers also saw jugglers, acrobats, comics, trained animals, singers, dancers, and other variety acts performed *between* the acts of the play. Besides all that, a farce closed the show, leaving the audience laughing. Reflecting the same trend, when the first uniquely American entertainment form, the minstrel show, developed in the 1840s, it packed in as many popular features as possible and made no pretense of doing anything but catering to the broad tastes of the new audience. The white minstrel men wearing burnt cork makeup and masquerading as blacks not only provided northern whites with entertaining caricatures of black people in the era when slavery was threatening to tear America apart, but they also provided the public with a fast-paced blend of popular music, comedy, dance, novelties, parodies, and production numbers. In the 1840s and 1850s the public could not get enough of this blackfaced variety entertainment.

Show business, always taking its cues from its audiences, grew up with the country. Before 1860 the bulk of the American people and the bulk of American show business were still concentrated in the big cities of the East, where the demand for entertainment was high and the supply was low. After the Civil War, as urban areas grew ever larger, so did the potential audience and the supply of popular entertainment. The growing competition not only improved the quality of productions but also generated a number of separate entertainment forms—musicals, popular plays, extravaganzas, circuses, burlesque, drama, Wild West shows, and vaudeville. By the late nineteenth century the urban public had incredibly rich entertainment choices.

As the population shifted westward, as show business competition intensified, and as railroad transportation became faster and cheaper, major shows and stars began to travel regularly. The popular stage was becoming a road show. At first acting stars traveled alone, playing standard roles with local acting groups, as many major opera stars do to this day. But in the 1880s entire dramatic and musical productions also began to tour. The melodrama *Hazel Kirke* scored a great hit in New York in 1880, and while it was still running there, duplicate troupes began to tour with the show. In 1881-82 four *Hazel Kirke* companies were on the road; the next year there were fourteen. When other shows followed *Hazel Kirke*'s example, the number of touring productions exploded from about fifty in 1880 to over 500 in 1900, an estimate that does not include the many traveling circuses, variety troupes, vaudeville, Wild West, burlesque, and minstrel shows. This vast number of productions was one of the most important characteristics of the heyday of live entertainment.

All over the nation people clamored for professional entertainment. And they got it. Actors, actresses, musicians, singers, dancers, comedians, sharpshooters, chorus girls, acrobats, lion tamers, and many other types of barnstorming performers gave America the widest variety and greatest number of live shows ever seen in one country at one time. Americans almost everywhere had the chance to see good shows although possibly not the productions and stars they may have wanted to see. Small, hard-to-reach towns did not get the top attractions. It was simply not financially feasible. Naturally, the biggest hits, seeking to earn the greatest profits, preferred to play in cities that were close together and large enough to sustain long runs. This generally meant the big cities of the East and Midwest, but some itineraries did include brief stopovers in small towns and cities en route to major bookings. In the age of live entertainment the number and quality of shows available to individual citizens usually depended more on where they lived than on how much money they had.

Besides the uneven distribution of top attractions, the huge number of productions also meant that people around the country who saw shows with the same title often saw very different productions. In addition to normal variations in casts, costumes, sets, and acting abilities, traveling troupes freely adapted scripts to suit the special talents of their performers and the special tastes of their audiences. The clearest example of this adaptation was *Uncle Tom's Cabin*, which opened in 1853 and ran well into the twentieth century. Probably performed more than any other play in American history, *Uncle Tom's Cabin* was so popular in the late nineteenth century that many acting companies, called "Tommers," performed nothing else. The Tommers actually staged a wide range of shows by varying their mix of stock scenes and features, sometimes emphasizing the saintly white child, Little Eva, sometimes playing up melodramatic action like the bloodhounds chasing Eliza as she flees to freedom with her son in her arms, sometimes preaching about Uncle Tom's Christian martyrdom, sometimes stressing comedy or changing to a happy ending with Uncle Tom being rescued in the nick of time. Usually the Tommers blended several of these scenes together and then added novelties such as trained mules, dancers, jubilee singers, or almost any other act that audiences liked.

Few other shows were as frequently or as substantially changed as *Uncle Tom's Cabin,* but touring productions were regularly adapted because producers and performers were acutely aware that New York and Nebraska were not just miles apart, but were worlds apart. Until well into the twentieth century there were *several* American publics with differing values, interests, and tastes. What was considered tame, humdrum, or innocuous in big cities often seemed daring, exciting, or scandalous in small towns. With its many different productions, live show business could tailor its shows to suit each audience. The principal concern of popular entertainers was not innovation, experimentation, or originality, but pleasing audiences. "I've got only one method," explained J. H. Haverly, a successful late-nineteenth-century producer, "and that is to find out what the people want and then give them that thing. There's no use trying to force the public into a theater."[3] In most areas there was no problem finding enough of the public to watch performers; the problem was finding enough performers for the public to watch.

Because of this great demand for entertainment, almost anyone with talent could get a chance to work in show business. There were abundant entry level opportunities for entertainers and plenty of time for them to perfect their crafts as they worked their ways up from the small-time to the big-time. While serving their apprenticeships on the road, would-be entertainers could study in the best of schools, the country's theaters, learn from the best of teachers, the old pros, and be evaluated by the best of judges, the American people. Out of this process came thoroughly professional performers with a keen sense of the business of entertaining.

Touring performers had the advantage of being able to use the same material or to play the same part for years because there were long intervals between repeat engagements and because audiences wanted to see their old favorites over and over again. Actor Frank Mayo excited the public as the frontier hero Davy Crockett for nearly twenty-five years; James O'Neill thrilled audiences with his portrayals of the dashing Count of Monte Cristo for decades; and Joseph Jefferson Jr.'s nostalgic Rip Van Winkle charmed America for nearly forty years until Jefferson's retirement in 1904. Similarly, early musical extravaganzas such as *The Black Crook* and *Evangeline,* initially staged in the 1860s, remained popular throughout the nineteenth century, outdrawing many of the shows designed to emulate them. Variety audiences would have felt cheated if stars like the comedy team of Joe Smith and Charlie Dale had performed anything other than their "School Act," "Dr. Kronkhite," or "Hungarian Restaurant" routines, which they did several times a day decade after decade to laughter that only got longer and louder as time passed.

Because they could use the same material for years, entertainers could concentrate on honing their performance skills. In vaudeville, which in many ways epitomized live show business, the key problem for performers was less what they did than how they did it. Every vaudevillian, no matter how famous or highly paid, appeared only *once* in each show for no more than twenty minutes. The act had to grab the audience immediately, hold its attention, and leave it wanting more. There was absolutely no time to waste and no second chance to win over that crowd. Every gesture, intonation, and phrase had to be carefully calculated, meticulously rehearsed, and masterfully delivered, so that the act—whether juggling or slapstick—was as flawless as possible. "The materials, they are trivial, yes," observed Gilbert Seldes in praising the performing artistry of vaudevillians, "but the treatment must be accurate to a hair's breadth."[4] This made vaudeville an unequaled medium for perfecting comic timing and delivery. It was no accident that many of the top comedians who learned to make America laugh while touring in vaudeville, comedians like W. C. Fields, Ed Wynn, Will Rogers, Fred Allen, Jack Benny, George Burns and Gracie Allen, Milton Berle, and Bob Hope, dominated American comedy in every medium until they passed from the scene.

The vaudevillian's obsession with perfect delivery differed only in degree from the concerns of entertainers in shows that allowed repeated appearances. As a result of this focus on performing artistry, all forms of live show business produced superlative performers. Burlesque nurtured top comics such as Bud Abbott and Lou Costello, Bobby Clark, Fanny Brice, Phil Silvers, Red Buttons, and Bert Lahr, who made generations of Americans laugh. Out of years of hard work on the stage also came many great singers and dancers with enduring appeal, from Sophie Tucker to Bing Crosby, from Bill "Bojangles"

Robinson to Gene Kelly. Those who rose to the top echelons of live show business, by the very nature of the medium, had to be able to please people all over the country and to do it year after year.

Al Jolson, who by about 1915 was almost unanimously recognized as "Mr. Show Business," represented live entertainers at their best. Like other stage performers who reached the big-time, Jolson had had a lot of theatrical experience before becoming a star. At the turn of the century the fourteen-year-old son of immigrants ran away from home to join a small-time circus that soon folded. But Jolson stayed in show business, moving to burlesque, vaudeville, minstrel shows, and musicals while learning to entertain. "I am a salesman of songs and jokes. Just as any other man sells merchandise, I have to sell my goods to the audience," he explained in 1919. "I got selling experience in small stores; these stores were called vaudeville." In 1911 after over ten years on the road Jolson rose quickly to stardom after he got a small part in the opening show at the new Winter Garden Theater in New York. The Winter Garden's runway, which extended out into the seats and normally would have been used only by promenading chorus girls, allowed Jolson to take his supercharged performances out into the audience and to establish the intimate relationship with his fans that became one of his trademarks. Like other great live entertainers, Jolson had an undefinable, but unmistakable quality that made even the people in the last row of a huge theater feel that Jolie was playing to them. Like others, then and since, Jolson felt, but did not know how to explain, the phenomenon. "When you have a crowded house," he observed, "you can feel the electric what-do-you-call-'em surging across the footlights between your audience and yourself, and you know you've got 'em."[5]

Although the vast national market for live shows allowed entertainers like Jolson to make mistakes, learn their trade, and polish their style, it also forced performers to travel almost continually. Beginning in the 1880s, when touring became common and continuing through the golden age of live entertainment, even the biggest stars faced ordeals on the road because of the size of the country and the limitations of the best transportation system available, the railroad. Between September 1887 and May 1888, for instance, Edwin Booth, the most renowned American actor of his time, traveled over 15,000 miles to give 258 performances in 72 communities from coast to coast and border to border. In eight months Booth spent more than 600 hours on trains, the equivalent of riding day and night, twenty-four hours a day for nearly a month. Though he had the luxury of a private railroad car, he still had to spend freezing nights sidetracked at rail junctions and hot, sweaty days bouncing along with dirt and cinders blowing in his face. He often spent more time traveling to a booking than he spent there. But at each stop he was treated as visiting royalty and given the best of everything, though in many places the best was none too good. For Booth the trip was well worth the effort—for the adulation he received and for the nearly quarter of a million dollars he earned on that one tour.

Few other traveling performers were treated so well. Riding on trains was the least of the problems for most entertainers. Even those on their way to top billing continually had to worry about getting bookings and about the bookings being abruptly cancelled, which could mean no pay, no work, and no prospects. Many small-timers, whom vaudeville veteran Fred Allen called "part gypsy, part suitcase," had no choice but to live out of their trunks. Generally they stayed in small rundown hotels or boarding houses, performed in poorly equipped theaters, received low pay, and then moved on. For most of the year they had no homes and often had to put their babies to sleep in bureau drawers, to wake up to canned beans warmed over sterno, and to sneak out of hotels without paying. What kept many of them going were the moments when they basked in the warmth of the footlights and the warmth of the applause and the moments when they fantasized about their cherished dreams of stardom, fame, and playing the big-time.

In the late nineteenth century as the number of entertainers, theaters, and performing companies increased every year, show business became too complicated for individual theater and troupe managers. Almost inevitably theater managers in the same areas and on the same transportation routes began joining together to offer performers series of dates. At the same time troupe managers were trying to get their clients the best possible schedules. Soon circuits of theaters, grouped as much by their seating capacities and the salaries they paid as by their location, and booking agencies, representing a number of performers and companies, began to bring order to the far-flung American entertainment world. Businessmen, rather than showmen, began to take control of the popular stage. Show business was becoming big business.

By the turn of the twentieth century a handful of business entrepreneurs controlled the most popular and profitable entertainment forms. In 1887 Boston vaudeville producers B. F. Keith and E. F. Albee, who pioneered continuous, inexpensive, and wholesome variety shows, began to expand their operation. By the 1920s their organization controlled over 400 vaudeville houses, and performers either signed with the Keith-Albee United Booking Office and paid it a substantial fee, or they did not work in those theaters. Similarly, in the 1895-96 season six powerful theatrical producers, including Charles Frohman, Marc Klaw, and Abraham Erlanger, who controlled theaters and booking agencies all over the nation pooled their resources to establish a virtual monopoly over major dramatic and musical productions, bookings, and theaters. But after 1900 the Theatrical Syndicate, as the monopoly was called, began to face major competition from the Shubert brothers who were on the rise as producers and theatrical businessmen. By 1924, *Billboard* reported, the Shubert organization owned or controlled 86 theaters, including more than half the seating capacity on Broadway, and handled the bookings for another 750 houses about the country. Similar consolidation took place with circuses and burlesque.

The few large companies that controlled the bulk of big-time show business confronted the major problems of other big businesses in the national consumer-goods industry, the problems of supply, quality control, and distribution of their products. By the early twentieth century, inexpensive, standardized mass production and efficient national distribution allowed consumers all over the country to buy the same quality Ivory soap, Gillette razors, and Campbell soup. But live entertainment presented much more difficult problems. Although there was no lack of performers, stage shows could not be mass produced, talent could not be standardized, and productions could not be cheaply produced and shipped. Besides these inherent problems, show business producers also had to try to satisfy the public's rising entertainment expectations.

Americans traditionally prided themselves on having the biggest and best of everything. Show business was no exception. The people who lived in small towns wanted bigger and better shows just as city dwellers did. The first entertainment form to satisfy that demand had also been the first on the road. Until the 1870s, circuses had been one-ring shows, basically like outdoor variety entertainment in a tent.

When the public developed a taste for large-scale productions, circuses, which carried all their facilities with them, responded quickly by enlarging their tents, adding a second and then a third ring, and becoming lavish extravaganzas with herds of elephants, gaggles of clowns, and detachments of daredevils. The modern circus dazzled audiences with literally more entertainment than anyone could absorb. Their huge canvas cities added to the wonder by appearing and disappearing overnight on the outskirts of American towns, as if some wondrous wizard had waved his wand, said the magic words, and made people's wildest fantasies materialize for a day or two.

Unlike circuses, which carried their theaters with them, stage shows were limited by the resources they found in local theaters. In big cities as popular tastes for lavish, realistic productions grew, theaters added elaborate machinery to improve their staging and special effects. In 1880, for instance, Steele MacKaye remodeled the Madison Square Theatre in New York so that it boasted the very latest, most advanced technology, including overhead electric lighting and an elevator stage containing two entire sets that could be raised and lowered in less than a minute. But country theaters changed little. In fact, many of them were nothing more than poorly equipped, multi-purpose rooms with small stages, no wings, a few standard props, and two double-sided drops with matching side flats. These drops and flats provided four basic sets—typically a kitchen, a forest, a parlor, and a prison. On the right night with the right players and the right audience, those simple sets could be transformed into Uncle Tom's cabin, Sherwood Forest, the Capulets' ballroom, or the Count of Monte Cristo's dungeon. But on most nights, the small and modest productions looked exactly like what they were.

Although producers who mounted shows for small towns tried to make their productions more appealing by enlarging their casts, big sets and elaborate props were too difficult and too expensive to move from place to place for short bookings in little theaters. Yet by the 1880s people all over the nation were treated to spectacular new scenery developed by actor-playwright Clarence Bennett, who originated the technique of applying vibrantly colored diamond dyes to lightweight cloth scrims which could easily be folded and carried. The lustrous, light-catching diamond dye drops not only brought a dazzling new brilliance to small theaters, but they also made it possible to stage convincing productions of shows with exotic settings, like

Bennett's own *A Royal Slave*, which was set in Mexico during Aztec times.

Each theatrical innovation, no matter how stunning, only whetted the public's appetite for ever more elaborate and realistic productions. In the late nineteenth century some urban shows grew so big that they had to move outdoors. In 1888 the Kiralfy brothers, who had been producing larger and larger stage extravaganzas in New York theaters, opened *The Fall of Rome*, with elephants, chariot races, tons of armor, and a cast of 2000 in an outdoor Staten Island arena. Such spectacles of ancient history proved to be only sporadic attractions, but a new American show business genre took shape in the open-air arenas of the period because of the enormous popularity of the saga of the American West. Even the biggest, best-equipped theaters could not convey the vast scale of the western epic. In 1872 Buffalo Bill Cody, a genuine western scout and Indian fighter, starred in a stage production which had him spinning yarns and shooting Indians. Cody could not act, but he could ride, shoot, and re-create his version of the winning of the West. Once he turned his shows loose in outdoor arenas and brought western action to life with hard-riding, fast-shooting cowboys, cavalry, and Indians, the public would not let Cody corral them in conventional theaters. For decades thousands upon thousands of people went to see his freewheeling, outdoor Wild West shows play out a central American myth.

But outdoor arenas were not a general answer for producers of realistic entertainment. In cities few arenas were centrally located, and even when they were they were at best uncomfortable seasonal facilities. So, large urban theaters, doing their best to please the public, spiced up their shows with special attractions such as explosions, waterfalls, fires, hurricanes, and railroad locomotives. In 1899 a large-scale New York production of *Ben Hur* even featured a chariot race with eight horses galloping on eight treadmills hidden in the floor while three painted panoramas rolled in the background to accentuate the sense of movement. In 1905 the New York Hippodrome opened with the largest stage and the best theatrical machinery in the world. A huge apron in front of the proscenium contained a water tank some 200 feet long, 60 feet wide, and 14 feet deep, which was used for spectacular marine productions including mock naval battles. Even with seating for 5000 patrons, the Hippodrome's vast, stunning productions—circuses, automobile races, battle scenes, Wild West Shows, and airplane dogfights—were so costly that the producers could make a profit only by running a bill for an entire year. Though the Hippo-drome was one of a kind, its realistic, monumental productions were the types of shows the American public loved by the early twentieth century, shows that could be staged only in the nation's largest big-city theaters.

In the 1920s show business was booming in New York City. In 1917 some 126 stage productions had opened on Broadway; in 1928 the number had more than doubled. In the 1927-28 season New Yorkers could choose from over fifty musicals alone. The eleven revues in-cluded Fats Waller playing piano in the all-black *Keep Shufflin'*, nudes in the Shuberts' *Artists and Models,* and the sophisticated glamor of the most expensive *Ziegfeld Follies.* Besides three romantic operettas by Sigmund Romberg and one by Rudolph Friml, fans of musicals could enjoy: jazzy, collegiate *Good News,* with the new dance the "Varsity Drag"; *Funny Face,* with a Gershwin score and the singing and dancing talents of Fred and Adele Astaire; the last performances of George M. Cohan in one of his own shows; Beatrice Lillie, Clifton Webb, and Irene Dunne performing songs by Richard Rodgers and Lorenz Hart; the choreography of Busby Berkeley in *A Connecticut Yankee* or in *Present Arms;* Ed Wynn's clowning antics in *Manhattan Mary;* or the singing and dancing of beautiful star Marilyn Miller in *Rosalie.* Devotees of drama could watch such stars as Katharine Cor-nell, George Arliss, Billy Burke, Mrs. Fiske, and Otis Skinner in plays ranging from Shakespeare's *The Merchant of Venice* to Noel Coward's *The Marquise.*

The 1927-28 Broadway season also offered the public *Show Boat,* the show that represents the maturation of the American musical as a popular performing art. Lavishly produced by Florenz Ziegfeld, *Show Boat* featured a great cast which included Charles Winniger, Jules Bledsoe, and Helen Morgan; marvelous sets by Joseph Urban; and Oscar Hammerstein II and Jerome Kern's "Ol' Man River," "Can't Help Lovin' Dat Man," "Bill," "Why Do I Love You?" and "Make Be-lieve." The truly wonderful score was in every sense the heart of this beautiful, emotionally moving show, which blended romance and old-time entertainment with the inherently American theme of the inter-action of blacks and whites on the Mississippi River. *Show Boat,* which became a beloved American classic, possessed all the glorious quali-ties of a top-flight live show, but its original production also demonstrated the major limitation of the live stage. During its nearly two-year Broadway run, the superb *Show Boat* could be seen only in New York. When it finally toured in mid-1929, it reached only ten cities and went no further west or south than St. Louis.

For the audience the greatest strength of live show business is the exhilarating experience of watching and becoming part of a great performance. The experience is indescribable and mysterious, and it is unforgettable. In the best live performances, whether opera or blues, ballet or burlesque, something happens that bridges all gaps between patron and performer and makes audience and artist one. It is an experience that seems to occur only when live performers play to live audiences. Ironically, the greatest weakness of live show business is that its greatest strength is available to relatively few people.

When the live stage was America's major entertainment medium, there was an almost unlimited demand for good, affordable performances. But there was only one Al Jolson and one *Show Boat*, and each could play to only one audience at a time. There were simply not enough accomplished live productions to reach a people scattered over more than three million square miles of territory. In big cities the humblest person had truly fabulous entertainment choices whereas in small towns even the wealthy were lucky to see any show at all, let alone a great one. As long as entertainment-hungry people had available to them only poor performers and productions, they went to them. But in the late 1920s, while Broadway boomed, the demand for modest road shows declined. The number of theaters in operation around the country plummeted from more than 1500 in 1910, by *Billboard*'s count, to fewer than 675 in 1925. American popular entertainment was changing fundamentally and radically.

1

The Entertainment Machine
in the Theater:
The Motion Picture as Medium

On April 23, 1896, Koster and Bial's Music Hall was filled with a typical vaudeville audience. The crowd had been lured partly by curiosity about one of the novelty acts on the bill—the New York debut of projected motion pictures. Fans knew something different was coming when the entire theater, including the stage, went dark during the show, and "an unusually bright light fell upon the screen. Then," reported a *New York Times* reviewer, "came into view two precious blond young persons of the variety stage" doing an umbrella dance. The lights flicked, and suddenly ocean waves crashed, something no one expected in a theater. "Some of the people in the front rows seemed to be afraid they were going to get wet," observed the *New York Dramatic Mirror* critic, "and looked about to see where they could run to, in case the waves came too close." After the surf, came a parody of a boxing match, a salute to the Monroe Doctrine, a scene from a stage show, and the flowing movements of a tall blonde doing a skirt dance. Except for the stunning surf footage, these moving pictures depicted standard vaudeville fare. But even the familiar seemed extraordinary when presented by this new entertainment machine. "The emotion produced upon the spectator is far more vivid than the real scene would be," wrote critic Henry Tyrrell of early movies in 1896, "because of the startling suddenness with which it is conjured up and changed, there in the theatre, by the magic wand of electricity . . . while the audience sit spell bound in darkness."[1]

The entertainment revolution had begun. From a modest start as novelties on vaudeville bills, movies eventually were to mature into a distinctive art form and to displace live shows as America's most popular theatrical entertainment. But the motion picture did not become a well-developed entertainment medium overnight. It evolved through five major phases.

Moving picture films, which began inauspiciously in California during the 1870s with the pioneering experiments of Eadweard Muybridge, were made practical by Europeans and by work undertaken in Thomas A. Edison's laboratory in the 1890s. Edison's first movie machine, the kinetoscope, ran a loop of film in a self-contained, coin-operated, "peep-show" cabinet, which proved very popular in penny arcades even though only one person at a time could watch the film. But in 1896 motion pictures became entertainment for large audiences when Edison and Biograph each marketed motion picture projectors. After that, movies rapidly became part of American show business as an "act" on vaudeville bills.

Motion pictures began as curiosities. "It did not make very much difference what moved or why; the important thing was that movement occurred," recalled early movie fan Edward Wagenknecht. "Nobody had ever seen a picture move before, and unless you keep this in mind you will be puzzled by our response to the Empire State Express rounding a curve or R. W. Paul's pictures of the surf breaking."[2] The examples Wagenknecht cited—outdoor action scenes—indicated the appeal of early movies, which were merely brief glimpses of scenes of all sorts. Moviemakers, quickly realizing one of the major advantages film had over stage shows, took their cameras out-of-doors to record everything from seashores to mountain tops, from snow falling to waterfalls, from boxing matches to bullfights. Many average Americans, seated in the comfort of theaters caught their first glimpse of the wonders of the world through the wonders of film. Capitalizing on the early appeal of these realistic pictures, George C. Hale in 1903 outfitted a small theater like a railroad car, dressed the ticket-taker as a conductor, and took patrons on "Hale's Tours and Scenes of the World" by projecting films that had been shot from the front of a moving train. Beginning in 1903, Hale's Tours traveled the country for years and earned Hale some two million dollars.

Motion pictures proved so popular with the American public by the turn of the century that penny arcade operators began to switch from kinetoscopes to movie projectors. They curtained off a section of the arcade, set up a screen and some chairs, and charged low admission fees. This approach was so successful that many arcades, dance halls, pawn shops, and other small stores were converted into makeshift movie theaters by pulling out counters and showcases, putting in wooden folding chairs, a screen, a projector, and a ticket booth, and hanging up garish posters to lure customers inside. Often called nickelodeons because of their cheap ticket prices, these early storefront movie houses might, at their classiest, boast a potted palm or some gilding, but most offered little comfort and less decor. "The ideal location," advised a handbook for would-be nickelodeon operators, "is a densely populated workingmen's residence section."[3] Besides appealing to working-class Americans, early movies also attracted a great many of the immigrants who flooded into the country in the early twentieth century since silent pictures required no knowledge of language and cut across all cultural and national bounds. Often located near vaudeville theaters, nickelodeons operated all day long, making it possible for women out shopping, children after school, and anyone else with a little spare time and money to see movies. Nickelodeon shows often began with patrons singing along to a piano and magic lantern slides provided by sheetmusic publishers. There might also be a vaudeville act or an illustrated lecture, sometimes both, but there was always a series of short movies of actual occurrences. Then the show was repeated. People packed into nickelodeons, and business boomed. "Store shows and five-cent picture theatres might properly be called the jack-rabbits of the business of public entertainment—they multiply so rapidly," quipped a writer for *The Billboard* in 1906.[4] By 1908 there were an estimated 8000 to 10,000 nickelodeons in the country. New York City alone contained some 600 movie houses with an estimated daily attendance of 300,000 to 400,000. By 1910 nickelodeons around the country reportedly drew twenty-six million patrons every week—nearly one in every five Americans.

Once movie theaters were established around the country and a regular clientele developed, changes in pictures themselves were inevitable. Short, realistic moving pictures of everyday life, special events, and natural wonders had fascinated audiences at first, but the novelty soon wore off. "These have lost their interest for the general public," noted the *Complete Illustrated Catalog of Moving Picture Machines, Stereopticons, Slides, Films,* a 1905 catalog for exhibitors, "and several of the most beautiful panoramas as well as scenes of travel that have been made recently are being rejected in favor of the story film."[5] Audiences and producers were learning that motion pictures need not be limited to documentary footage but could combine drama and the special qualities of film to tell stories.

Edwin S. Porter, a cameraman for the Edison Company, began to develop the special visual potential of film. In 1903 Porter made *The Great Train Robbery*, a story of outlaws robbing a railroad telegraph office, tying up the clerk, holding up a train, racing away in the locomotive to their hidden horses, riding off on horseback, and finally being captured. Using actors, costumes, sets, and scripts, Porter *staged* the scenes, rather than just filming what was already happening as the first moviemakers had done. Once Porter decided to film exterior scenes in the countryside, he was nearly forced to use innovative camera work. To keep the horsemen in view as they rode off, for instance, Porter had to break from the usual fixed camera angle and swing, or "pan," his camera to the side and tilt it to follow the riders down the hill, which gave his picture an interesting, new look. Porter also made effective use of film's potential for editing by taking footage shot at different times and places and splicing it to take the viewer back and forth from the train, to the telegraph office, to a western dance hall, and then back to the outlaws on horseback. This editing, which audiences easily followed even though the movie jumped around chronologically and geographically, was Porter's most important innovation. But it, too, seems to have been more the result of an instinctive drive to tell a story than of a concern with film artistry. Whatever Porter's intentions, the picture excited audiences, and young moviemakers. "When I saw *The Great Train Robbery*," Cecil B. DeMille recalled, "I discovered that you could tell a story in this medium and, in the telling, achieve both greater speed and greater detail than the stage allowed."[6]

Porter's innovations in film technique did not become general in early movies, even his own, primarily because the first generation of moviemakers was still discovering the potential of film and had little time to be concerned with movies as art. They were consumed with trying to produce enough movies to satisfy the rapidly growing nickelodeon audiences. But even before the medium developed its full potential, it was clear that movies were fundamentally different from stage shows.

The major problem for American producers had always been sup-
plying enough shows to satisfy the American people's seemingly endless demand for popular entertainment. Movies were the first answer
of the age of technology. "Just as McCormick solved the problem of
wholesale farming by the invention of the harvester machine," film actor Morton Sills observed, "so Edison and Eastman solved the problem
of the wholesale manufacture of amusement by the motion picture and
its retailing at prices within the reach of all."[7] Unlike a live show, a
movie could be reproduced any number of times, cheaply transported,
and shown almost anywhere, which meant that people all over the
country could see the same production with the same performers.

The public's appetite for realistic action, adventure, and suspense
had long challenged producers of popular plays to find new production techniques that could expand traditional stage effects. With lime-
lights and spotlights theatrical directors focused audience attention on
important props and characters; with two complete sets on stage at
once and fast light changes, directors cut back and forth between separate lines of action; and with rolling painted backdrops they made
characters and props seem to move through the countryside. Directors
also filled their stages with exciting eye-catching gunfights, buzz saws,
forest fires, horse races, and thunder and lightning. Audiences loved
these special effects and continually demanded new, even more exciting innovations. By the end of the nineteenth century stage producers had stretched theater walls, technology, and ingenuity to their
limits in an attempt to meet those demands.

But all these crowd-pleasing devices seemed transparently artificial
once the public got a glimpse of movies. Even the most elaborate stage
productions could not portray action and spectacle as convincingly as
crude, early movies. Reviewing a lavish New York stage production of
Ben Hur, critic Hilary Bell observed in 1899 that "in the play we see
merely several horses galloping on a moving platform. They make no
headway, and the moving scenery behind them does not delude the
spectators into the belief that they are racing." Bell felt only "Mr. Edison's invention," the motion picture, could do justice to this great action scene.[8] Only four years earlier, before motion pictures had been
shown in New York, such dissatisfaction with a major stage production
would have been most unlikely.

Movies, even in their first phase of·development, had demonstrated
their broad appeal to mass audiences and had begun to compete with

popular plays—not just in action and spectacle, but also in melodrama, which had been a stage staple for well over fifty years. Besides using outdoor shots for their melodramas, early moviemakers also used closeups, quick scene changes, and other techniques that intimately involved viewers in the plight of the players. "Popular (stage) melodrama, since moving pictures became the rage," critic W. P. Eaton noted in 1909, "have decreased fifty percent in number."[9] Within a decade, projected motion pictures had become part of American show business.

In the second phase of their evolution, motion pictures would develop their full potential as a visual, storytelling medium. Working without sound, movie directors had to learn to maximize the visual impact of their work, which meant learning to use film's unique qualities as Edwin Porter and other early directors occasionally had done. It remained for someone to take these sporadically used techniques and consciously mold them into the art of film. The man was David W. Griffith, who entered moviemaking in its undeveloped infancy and in less than ten years transformed nickelodeon fare into feature-length theatrical entertainment that rivaled live drama in its artistry and for its audiences. By World War I Griffith would establish the basic film techniques and structures that moviemakers have used ever since. With only slight exaggeration director Frank Capra could state as late as 1959 that there had been no major improvement in film direction since Griffith. "Not a picture has been made since his time," agreed Cecil B. DeMille, "that does not bear some trace of his influence."[10] The story of Griffith's innovations is the story of the development of film as an entertainment and artistic medium.

Griffith entered movies reluctantly in 1907 when he could find no work as a stage actor in New York and had to take acting roles in what he and many other stage actors then considered the demeaning, disreputable field of movies. But in motion pictures, Griffith found his calling. In 1908 he directed a typical one-reeler for Biograph and quickly fell into the mass-production pace of the industry in the salad days of the nickelodeon business. Griffith turned out 151 movies in 1908-09 and completed nearly 400 short movies by 1914. From this flurry of production, Griffith emerged as a master of film technique and the greatest American storyteller with film. Making so many pictures in such a short time stimulated Griffith's growth because it allowed him to experiment and to see the results quickly. His hundreds of short films were like the many canvases that a painter uses to perfect his form and technique. Visual art must be worked out in practice, which is what Griffith did. He built his style from an intuitive sense of good visual storytelling and a discovery of the unique properties of the film medium.

The major differences between motion pictures and live shows came from one basic fact—motion pictures were illusions created with film. At live shows, audiences watched performers at work with nothing intervening between entertainer and viewer. At movies, audiences watched the end product of a complex series of decisions that filtered the performance. The eye of the cameraman and the eye of the editor determined what the eye of the audience would see. The first major filtering took place when the camera recorded the action on film. By adjusting the lens, directors could photograph subjects from far away or close up. With different camera positions, they could film the same scene from many angles and distances. They could also take the camera out on location to film breathtaking panoramic vistas and wide-ranging action. By stopping the camera, changing the scene, and restarting the camera, directors could create special effects like changing a frog into a prince. The visual opportunities of film, unlike the stage, were almost limitless. The second major filtering came after the filming when editors cut up the diverse footage and spliced it back together to tell the story by blending film taken at different times, places, angles, and distances. As a result, editors not only gave audiences far greater visual variety than was possible in live shows, but they also achieved artistic, dramatic, and emotional effects that were not present in the original performance. Film, in short, differed fundamentally from the stage.

Before Griffith revolutionized filmmaking, other directors had used closeups, cross-cuts, dissolves, fades, scenes composed of multiple shots, and the other techniques that made watching film basically different from watching stage shows. But Griffith raised movies to the level of art by concentrating on the unique qualities of the medium—the camera, the film, and the editing. While virtually creating the language and structure of film, Griffith also made it a powerful, popular entertainment medium that could compete with the stage for the mass audience even when the motion picture was a medium without a voice.

Griffith began by freeing the camera from the fixed perspective of the theater seat, which early movie directors had commonly used. By moving the camera closer to players during scenes and by blending closeups with mid-range shots, Griffith created a greater sense of intimacy between viewer and player that changed movie acting styles. "We were striving for real acting," he explained of his use of the closeup. "When you saw only the small full length figures it was necessary to have exaggerated acting, what might be called 'physical' acting, the waving of the hands and so on. The closeup enabled us to reach real acting, restrained acting that is a duplicate of real life." "Above all," Cecil B. DeMille observed of Griffith, "he taught us how to photograph thought, not only by bringing the camera close to a player's eyes, but by . . . focusing it on a pair of hands clasped in anguish or on some symbolic object that mirrored what was in the player's mind."[11]

Many early silent movie stars had limited stage experience, if any, which meant they could learn the most effective *motion picture* acting style without having to make the difficult adjustment between fundamentally different media. Silent movie players had to learn to convey meaning and emotion without words and to make maximum use of the intimacy of the screen closeup through subtle expressions and movements. Many experienced stage stars, accustomed to gesturing and projecting to reach the last rows of huge theaters, found it difficult to adjust to the intimacy of film. In 1916, when Griffith produced a film of *Macbeth* starring the great stage actor Sir Herbert Beerbohm Tree, the actor simply planted his feet as he would on stage and declaimed grandly in his expressive voice, which was useless in silent movies. Tree was shocked when he saw the rushes. "Mr. Griffith," he reportedly said, "do you think you could teach me something about this new medium?"[12]

Griffith ultimately taught everyone about the new medium. But he faced strong opposition, even from Biograph, his own studio, which objected to Griffith's "jerky and distracting" technique of editing his movies so that they cut back and forth between subjects, settings, and lines of action. "How can you tell a story jumping about like that?" the studio asked. "People won't know what it's all about." Griffith replied that Dickens and other great novelists did the same thing, except that "these stories are in pictures, that's all." "The reason for the switchback," he briefly explained, was "to draw the threads of the narrative together, to accelerate the action, to heighten the action." Biograph also complained that his frequent use of closeups, which showed "only the head of a person," violated "all rules of movie making." In 1909 the *Moving Picture World* and other periodicals that still measured movies by stage standards protested that closeups made players look like "a race of giants and giantesses" and that the variety of camera angles created "an infinite variation in the apparent sizes of things as shown by the moving picture." "On the vaudeville or talking stage," the writer continued, "figures of human beings do not expand or contract irrationally or eccentrically. They remain the same size."[13] That critic was absolutely right. Motion pictures and stage shows *were* basically different viewing experiences, as Griffith fully understood.

Griffith prevailed with his innovative techniques because of the great popularity of his one-reel motion pictures, but when he wanted to expand to two-reel movies, the studio again opposed him. In retrospect it is astonishing that as late as 1911 the American film industry felt that anything longer than one reel—fifteen minutes at most—was too long for audiences. It was the success in America of elaborately produced, multi-reel foreign films that established the popularity of long pictures. In 1913 the nine-reel Italian epic *Quo Vadis* created a sensation in America with its unprecedented spectacle of ancient Rome. The two-hour film played in first-class theaters, drew huge crowds, and opened the way for such other European epics as the Italian *The Last Days of Pompeii* and the French *Les Miserables*. Determined to surpass the foreign films, Griffith left Biograph, taking many of his best players and his best cameraman, Billy Bitzer, with him.

In 1915, Griffith produced an American epic to challenge the European epics. He based his story of the Civil War and Reconstruction on the novels and drama of Thomas Dixon, who captured the heroic grandeur, massive scale, and human tragedy of the period, but also expressed the extreme pro-Confederate, anti-black biases that Griffith shared. In this view, vanquished white Southerners were saved from oppressive black rule, plunder, and rape only by the "heroic" Ku Klux Klan, a perspective which grossly distorts history. But *The Birth of a Nation,* despite its biased messages, was a great film that captured the vast panorama of the Civil War. It pulsated with emotion, built tension to cathartic climaxes, and moved viewers to the edges of their seats and to the verge of tears. Blending long, medium, and close shots, varying the lengths of time that shots were held on screen, contrasting vivid, emotionally moving images, and repeatedly switching among locales, Griffith made even relatively ordinary scenes like troop movements throb with action and feeling. "Every little series of pictures, continuing from four to fifteen seconds symbolizes a sentiment, a passion, or an emotion," observed Henry MacMahon in his *New York Times* review. "Each successive series, similar yet different carries the emotion to the next higher power, till at last, when both of the parallel emotions have attained the nth power, so to speak, they meet in the final swift shock of victory and defeat."[14] Like the composer of a symphony, Griffith orchestrated all the resources and artistry at his command to move his viewer emotionally, to make his audience *feel* what he wanted it to feel. At least for the moment, he made audiences experience the humiliation of being conquered, the terror of being menaced by an alien race, the relief of being rescued by brave, courageous heroes, and the exhilaration of returning to power.

President Woodrow Wilson, who had the film screened at the White House, praised *The Birth of a Nation* as "like writing history with lightning." Griffith had harnessed the full power of "the magic wand of electricity" and used it to touch people's hearts and to enflame their passions. The film was used to justify racial segregation and anti-black mob violence; it heightened black consciousness; and it prompted organized boycotts and censorship campaigns by civil rights groups. *The Birth of a Nation* proved beyond any doubt that an entertainment machine could be a powerful social and political force. The film also firmly established feature-length motion pictures as a respectable, popular art form for audiences of all sorts and classes. The combination of *The Birth of a Nation*'s artistry, impact, and timing prompted film historian William K. Everson to call it "quite possibly the single most important film of all time."[15] By 1915, then, Griffith's pathbreaking innovations had clearly demonstrated the potential of the new medium. Even without dialogue or sound track, film was becoming America's most popular theatrical entertainment. It was also about to become a vast industry with its own capital, features, and institutions.

Since early in the twentieth century, moviemakers had searched widely for areas with more sunshine than existed around New York. The search led them to Cuba, Florida, Colorado, San Francisco, and many other places. But Southern California seemed to offer the most advantages—good weather nearly year round, cheap labor, and a landscape that within a few miles varied from ocean to mountains to desert. After film-makers began to set up shop in Southern California in 1906, their numbers grew steadily, but slowly. In 1914 ex-vaudeville

manager–turned–moviemaker Jesse Lasky left New York to visit the
Lasky studio that Cecil B. DeMille had set up in a Hollywood barn. At
the Santa Fe depot in Los Angeles, Lasky's cab driver did not even
know where *Hollywood* was, but he somehow got Lasky to the Hollywood Hotel where the clerk finally remembered a barn where "movie
folks" were working. "Drive down this main road," he said of Hollywood Boulevard, "till you come to Vine Street. You can't miss it—it's a
dirt road with a row of pepper trees right down the middle."[16] The
movies made in that barn at the crossing that was to become one of
the more famous intersections in the world were so successful that the
studio expanded rapidly, ultimately evolving into Paramount Pictures.
Other studios in Southern California also prospered. By 1916 half of
American movies were made in California; a few years later the figure
reached 90 percent. For the first time since the birth of American show
business, New York was no longer the unchallenged center of the nation's popular entertainment.

Hollywood movie studios became huge cities within cities with vast
resources. Carl Laemmle's Universal City, for instance, had its own
houses, post office, and police force, as well as all the facilities for
movie-making. Within the walls of the major studios which had become self-contained film factories by the 1920s were all the resources—
topographical, technical, and human—needed to make movies. Besides
covered stages for filming interiors, studio lots contained landscaping
and permanent clusters of false-front buildings that with minor modifi-
cations could represent exotic jungle lagoons, white-columned planta-
tions, frontier forts, medieval castles, quaint country towns, water-
front wharves, western towns, and street scenes from San Francisco to
Singapore. Studios also had on the permanent payroll huge staffs of
costume designers, seamstresses, carpenters, plumbers, makeup artists,
writers, cameramen, extras, lighting experts, set designers, and many
other specialists. By the mid-1920s, studio overhead accounted for
about 40 percent of every picture's budget.

Hollywood, virtually the creation of the movie business, became a
relatively isolated, self-centered world, cut off from the artistic, cultural, and intellectual ferment of New York. Even the fastest express
train took three full days to travel from coast to coast, and since moviemaking in Hollywood was a full-time, year-round business, most motion picture people did not have the stimulating, broadening experiences of their counterparts on the live stage. Movie people did not play

to live audiences and did not tour with their shows. While movie-makers had the great advantage of establishing permanent homes in a community they could call their own, they did not get a direct feel for popular tastes and concerns. "In Hollywood," director Frank Capra observed with possibly only slight exaggeration, "we learn about life only from each other's pictures." Set off from the rest of the country and aloof from the general affairs of Los Angeles, Hollywood's life centered almost totally on movies and moviemakers. "I've often thought that whoever dubbed us the movie colony hit on an apt term," observed silent movie star Colleen Moore. "In my years there it was a tight, provincial little world enjoying the society of its own people, wanting no other."[17] Hollywood became synonymous with glamor, beauty, and extravagance, on screen and off. Important movie people, who lived like pampered royalty in a sheltered enclave, often found it easy to forget what the real world was like. This self-indulgent insularity made it much easier for moviemakers, removed from current thought and social conditions, to create a world of fantasy. Movies might have been quite different if the studios had remained in New York or had been scattered around the country instead of being concentrated in the relatively undeveloped, isolated area of Southern California in the late 1920s.

Hollywood and movies would also become synonymous with stars. But before 1910 actors and actresses were not even given billing on their films. Still, audiences began to recognize them and to write to studios and movie magazines asking the players' names. Established studios, like Biograph, refused to supply the names, arguing that good pictures were the result of the story, director, studio, and "competent people as a class and not as individuals."[18] But ambitious new moviemakers in search of audiences for their films were pleased to give the public what it wanted. In 1910 Carl Laemmle of Independent Motion Pictures (IMP), who later founded Universal Studios, hired away "the Biograph girl," Florence Lawrence, by offering her a larger salary, extensive promotion, and name billing. When fans clamored to see Lawrence, the movie star was born.

The career of Mary Pickford, America's most popular early movie star, symbolized the development and maturation of silent motion pictures. Born Gladys Smith in 1893 in Toronto, she became a child stage actress, playing major roles and touring at age thirteen with a production directed by David Belasco, the greatest American stage producer and director of the age. She was with Belasco, who gave her the name Mary Pickford, for three years. But stage roles were hard to find, and, in desperation, her mother asked Mary to lower her standards and act in movies for Biograph, promising her that she could wear silk stockings and high heels for the first time if she took the movie job she felt was "beneath my dignity as an artist."[19]

In 1909, the sixteen-year-old Pickford went to work for Biograph, and D. W. Griffith, who realized that the pretty, fresh-faced girl-woman would photograph beautifully, signed her to a contract at forty dollars a week, a figure that angered Biograph. But, again, Griffith was right. Even before movie fans knew her name, they were drawn to her, calling her "Little Mary" and "Blondilocks" after roles she played. But Pickford, like many devotees of the legitimate stage, still looked down at motion pictures. When people in a subway recognized her as a movie player, she was outraged. "If I'm going to be embarrassed that way in public," she told Griffith, "I'll have to have more money." The low status of early movies may have bothered her, but the high pay did not. In 1911 she followed Florence Lawrence in taking advantage of the growing competition in the movie business and signed with Carl Laemmle for $175 a week, a salary increase of over 400 percent in two years. She rose to fame and higher salaries, but remained dissatisfied with movies. In 1912 she returned to the stage, winning applause and critical acclaim in another Belasco production. But she was no longer happy on stage performing the same role in the same way night after night. In spite of herself, she missed "the exciting jigsaw puzzle of a motion picture in progress—the novelty, the adventure, from day to day, into unknown areas of pamtomime and photography."[20]

Movies were as exciting for Pickford to make as they were for audiences to watch, and in 1913 she returned to motion pictures to stay, signing with ex-nickelodeon operator turned movie entrepreneur Adolph Zukor and his Famous Players for $500 a week. Pickford proved that she was worth that and more with a series of hit movies between 1913 and 1916, including *Tess of the Storm Country, The Foundling,* and *Rebecca of Sunnybrook Farm.* Her portrayals of what she described as "the gawky, fighting age of adolescent girlhood" made her "America's Sweetheart."[21] In a March 1917 popularity poll by *The Ladies' World,* she beat her closest rival by half a million votes. Her salary jumped with her popularity. In 1918 she left Zukor for a contract with First National paying her $675,000 for three pictures, plus a bonus and other benefits. These astronomical figures testified to the high profits and intense competition in the movie business prior to 1920, as well as to the importance of Pickford and other movie stars. Pickford moved into the ranks of studio bosses in 1919, joining with D. W. Griffith and the other two most popular stars of the day, Douglas Fairbanks and Charlie Chaplin, to form United Artists, which would distribute the movies each partner made and give them total control over their films and their finances. Clearly, stars had become major forces in the motion picture business by 1920, a position that only grew stronger as the movie business matured.

Between World War I and the advent of sound motion pictures in the late 1920s the most important business development in the film industry was the consolidation of the three major facets of the business—production, distribution, and exhibition—in vertically integrated companies with great power. Originally, moviemakers produced and then sold their films to distributors, who rented them to exhibitors. Each was an independent operation. But as movies became a big profitable business, the advantages of controlling all facets of the industry became increasingly obvious. The large profits distributors made from popular movies they had purchased prompted studios to branch out into distribution. At the same time, distributors used their earnings to expand into moviemaking to ensure themselves a steady and inexpensive supply of films, and theater operators tried to cut their costs and raise their profits by moving into distribution and then production. By 1920 a number of powerful movie companies controlled several facets of the business and fought for dominance.

The studio that led the way to consolidation was Paramount, built by Adolph Zukor, who handled business affairs in New York, and Jesse Lasky, who supervised production in Hollywood. Zukor developed his power by signing popular stars like Mary Pickford and then insisting that theaters book blocks of Paramount pictures, sight unseen, in order to get films with stars. In 1917 Zukor acquired a huge chain of movie theaters which guaranteed Paramount pictures outlets and publicity in all the major markets. With that base and the threat that he would add more movie houses to his chain and force independent exhibitors out of business, Zukor put even greater pressure on theater managers to sign with Paramount, which meant taking an entire year's supply of 104 of the studio's pictures, enough films to change the theater's bill twice a week. Zukor's power play worked. In 1920 the Federal Trade

Commission charged that "more than 6,000 American theaters or approximately one-third of all motion pictures in the United States showed nothing but Paramount pictures."[22] This was not just a theoretical problem of monopolistic practices or just a business matter of concern only to moviemakers and theater owners. For movie fans the block-booking system meant that for every picture with a top star that played at a neighborhood theater there might be a dozen inferior movies with unknown players.

In the 1920s, through mergers, purchases, and manipulations, a relatively few large studios controlled the movie business with vast empires that produced, distributed, and exhibited their own movies. Carl Laemmle's Universal added theaters; First National, a studio created by theater owners, expanded production; William Fox, who moved from running movie houses to distribution and then production, expanded his operation at every level; Marcus Loew, owner of a large theater circuit, purchased the Metro studio, the forerunner of Metro Goldwyn Mayer (MGM). Cutthroat competition eliminated many fledgling studios and forced continued consolidation, leaving a group of shrewd businessmen who thoroughly understood motion pictures and their appeal. MGM, for instance, emerged as one of the giants of the industry when Marcus Loew and Nicholas M. Schenck added Samuel Goldwyn's studio to Metro in 1924 and Louis B. Mayer Pictures in 1927. With Schenck controlling finances from New York, Irving Thalberg overseeing film-making in Hollywood, and Louis B. Mayer anticipating popular tastes, MGM became the most successful movie studio. The founding fathers of modern Hollywood studios, who came from the same immigrant and working-class groups their early movies entertained, learned the movie business from the ground up. They acquired a keen sense of the public's tastes from their early years as nickelodeon operators, distributors, or small-time moviemakers and an acute sense of business from their brutal battles against each other. Based on those experiences they built the movie industry. In many cities, as the flagships of their glamorous empires, the studios built huge, ornate movie theaters that expressed American fantasies of opulent, often Oriental, palaces. They made lush surroundings and attentive servants available to anyone who could afford a ticket—as vaudeville palaces had been doing since the 1880s. The rococo movie palaces promised America dreams, and they delivered.

Hollywood may have been America's "dream factory," as anthropologist Hortense Powdermaker labeled it, but it was first and foremost a film factory. In the mid-1920s the major studios turned out a total of some 700 to 800 feature-length pictures a year, which meant that each big studio *finished* one or two feature-length movies *every* week. In Jesse Lasky's words that was "mass production with a vengeance, and need I mention that, if we had been fabricating aircraft, some of them would have been a menace to life and limb."[23] For their lead pictures, studios concentrated on making movies with big-name stars, elaborate productions, and popular themes, movies with enough advance appeal to sell the studio's block of mass-produced, formulaic "program pictures." Even the quickly made, low-budget pictures stamped from familiar patterns had a rather high degree of polish because studios were also training grounds for directors, technicians, and editors who learned to tell their stories with great technical finesse. As early as 1919 the *New York Times,* in reviewing an exciting auto race in *The Roaring Road,* an ordinary action picture, praised that skill. "Just jumping from the train to the automobile and back would never have made the race real," the critic observed, suggesting that simple cross-cutting was already losing its effect. "But by showing now a glint of the smooth tracks ahead of the train, now the beam of the automobile's headlights, now the expressions on the faces of the passengers, now the engineer and fireman at work in their cab, first one almost instantaneous picture and then another, the director succeeded in giving the spectators such a comprehensive view of all the action that they felt themselves a part of all of it."[24] Even program pictures that had such exciting editing had to be made quickly, which meant using stock genres and themes—melodrama, westerns, comedies, action, romance, and mystery. The formulas existed not only because audiences liked them, but also because movie studios *needed* them to be able to crank out enough pictures to fulfill their commitments to the block-booking contracts and the theater chains that kept the studio system going.

The star vehicle was perhaps Hollywood's most successful and dependable formula. The name on a theater marquee of stars such as Mary Pickford, Charlie Chaplin, Douglas Fairbanks, Rudolph Valentino, Gloria Swanson, William S. Hart, or Clara Bow was enough to draw a crowd. Movie fans wanted to see their favorites playing the kinds of roles that had made them famous, much as readers of series books looked forward to the further exploits of their favorite characters or as nineteenth-century theater audiences lined up year after year to see Joseph Jefferson, Jr. as Rip Van Winkle, James O'Neill as the Count of Monte Cristo, Lillian Russell in her latest role, or any number of popular actors, singers, or comedians who kept the same image, style, and material. Many people criticized movie stars for merely projecting images that appealed to the public rather than really acting, as did the great stars of the stage. But movie stars should be compared not with serious dramatic actors and actresses but with the popular stage performers who attracted mass audiences. Popular stars of all the entertainment media seem to have projected *personal* qualities or images that touched the public, qualities that did not derive from the roles they played or the material they used. It was, after all, audiences accustomed to live shows who demanded the names of early movie players. The public wanted stars. It found them in compelling movie personalities as it had found them in compelling stage personalities.

Screen stars differed from stage stars primarily because they worked in such different media. Unlike stage performers who took years to gain national exposure and popularity, years in which they could sharpen their talents, performances, and images, movie performers could become national stars in a matter of weeks because they appeared in mass-produced entertainment that could be seen throughout the country at almost the same time. Also, different media demanded different qualities. Stage performers had to have special rapport with audiences and be able to project their personalities to the last row of the top balcony. In large theaters without microphones and amplification, that often meant acting with grand gestures and booming voices. Movie stars, on the other hand, played to the camera, which, with its closeups, could make stars of people whose only attribute was how they looked on screen. Many instant stars disappeared almost as quickly as they appeared. "Careers became full-blown in a matter of months instead of years," explained Jesse Lasky. "They lost their luster much faster, too."[25] But some movie stars had long careers because of their great screen presence, the enduring appeal of their central images, and the varied nuances they brought to similar roles such as Charlie Chaplin's little tramp, Douglas Fairbanks's dashing adventurer, and Mary Pickford's spunky adolescent.

By the 1920s the new entertainment medium had matured and had taken the audience for action and adventure productions away from the stage. But the silent screen did have disadvantages that live shows could exploit. Directors of plays tended to concentrate on shows with involved dialogue and on sophisticated, introspective drama. Although such serious productions had only limited appeal, comedy and music both remained popular stage fare. Silent movies, of course, produced great pantomime and sight-gag comedians such as Charlie Chaplin, Harold Lloyd, and Buster Keaton, but they complemented rather than replaced the verbal humor of live vaudeville, burlesque, revues, and musicals, which produced stars such as Will Rogers, Fanny Brice, W. C. Fields, and the Marx Brothers. Silent pictures also could offer no competition for tremendously popular musical comedies and revues. Operators of silent movie palaces often added live musical entertainment to their bills in order to fill their large houses, an acknowledgment of a major weakness in the appeal of silent films. It was no accident that the golden age of silent movies was also the golden age of stage musicals and revues. The nation's most talented singers, composers, dancers, choreographers, musicians, and musical directors were still concentrated on Broadway. That changed when the motion picture added the last major element it needed to displace the live performance as America's most popular theatrical entertainment medium.

The fourth period of motion picture history began in the late 1920s with the popularization and perfection of sound movies. The idea of films with synchronized sound was virtually as old as motion pictures. As early as 1888 Edison had attempted to match recorded sound with filmed action. But the early phonograph's poor sound quality and weak volume and the difficulty of synchronizing sight and sound proved insurmountable until the early 1920s. By 1923 both problems had been solved, the first with electrical recording and amplification, the second with Lee De Forest's successful recording of sound on movie film, which physically bonded sight and sound together. At about the same time, the Bell Telephone Laboratories unveiled Vitaphone, an efficient phonograph record-film combination for sound movies. But the movie industry did not rush to capitalize on these important technological innovations. The major studios had too large an investment in silent pictures, stars, and theaters and were doing too well with them to jump into an expensive venture that had yet to prove its popularity.

The break came when Warner Brothers, a small studio near the bottom of the movie business, decided to gamble on sound as a way to spring to the top. In 1925, when the Warner brothers saw sound movies at the Bell Laboratories in New York, they committed themselves to the new technology. Skeptical Harry Warner embraced sound movies because they could provide small theaters with excellent vaudeville acts and musical accompaniment for their pictures. When his brother Sam explained that the system could also make actors talk, Harry shot back, "Who the hell wants to hear actors talk?"[26] Warner Brothers' first sound movies reflected Harry's bias. In 1926 the studio released a number of short musical pictures and the feature film *Don Juan* with John Barrymore and a coordinated sound track. The New York Philharmonic Orchestra played the score, but the film did not contain a single word. Warner Brothers installed sound equipment in Chicago, Boston, St. Louis, Philadelphia, Hollywood, Detroit, and New York. But big city audiences were accustomed to hearing excellent music with major pictures, so *Don Juan* did not generate great excitement.

Sound motion pictures caught the public's fancy only when producers found the right material for the new entertainment medium. Vitaphone shorts featuring such popular entertainers as George Jessel, Irving Berlin, Elsie Janis, and Al Jolson excited much more interest than classical music because they brought dream bills of famous vaudeville acts to moviegoers around the nation at low prices. By early 1927 the Warner studio had filmed over fifty acts and was moving ahead with plans for a new Vitaphone feature-length picture. With its emphasis on music, Warner Brothers naturally looked to the Broadway musical stage for material and stars. The company bought the rights to the hit musical *The Jazz Singer*. After failing to come to terms with George Jessel, who originated the lead role on stage, the studio signed Al Jolson as its star. The movie script contained no dialogue, just songs, but during filming the irrepressible Jolson burst out with his trademark, "You ain't heard nuthin' yet, folks! Listen to this." Sam Warner, supervising the recording, realized the impact of Jolson's words and added a sentimental soliloquy for Jolson to deliver to his mother. This inspired improvisation, a total of only about 250 words of dialogue, and Jolson's exciting performance created a sensation that permanently changed motion pictures.

Warner Brothers rose to the top ranks of the industry as soon as it realized that Harry Warner had been wrong. People *did* want to hear actors talk. After adding dialogue to three of its other 1927 movies, Warner in 1928 released the first full talkie, *The Lights of New York*, which reportedly cost about $75,000 to produce and made $1 million. Warner Brothers' 1928 profits of $2 million jumped to $14 million in 1929, which enabled the company to purchase First National Studio.

In 1925 Warner had had total assets of about $5 million; by 1930 its assets had reached $230 million, making it one of the largest studios in Hollywood.

The major studios had all converted to production of sound motion pictures by 1930, but the conversion, a thorough redesign and retooling of the industry, deeply affected every phase of the movie business, from searching for material to editing film. Writers accustomed to conveying meaning entirely with visual images were poorly equipped to produce the dialogue that talkies needed, so Hollywood turned to stage writers for scripts. With their limited action and concentration on dialogue, stage plays proved just the right vehicles for early sound movies, which had to give up most of their location shooting and mobile, diverse camerawork. The initial shooting problem was that early microphones picked up all sounds indiscriminately, forcing actors and cameras to move as little as possible to avoid making noise. Sound engineers virtually took over production of early talkies, even overruling directors. "How many times do I have to tell you, Mr. Hersholt?" a sound man hollered at actor Jean Hersholt in 1929, "You've got to talk directly into this mike in the flowerpot. You can't turn away and look at Mr. Cortez. And you can't talk between this mike and the one hidden in the desk drawer until you *get there*." Camera movement could not compensate for the static actors. "To kill the camera noise," Capra explained, "our wonderful mobile, moving cameras were mummified and entombed in thick padded booths."[27] Even costume designers fell under the stupefying spell of the early sound system. Rustling material like taffeta was out; petticoats were fashioned from felt or wool, not silk; and soles of shoes had to be covered with felt or rubber.

Shot on confined, indoor sets with a fixed camera, little action, and limited costuming, early talkies reverted to the days when movies were little more than filmed stage plays. Editing was also of little help at first. Because sound and image were recorded simultaneously, the sound being fixed on records for Vitaphone and directly on the film for other systems, film editing had to be very limited because it created crude, jarring jumps in the sound. But talkies had great initial novelty appeal. Movie attendance shot up from 57 million in 1927 to 95 million in 1929. As the novelty began to wear off, so did the appeal of visually uninteresting early talkies. In March 1929 *Photoplay* reported on a number of letters it had received about talkies. "Nine out of ten will say they would rather have a first-rate silent picture than a second-rate talking picture. They complain of the mediocre photography and static quality of acting in the talking versions."[28]

In 1929 sound movies improved greatly. "The end of *Broadway Melody* (1929) sounded much better than the beginning," recalled MGM star Bessie Love of the film that began the rage for movie musicals. The studio was so sure that the sound musical would be successful that it did not even bother to reshoot the early scenes to take advantage of a breakthrough that allowed sound and image to be recorded separately. *Broadway Melody* was indeed a great hit. Movie fans could now experience the joys of musicals, which Hollywood produced as quickly as possible, using the ready-made shows that had been audience-tested on the nation's stages. For subsequent musicals, Love noted, "we recorded the musical numbers first, and then acted to them on playback, like they do now."[29] With improved microphones and recording equipment that allowed players and cameras to move freely, film could be shot and edited as it had been for silent pictures, and the sound tracks could also be edited and added separately. Led by silent film veterans Ernst Lubitsch and King Vidor and by stage directors George Cukor and Rouben Mamoulian, creative directors soon retook control of production and began making talkies that had the visual artistry of fine silents with the added dimension of sound.

Sound had many obvious advantages for film-makers. It made dialogue, musicals, and verbal humor possible; it allowed characters to verbalize their inner thoughts; it added clout to actions like gunshots and explosions; and it intensified emotional scenes with musical and sound effects. But these were only the beginning. Off-screen voices or sounds could provide narration or other information without a change in the visual image. While watching a character's face, for example, the audience might hear a car pull up outside, a child scream, or rain begin to fall. The soundtrack could provide transitions between scenes by introducing the sound of the image to come, or it could create the equivalent of a sound closeup by riveting the moviegoer's attention on the sound of a clock ticking, a door creaking, or ominous footsteps approaching, while the visual focus remained elsewhere. Sound "flashbacks" could also recall past events, adding unexpected depth and meaning to ordinary-looking scenes. After the early thirties, the range of possibilities was limited only by the director's imagination, ingenuity, and artistry.

Some silent stars could not successfully make the transition to sound movies. But except for a few stars such as Pola Negri who were done in by their accents, performers' voices were rarely their major problem. Although John Gilbert—the dashing, romantic lover of the silent screen—supposedly flopped in talkies because of his high-pitched voice, there was much more to success in sound films than pitch. With established stars, such as Gilbert, audiences had formed notions of the voice that would go with the player's screen image. When the voice did not match the image, audiences were disappointed. So, even though Gilbert's voice was technically acceptable, it was not what the public expected from the lovers he continued to play. The silent stars who scored the greatest successes in talkies were those who developed *new* screen images, such as Greta Garbo who switched from playing the sexy temptress to the doom-laden heroine, or Joan Crawford who switched from the saucy flapper to the sophisticated woman. Another reason that a new generation of stars emerged with talkies was that the sound motion picture was a new medium requiring a new acting style. Many experienced players who for years had relied on visual images to move audiences could not be as effective in talkies as newer, more versatile actors and actresses.

The fading of established stars and the emergence of new stars in the early 1930s may have had as much to do with the wrenching change from the buoyant twenties to the depressed thirties as with the change from silent to sound movies. The birth of talkies coincided with the onset of the worst economic depression in American history. The changes the Great Depression forced in the content of popular entertainment are discussed in later chapters. The point here is that jarring dislocations in the lives of the great mass of Americans probably would have called for new stars with new images even if sound movies had not developed. When major social and economic changes coincided with major changes in the film medium, it is no surprise that there was a wholesale change in movie stars. Many of the new stars had stage experience which prepared them for talkies, stars such as tough guys James Cagney and Edward G. Robinson, sexy blondes Joan Blondell and Mae West, anarchistic comics W. C. Fields and the Marx Brothers, pert ingenue Ruby Keeler, and cocky leading man Clark Gable. But many others, like Robert Taylor and Jean Harlow, came directly into talkies with no stage background. All had qualities that appealed to Depression audiences.

After doing well in 1929 and 1930 because of the great initial popularity of talkies and because the stock-market crash of 1929 did not have an immediate impact on the masses of movie fans, studios and exhibitors lost a total of $85 million in 1932 and hit new lows in 1933. Nearly a third of all theaters closed; prices and attendance fell; and half of the eight major studios neared collapse—Paramount in bankruptcy, RKO and Universal in receivership, and Fox being reorganized and soon taken over by Darryl Zanuck's Twentieth Century. These studios were soon refinanced and reorganized by major banking interests, and in 1934 movies began to recover. To stimulate attendance, the industry enticed fans by dropping ticket prices, giving away door prizes, and staging games and lotteries. By 1938 roughly half of American movie theaters used some sort of inducement other than film to attract audiences. But perhaps the new incentive with the greatest impact on audiences and studios was the double-bill, which became widespread by 1935.

Double-bills, offering two movies for the price of one, not only stimulated attendance, which jumped from about 70 million a week in 1934 to 88 million in 1936, but they also stimulated production and contributed to the full maturation of major movie studios as film factories, a process begun in the 1920s. For the second feature on the double-bill, studios produced low-budget, "B" movies, which helped maintain full production during the Depression and also served as training grounds for studio personnel. As self-contained mass-production units, major studios signed exclusive contracts with actors, technicians, and directors, who were paid regular salaries and could work only for that studio unless it "loaned" them to another producer. For beginners a contract with a major studio meant the chance to make a lot of pictures, to learn their trade by doing, and to develop the images the studio chose for them.

Novices usually began in "B" movies. Performers and directors who did well in "Bs" were moved up to larger responsibilities in films with bigger budgets. Some finally became major directors and stars. This system allowed movie fans to follow the development of favorite performers through a great many roles and movies. For performers it was as if the many theatrical circuits, which had provided live entertainers with experience and the chance to move up through the ranks, were all contained within the walls of a big studio. Players also shared something of the status of professional athletes, who were "owned" by their

teams and had to play where they were told and what they were told—
or not play at all. Even the most famous, highly paid movie stars had
to take roles their studios assigned to them or face suspension without
work or pay. The studio system lacked freedom, but it had important
advantages for performers, as well as for the fans who enjoyed its great
output of films. No star fought the dictatorial quality of the system
harder than Bette Davis, which makes her praise for its advantages all
the more powerful. "The *great* side of the contract system," she reflected in the 1970s, "was the constant work and the investment by the
studio to further your career. Publicity departments in those days
made your name known all over the world." Looking back on that by-
gone era, she concluded: "I thank God I was brought up in the films
under this system."[30]

By the mid-1930s motion pictures had regained their popularity and
profitability. At the same time, the triple wallop of the Great Depression, the development of professionally produced national radio shows,
and the perfection of sound movies delivered a knockout blow to popular stage entertainment. Radio brought the sounds of the nation's stars
to everyone, and talkies brought the sights and sounds of the greatest
stars, shows, and productions to people in even remote, small towns
throughout the country—something live show business could never do.
But even when live show business could match motion pictures production for production and star for star as it sometimes could in cities like
New York, it could not match their prices. Both movies and live shows
had high initial production costs. But while live shows had huge op-
erational expenses for casts, musicians, and crews, the movie industry
needed only projectionists and projectors to give unlimited performances of its mass-produced shows. When sound movies preempted
the stage's last unique attractions—musicals, vaudeville, and revues—
live shows would have been seriously wounded in the best of economic
times. But coming when they did, sound movies crippled stage shows
as mass entertainment. Even the Palace Theatre in New York, the most
prestigious vaudeville house in the capital city of live show business,
became a move theater in 1932, symbolizing the end of an era. The battle for mass audiences now became a battle between entertainment
machines.

The 1930s and 1940s were the golden age of movies. Working in
their new sound stages, directors, performers, and technicians busily
turned out 400 to 500 movies every year, while the studios' efficient

organizations distributed them throughout the nation to studio-owned chains of theaters and to the "independents" that signed up for block bookings. Fueled by the predictable receipts from these guaranteed bookings, Hollywood's well-oiled moviemaking machine hummed along in high gear. Between 1936 and 1949, average attendance at movie theaters never fell below 80 million a week. It was the era of stars and pictures of all sorts, of Bette Davis and Ginger Rogers, of Humphrey Bogart and Fred Astaire, of Greta Garbo and Shirley Temple, of Clark Gable and Mickey Mouse, the era of *Stagecoach* and *Bringing Up Baby*, of *The Grapes of Wrath* and *The Great Ziegfeld*, of *Casablanca* and *The Wizard of Oz*. Two great, roughly contemporary, but far different films—*Gone with the Wind* (1939), perhaps the most popular picture of all time, and *Citizen Kane* (1941), widely considered one of America's finest sound films—indicated the variety and artistry of Hollywood in its golden age.

Gone with the Wind, a meticulously made, opulent epic, in many ways represented the culmination of the vast resources of Hollywood at its height. Beginning with a best-selling romantic novel set amidst America's greatest tragedy, the Civil War, producer David O. Selznick started building public interest in the film even before it was begun. For a large percentage of the picture's profits, Selznick "borrowed" tremendously popular Clark Gable from MGM to play dashing, cynical Rhett Butler, and conducted a well-publicized search for the actress to costar as fiery, headstrong Southern belle Scarlett O'Hara, a search that finally settled on Vivien Leigh. Besides this great casting and such other stars as Olivia De Haviland and Leslie Howard, the lavishly produced film also boasted: stupendous productions including monumental battle scenes and the spectacular burning of Atlanta, beautiful costumes and sumptuous sets, a lovely, rhapsodic score, and gorgeous photography exploiting the stunning potential of the newly perfected Technicolor process. From casting to camera work, *Gone with the Wind* epitomized the lush, big-budget Hollywood blockbuster at its glittering best.

In contrast, *Citizen Kane,* a moody, iconoclastic character study of William Randolph Hearst, was the experimental film debut of little known, twenty-five-year-old actor-director Orson Welles. The rest of the cast, which included Agnes Moorehead, Everett Sloane, and Joseph Cotton, came largely from the acting company Welles worked with on stage and on the radio show *The Mercury Theatre on the Air.* Drawing on his radio and stage experience, especially for the evocative values of sound and of dramatic lighting, Welles explored the artistic potential of sound motion pictures with the fresh inventiveness of the talented outsider. Using somber lighting and deep shadows, frequent cuts back and forth between different times and places, overlapping dialogue, an omniscient narrator, a powerful score that punctuated the plot rather than just providing background music, and Gregg Toland's masterful photography with its unusual camera angles and deep focus shots, Welles, as director and star, said as much with the film's form as with its content. Though it was not a top-grossing picture, *Citizen Kane's* striking innovations made it one of America's most respected and most influential films. Hollywood studios in their heyday could afford to explore some such unusual approaches to film-making, which generated new ideas, techniques, stars, and directors, because of the dependable revenues generated by the self-contained studio empires.

The fifth phase of motion picture history, the period from the late 1940s to the present, has been one of upheaval and radical change. In the 1940s the U.S. Justice Department, long concerned about the monopolistic practices of the industry in controlling everything from production to exhibition, pressed new anti-trust charges against the major studios. In 1949 the federal courts ordered the studios to end block booking and to sell off their theaters. As a result, studios could no longer bank on automatic rentals for all the pictures they could make, which caused a sharp decline in production. Low-budget movies without name attractions were the first to be cut because they simply could not get enough bookings in open market competition. Reducing production meant studios were unable to make efficient use of their big backlots, vast resources, and large stock companies. When the studios were forced to reduce the number of their players, the contract system that had trained and developed the industry's new stars disintegrated. The court orders by themselves would have forced a basic restructuring of the studio system.

At the same time that the motion picture industry had to contend with its first fundamental reorganization since the early 1920s, it also had to contend with a formidable new competitor—television, an entertainment machine that for the first time seriously challenged movies for audience allegiance. Television brought the sights and sounds of show business directly into American homes for the first time. Radio and talkies had coexisted through the 1930s and 1940s because radio's one-dimensional entertainment complemented, rather than challenged, talkies. In the late 1940s when television began to improve markedly in quality, distribution, and programming, when stars such as Milton Berle, Ed Sullivan, and Arthur Godfrey began to attract growing audiences, television ceased to be a novelty. In the postwar baby boom when many young married couples were buying houses and raising children, television had the added attraction of providing free shows in people's homes. Television ownership jumped from about 3 million in 1950 to over 21 million in 1953, while average movie attendance plummeted from 90 million a week in 1948 to about half that in 1953. There was a direct correlation between the increase in television viewing and the decrease in moviegoing. In 1951 movie attendance held firm in cities without television stations, while it fell 20 to 40 percent where there were television broadcasts. "It is a certainty," Samuel Goldwyn observed in 1949, "that people will be unwilling to pay to see poor pictures when they can stay home and see something which is, at least, no worse."[31]

Crippled internally by a loss of the captive markets that had provided its financial underpinning and challenged externally by a new entertainment machine, the motion picture business changed greatly. By 1954 American movie production had fallen to 250 films a year, down from over 400 only ten years earlier. Television, already a well-established entertainment medium, preempted the modest-budget entertainment staples that had been the foundation of the movie industry. "The studios don't want ordinary stories any more," screenwriter Daniel Taradash complained in 1956. "Themes like the one about the husband getting into trouble because the box of flowers he intended for his wife were delivered to his girl friend—these are on television."[32] As television grew more popular, moviemakers responded by mounting lavish, big-budget films featuring the most famous movie stars, exploiting sexuality, and developing new technical systems, from high fidelity sound to such novelties as three-dimensional pictures, and the wide movie screens of Cinerama and CinemaScope. All these drew the greatest possible contrast between the grandeur of the movies and the small scale of television. But such innovations were exceedingly expensive and sapped already diminished studio resources. Reflecting modern corporate realities, many studios became subsidiaries of large conglomerates. Gulf and Western bought Paramount; Kinney absorbed

Warner Brothers; Trans-America acquired United Artists; and M.C.A., Inc., took over Universal.

Whether they became parts of conglomerates or remained independently owned, as Twentieth Century-Fox and Columbia did, major studios by the 1960s and 1970s became more important as distributors than as film-makers. Increasingly, independent producers—sometimes stars, sometimes directors, sometimes agents—put together individual packages of financing, stories, directors, and casts to make the blockbuster movies that the industry had come to rely on to attract audiences. The independently produced movies were then distributed by the major studios which had the resources to do the job. The huge cost of these movies also required high promotional and advertising budgets, which accelerated the process of the industry spending more and more money on fewer and fewer pictures. The trend intensified in the 1970s because it was so successful. In 1971 *Love Story* grossed $50 million, while the next most popular picture, *Little Big Horn*, earned $15 million; in 1972 *The Godfather* exceeded $80 million, more than triple its closest rival, *Fiddler on the Roof*; and in 1975 *Jaws* shattered the $100 million mark. In 1977 one out of every twenty moviegoers in the United States bought a ticket to see *Star Wars*, which grossed $127 million.

The great earning power of these and other top films demonstrated that movies remained America's most popular theatrical entertainment medium. But the nature of the movie audience and thus of the movies had changed markedly since the 1930s and 1940s. Television had won much of the family audience that had been the bulwark of the movie business in the days of the big studios. In the 1970s few families went out to their neighborhood movie theater every week or every other week to see whatever movies happened to be playing there, as families often had done in the thirties and forties. Instead, families in the 1970s tended to stay home for their regular entertainment, only occasionally venturing out to see one of the spectacular movies they had seen promoted on television. To replace its traditional family trade, the movie business had to find a new clientele. Beginning in 1969 with *Easy Rider*, a movie about young wanderers, which was made by young film-makers for about $400,000 and grossed over $7 million, the industry discovered the huge potential of the youth market. Many young people had money to spend and welcomed the chance to go out for their entertainment. Accustomed to television, they went from one entertainment machine to another. Some were drawn by motion pictures' greater scope and scale, others by their content, and still others by their status or their artistry. Whatever the reasons, young people became the new backbone of the movie audience.

In the 1970s the movie business in one sense had returned to its pre-1920 institutional structure. Production, distribution, and exhibition were again separate businesses within the industry. Independently minded film-makers such as Francis Ford Coppola, Woody Allen, and George Lucas crafted films that combined film artistry with audience appeal, just as Griffith had done. Major companies rented and distributed the films to independently owned theaters that selected each picture. Yet monumental differences divided the periods. In the 1970s the amount of money involved in each major picture had become an immense sum. Careers rose and fell with the fate of a picture or two, rather than with a large body of work as had been the case in the past. In the world of high stakes, shoot-the-works productions, there was no longer time for actors, actresses, and directors to make a great many films, to learn by doing, and to develop their abilities over a period of time.

The absorption of the studios by conglomerates also greatly affected many facets of the movie business. The parent organizations had vast resources for financing big budget films and for absorbing losses. But profits from successful films went into general corporate coffers and were as likely to be used to buy candy companies, hotel complexes, or shoe stores as to make more movies. Corporate decision-making often placed authority in the hands of people who knew little, if anything, about movies, which accentuated the tendency of movie-makers to imitate rather than to innovate. Gone were the founding fathers of Hollywood, the "committees of one," men like Louis B. Mayer who built MGM into a giant by making the kind of family movies he and America liked. Film technology had also grown incredibly complex and sophisticated, which put part of the creative process into the hands of highly specialized technicians who could achieve stunning special effects but could not necessarily tell entertaining stories with film.

Motion pictures also faced intensified competition from the proliferating entertainment machines in the home, especially telvision sets with huge screens and video machines that showed the latest movies. Such in-home entertainment offered serious, new challenges to the movie business, which was based on the assumption that people would leave the comfort of their homes and pay for entertainment.

But there has always been something compelling and magical about going into a theater, leaving control and skepticism at the door, seeing the lights go out, hearing the audience hush, and feeling a sense of union with the strangers who share the experience of sitting, in the words of 1896 critic Henry Tyrrell, "spell bound in darkness." In the age of technology, the theatrical experience of motion pictures preserves some of the transcendant qualities of ancient rituals in which common people leave behind the concerns of their ordinary, daily lives to participate in something greater and grander than themselves. Whatever the structure of the movie industry, whatever the content of the pictures, whatever the film techniques used, as long as moviemakers continue to work their magic and make audiences feel that the illusion of motion pictures is, for the moment, the only reality that matters, people will pay to experience the entertainment machine in the theater.

2

The Entertainment Machine in the Home: The Phonograph, Radio, and Television as Media

"The machine that talks—and laughs, sings, plays, and reproduces all sound," boasted advertisements for the Columbia Phonograph Company in 1896. The company bragged that its new entertainment machine was "so simple that even a child can make it pour forth the most enchanting selections of the world's greatest Musicians, Singers, Actors, and Speakers." To illustrate the joys of the "entertainer of which one never tires," Columbia pictured three generations of a model American family enjoying music in their parlor. This was certainly nothing new in the 1890s. What *was* new was that the family was not gathered around a piano making its own music, but was seated quietly, its attention fixed on the horn of the phonograph that was providing the family's entertainment.[1]

For the first time an inexpensive, easy-to-operate entertainment machine was bringing professional performances into the average American home. This development signaled the beginning of changes in entertainment that were to be even more fundamental and profound than those caused by motion pictures. Late-nineteenth-century Americans had become accustomed to going to theaters for an incredibly rich variety of live entertainment. When movies replaced live performances, people continued to leave their homes to get their entertainment. Until the late 1890s only members of the upper class could afford to hire entertainers to perform in their homes. But at about the same time motion pictures were being developed, the phonograph be-

46

gan to bring the sounds of show business into common people's living rooms. Ultimately, this had a great influence on American family life as well as on show business. But entertainment machines developed much more slowly in the home than they did in the theater. The story of entertainment machines in the home can be divided into three roughly equal twenty-five-year periods, each dominated by a different medium—the phonograph, radio, and television.

Like the motion picture, the phonograph—using that word as a generic term for a machine that replays recorded sounds—did not become a commercial product until twenty years after its invention. Thomas A. Edison had patented a "talking machine" in 1877, but it was not until the early 1890s that the phonograph was marketed for home entertainment, partially because Edison had originally conceived of it as a dictaphone-like tool for business. Early phonographs used wax cylinders that could both record and replay sound, but could do neither effectively. The range, quality, and diversity of early acoustic recordings were severely limited by the period's crude technology. People had to perform directly into a phonograph horn which vibrated a stylus that mechanically cut grooves into a wax cylinder. The clarity and volume of the recording depended totally on the intensity and pitch of the performance. Though people could make their own recordings at home with blank cylinders, the public quickly showed its preference for listening to professional performers who had the strong, clear sounds needed to record effectively on the period's limited technology. John Philip Sousa and his military bands, May Irwin, the hard-belting "Coon Shouter," Russell Hunting with his "Casey" monologues, black whistler George W. Johnson, and Enrico Caruso, the great operatic tenor soon became popular recording stars. When permanently grooved, easily handled, and conveniently stored disc recordings went on the market the public snapped them up even though discs could not be used to make recordings at home. By World War I discs marketed by Victor and Columbia were more popular than cylinders.

The popularity of records changed the popular music business. When the phonograph became a major source of music in the home, sales of sheet music plummeted, and popular songs became musically more complex but shorter to fit the three-minute playing time of records. Beginning in 1914 the record and phonograph businesses boomed as America was swept by new dance crazes such as the "Grizzly Bear," "Fox Trot," and "Tango," which were done to complicated ragtime and Latin rhythms. Although this music was difficult to play on a piano, it was easy to play on a phonograph. The public bought records and the new entertainment machines as quickly as they could be produced, and there was no lack of production. In 1912 only Victor, Columbia, and Edison made phonographs; by 1919 nearly 200 companies turned out some 2 million phonographs, a 400 percent increase in five years.

Business got even better after World War I when brassy Dixieland jazz, which recorded well, captured the public's fancy, and records provided the unfamiliar and difficult music for popular dances like the "Black Bottom" and the "Charleston." Besides serving the general, national market, record companies of the 1920s also discovered lucrative regional and ethnic markets in country music, which appealed primarily to white Southerners, and in blues and jazz, which appealed primarily to black people. Record sales exceeded 100 million in 1921 and held up until the late 1920s. But in the early 1920s, the static-laden sounds of radio were growing clearer, stronger, more ominous for the phonograph and record businesses, and more promising for the public.

At the turn of the twentieth century the air had begun to come alive with the transmissions of Guglielmo Marconi's "Wireless Telegraph," which at first broadcast only Morse code. Before World War I amateur radio enthusiasts around the country broadcast voices and records, but the companies that invested in radio were interested in wireless communication with ships, not in entertainment. Until 1920 radio in America remained essentially a telegraph without wires, a business dominated by a few major companies—Radio Corporation of America (RCA), General Electric (GE), Westinghouse, and American Telephone and Telegraph (AT&T), which had entered the field in case a wireless telephone developed. The only entertainment machines in the average American home were phonographs and pianos, particularly player pianos, which became very popular after 1900. Radio only began to take its familiar form in 1920 when, besides the many amateur radio stations, Westinghouse started daily broadcasts in Pittsburgh to gain publicity and to create demand for simple-to-operate, self-contained radio sets similar to those the company had made for the military during World War I. Professional broadcasting began when Westinghouse's KDKA took to the air. Envisioning "limitless opportunity" if it could interest the general public in radio, Westinghouse tried to attract the largest possible listening audiences. After a good initial response, the company expanded into other major metropolitan areas with powerful stations in Newark, Chicago, and Springfield, Massachusetts, where it manufactured its home crystal sets.

Radio became a popular fad in 1922. By the end of that year the federal government had licensed 670 stations, and sales of mass-produced radio sets and parts reached $60 million, a total that mushroomed to $358 million in 1924 and kept growing. The novelty of radio was probably its greatest initial appeal. Early stations broadcast almost anything they could get inexpensively. "The talent would come over to the office and tell us what they could do," a veteran of WWJ in Detroit recalled of the chaos of 1922. "We didn't rehearse them, we took their word for it."[2] Organizations of all sorts ran radio stations—newspapers, universities, churches, hotels, department stores, laundries, and even a poultry farm and a stockyard. But *none* of these stations directly earned *any* money for its owner. The owners paid the costs of broadcasting to gain the goodwill of listeners. The radio manufacturers—Westinghouse, RCA, and GE—opened powerful stations around the country to stimulate sales of their radio sets, which theoretically benefited all the companies by increasing general demand. But by 1923 with listeners in many areas able to choose among programs, stations began to compete for audiences by offering more appealing shows. The competition rapidly drove up the costs of broadcasting.

Once the initial burst of radio sales began to level off, the manufacturers had to find a new method of paying for the rising expenses of broadcasting. Several solutions to this problem were discussed within the industry in 1922. None was adopted, but the idea of selling advertising to pay the bills seemed repugnant to many people, including Secretary of Commerce Herbert Hoover, whose department controlled radio licensing. "It is inconceivable," Hoover argued in 1922, "that we should allow so great a possibility for service, for news, for entertainment, for education to be drowned in advertising chatter."[3] Yet the chatter was already beginning.

AT&T which initially had invested in radio in case it became part of the telephone business decided to enter broadcasting in 1922. The company had no radio equipment to sell, so when it announced it was entering "public radiotelephone broadcasting," it had another product in mind. "We, the telephone company, were to provide no programs," recalled one of its executives. "The public was to come in. Anyone who had a message for the world or wished to entertain was to come in and pay their money as they would upon coming into a telephone booth, address the world, and go out."[4] Just as AT&T provided the telephone facilities, not the phone calls, it would provide only the "toll-broadcasting" facilities, not the content of the broadcasts. AT&T's first station, WEAF in New York, went on the air in August 1922, and in its first two months sold $550 of broadcast time to businesses. It was $550 more than any other station had ever directly earned. The businesses—an apartment complex, an oil company, and American Express—used their time to talk to the audience. There was no other entertainment. But in its unsold time WEAF, using AT&T's long-distance telephone lines to pick up operas, concerts, stage shows, and football games from as far away as Chicago, provided programming that built a large listening audience and convinced more businesses to use radio to reach the public.

Concerned about the stigma of obvious advertising, AT&T insisted that its paying customers not mention their product's price or color or their store's location. No samples were to be offered, and nothing even potentially offensive was to be said. WEAF executives even postponed a talk by a toothpaste company while they decided whether anything as intimate as brushing teeth should be discussed on the air. But the station soon had to contend with professional pitchmen who bought radio time, resold segments to businesses, and used the purchased time to deliver their messages for them. Actor Bruce Reynolds made a lot of money doing this until WEAF found his pitches too blatant and urged him to "be more subtle so that the listeners won't realize it's advertising." WEAF finally refused to sell him time. When Reynolds suggested such sponsored talks to another station, its outraged executives replied, "We wouldn't prostitute our station by accepting outside advertising."[5] WEAF soon found a way to make money and to avoid objectionable sales pitches by persuading firms to buy air time and use it to broadcast entertainment that carried only the sponsor's name. There were no sales pitches. This discreet approach produced groups like the Clicquot Club Eskimos, Gold Dust Twins, A&P Gypsies, Best Food Boys, and Ipana Troubadours.

In December 1923 WEAF broadcast a new show that indicated the direction sponsored programs would take. The *Eveready Hour,* paid for by Eveready batteries, was a thoroughly professional, well-rehearsed program that evolved into a varied series of concerts, dramas, variety shows, and dance music. The show also had a major impact on the structure of broadcasting. Eveready got such favorable response to its programs on WEAF that the company sent the performers out to other stations to do additional broadcasts, which was like sending shows on tour and charging no admission fees. As the Eveready productions grew more elaborate and expensive this method of reaching more audiences proved impractical, especially when radio offered an inexpensive alternative. By linking stations with telephone lines, a single performance could be broadcast simultaneously on a network of stations with the sponsor buying time on each station. That is what Eveready did. By the end of 1923 AT&T had a six-station network in operation. This was a major step toward developing the unique capability of the new entertainment machine to blanket the nation with the same show at the same time. Unlike any previous entertainment medium, radio had the potential to be everywhere at once.

By 1925 at the end of the first stage of the development of entertainment machines in the home, phonographs and recordings had matured into a major popular medium while radio was still in an experimental phase, exploring the possibilities of selling advertising to businesses, broadcasting well-produced shows, and linking stations into networks. But it was on the eve of an explosion that would make radio a major force in popular entertainment.

The second major period in the development of entertainment machines in the home, a period dominated by radio, began in 1926 with the formation of the first national radio network. AT&T, which had created commercial broadcasting and the first radio network, left radio in 1925 when it sold WEAF to a new network, the National Broadcasting Company (NBC), which was owned by RCA, GE, and Westinghouse. In November 1926 NBC made a spectacular debut with a star-studded broadcast that showcased the unique potential of radio by originating parts of the show in New York, Chicago, and Kansas City, among other locations. The debut was broadcast by twenty-six stations to as many as 12 million people. Within a year NBC had expanded to two separate networks, designated as red and blue, with over 100 stations, most of them independently owned and voluntarily affiliated with NBC. NBC paid its affiliates to broadcast nationally sponsored shows and charged its affiliates for unsponsored shows that the stations could sell locally. But NBC soon faced outside competition.

United Independent Broadcasters, Inc. (UIB) began as a financially wobbly network in 1926. Within a year, the Columbia Phonograph

Company, pressured by radio's inroads into the record business, invested in debt-ridden UIB and formed the Columbia Phonograph Broadcasting System, which was reorganized and renamed the Columbia Broadcasting System (CBS). The new network barely survived until William S. Paley, the twenty-seven-year-old son of a wealthy family, bought it in 1928. After putting CBS on solid footing, Paley rapidly expanded the network. Unlike NBC, which charged its affiliates for unsponsored shows that they could sell to local sponsors, CBS *gave* these money-making programs to its affiliates in exchange for the right to preempt the affiliates' broadcast time which the network paid for. This system attracted stations and allowed Paley to guarantee sponsors national exposure on the entire CBS network, which NBC, unable to preempt affiliates' local time, could not do. From 19 stations in 1928 CBS grew to 79 stations in 1931 and for the first time made more money than NBC. The competition changed advertising policies. NBC, priding itself on its decorum, maintained a long list of taboo words and would not let sponsors mention prices. CBS had no such qualms. George Washington Hill of the American Tobacco Company, who believed listeners remembered irritating commercials, could say what he wanted on CBS. What he wanted to say was that his Cremo cigars cost five cents and that "there is no spit in Cremo!" NBC began to adopt CBS's policies. Advertisers were taking control of radio away from broadcasters.

Radio was a unique entertainment medium that required a completely new method of financing, a method that was another major step in the destruction of the once intimate relationship between audiences and performers. Before radio, producers had created entertainment and tried to convince the public to buy tickets or records. The revenues paid the bills and provided the profits. This was as true for Adolph Zukor's Paramount Pictures as it was for Barnum and Bailey's Greatest Show on Earth. The public paid the piper and called the tune. In the first stage of the modern entertainment revolution, phonographs and motion picture projectors presented previously recorded and mass-produced entertainment, which eliminated interaction between patron and performer. But the success of these entertainment machines still required producers who understood show business and popular tastes. Radio was *totally* different. Businesses, which had nothing to do with entertainment, bought shows and paid to broadcast them to people who received the entertainment free of charge. Like medicine shows radio programs were given away to draw crowds so a pitchman could sell his wares. "The play is not the thing," observed veteran radio actress Mary Jane Higby. "The sponsor's message is the thing and no radio or television actor can ever forget it."[6]

By the early 1930s radio was controlled by a new breed of experts who specialized in meeting the needs of the people who paid radio's bills—the sponsors. Since the purpose of the radio program was to draw a large audience to hear the sponsor's commercials, there had to be a new way to judge the size of a show's audience. Obviously it was impossible to count heads or ticket stubs. In 1930 Archibald Crossley formed the first radio rating service. Using telephone interviews of a small population sample, Crossley projected the size of shows' audiences. Over the years rating systems grew increasingly refined and sophisticated and exerted a powerful influence on sponsors' decisions about what radio time and shows to buy. But even at their best, even if ratings experts could determine precisely how many people listened to each show, they could not tell how well the shows helped sell the sponsors' products. There certainly were some striking examples of what radio advertising could do. La Palina cigar sales jumped from 400,000 to a million a day after a 1928 radio advertising campaign, and Pepsodent toothpaste tripled in sales within weeks of Procter & Gamble's sponsoring of *Amos 'n' Andy*, radio's greatest early hit. Even though there was rarely such clear evidence of radio's sales effectiveness, many businesses found advertising on radio irresistible because the entertainment machine reached into the homes of millions of people across the nation. But radio advertising was also filled with uncertainty, insecurity, and anxiety for sponsors who turned for help to the experts—in this case advertising agencies.

Since the purpose of paying for the production of programs and for the time to broadcast them was to sell their products, businesses in the 1930s came to rely on advertising agencies not only to design the best commercials and select the right broadcast time, but also to *create* shows that would attract the right sorts of audiences. Advertising agencies produced almost all sponsored network radio shows. When an agency interested a client in radio, the agency, whose expertise was advertising not entertaining, began to produce a show. After it had chosen the show's concept, writers, and actors, a producer-director, often a member of the agency staff, developed a "pilot" show, while the agency secured an option on a broadcast time and prepared ad-

vertising copy. When the entire production was completed and rehearsed, it was auditioned for the sponsor, adjusted to his tastes, and,
if accepted by the sponsor, was booked for thirteen weeks on a network. Although networks had to approve the programs the agencies
created for the sponsors, that approval had become virtually automatic by 1932.

The commercial basis of radio did not seem to bother the public. In
1945 a public opinion poll asked Americans: "If your radio programs
could be produced without advertising, would you prefer it that way?"
An astounding 62 percent of the people interviewed, nearly two out of
every three people, said *no*. They would *not* prefer programs without
advertising. About half explained that commercials did not interfere
with their enjoyment of the programs, and nearly a quarter of the people said they liked the advertising because "it tells me about the things
I want to buy."[7] But perhaps the major reason that the public preferred
radio programs with commercials was that most Americans first bought
radios in the late 1920s and early 1930s when commercially sponsored,
top-notch entertainment took over the airwaves. Many people probably felt that ads and good radio shows were inextricably linked and
that removing one might remove the other.

In 1928 network radio was dominated by music, especially popular
dance music, with a sprinkling of dramatic series. Then radio programming was permanently changed by the incredible popularity of *Amos
'n' Andy,* in which two white men acted out the comic exploits of two
black men, their families, and their friends. Though using exaggerated
black stereotypes, caricatures, and dialects that hearkened back to the
minstrel show, the show also portrayed trusting, hard-working Amos
and scheming, lazy Andy as appealing *people* with families and feelings, people fighting gamely to survive in the bleak despair of the
Great Depression. The plots unfolded slowly through months of daily
fifteen-minute episodes, a format that allowed far more time for characterization than was possible in self-contained single episode shows.
The serial became an enduring pattern for radio, one that capitalized
on the medium's intimate relationship with its regular listening audience by stressing the personalities of the characters rather than the action of the plots.

Between 7:00 and 7:15 every week night America stopped what it
was doing to listen to *Amos 'n' Andy*. In the 1930s an estimated 40
million people—about one out of every three living Americans—listened

to *Amos 'n' Andy*, a figure that demonstrated the incredible reach of national broadcast entertainment as well as the unprecedented popularity of this show. To avoid losing customers, movie theaters played *Amos 'n' Andy* in their lobbies, and Atlantic City merchants piped it onto the boardwalk; utility companies reported a drop in water pressure as the program ended and people flushed their toilets; when the show asked listeners to name Amos's baby, nearly 2.5 million people offered their suggestions. "There are three things which I shall never forget about America," observed George Bernard Shaw, "the Rocky Mountains, Niagara Falls, and *Amos 'n' Andy*."[8]

Freeman F. Gosden (Amos) and Charles J. Correll (Andy), the creators and performers of the show, instinctively knew how to use the new medium. "Listening to them," observed critic Gilbert Seldes, "you never felt that they wished people could see them or were afraid their comedy was not getting across because they were invisible." Instead, they used that invisibility as an asset. Changing their inflection, tone, dialect, and phrasing, Gosden and Correll portrayed scores of distinct, easily recognizable characters—men, women, and children. Characterization was the key to the show's success. "Most (critics) did not realize that we were after the creation of character, not gags," Gosden explained on the twenty-first anniversary of the show. "We believed then and believe now that once you establish your characters, if they're likeable, the public will become fond of them. All you have to do then is to put them into recognizable situations. You don't have to have a laugh in every line to be funny."[9] Following this pattern, *Amos 'n' Andy* defined and popularized situation comedy. After the show's astounding success, scores, then hundreds, of radio programs used *Amos 'n' Andy*'s formula, making situation comedy a basic staple of broadcast entertainment.

As advertising agencies tried to reach the largest possible audiences with their sponsors' commercials, they developed different types of shows for different times of day. At night, shows that appealed to the whole family filled the radio dial—situation comedies like *Amos 'n' Andy*, music of all sorts, mysteries like *The Shadow*, drama like *First Nighter*, adventures like *Death Valley Days*, quiz shows like *Kay Kyser's Kollege of Musical Knowledge*, and variety shows starring big-name vaudevillians Eddie Cantor, Ed Wynn, Al Jolson, and others who found new homes in radio when vaudeville collapsed during the Depression. The late afternoon and early evening hours were dominated by children's action and adventure serials, such as *Jack Arm-strong, The Lone Ranger,* and *Little Orphan Annie.* Mornings and afternoons belonged to housewives for whom advertising agencies developed domestic serials popularly called "soap operas" because companies such as Procter & Gamble and Lever Brothers sponsored many of them. Focusing on the family and personal problems of perpetually plagued heroines, soap operas used the continuing story, characterization, and personal involvement that *Amos 'n' Andy* had pioneered, but put their characters into perplexing rather than humorous situations. Embroiling heroines in seemingly endless anguish, torment, and worry proved so popular that by the end of 1938 thirty-eight women's serials were broadcast every weekday, and their number was still growing. But daytime programming was not limited to soap operas. In 1934 Mary Margaret McBride created the "talk show" format later adopted by stars such as Arthur Godfrey. She informally interviewed famous guests and chatted casually with listeners about her opinions, tastes, experiences, and feelings. "You bring the world into my little kitchen—the people, the sights, the sounds," an ex-working woman wrote to Mc-Bride.[10] That fan identified radio's single greatest appeal. It brought the world into kitchens, bedrooms, and living rooms throughout the country, making listeners feel that radio personalities and characters were people they knew.

As a unique entertainment medium, radio had to develop its own performance styles as well as its own shows. "Radio actors must achieve all their effects with their voices," explained radio veteran Joseph Julian. "They can't use gestures, expressions, stances, or other visual nuances." Radio performances had to spark the imagination of listeners. "What was needed," explained radio star Mary Jane Higby, "was a quick impression, given with broad, sure strokes. It bore the relation to a stage performance that a pencil sketch has to an oil painting."[11] Pencil sketches can have a directness, spontaneity, and immediacy that oil paintings lack, but they do not have depth, texture, and complexity. Neither did radio acting, because radio was one-dimensional, because there was little time to rehearse, and because there were no retakes or editing.

When Mary Jane Higby left the theater for radio, she quickly learned that she had to make major adjustments. After memorizing all her lines for her first radio role as she would have done for the stage, she arrived for the performance and was handed pages and pages of major revisions. Higby never memorized another radio script. But she did carefully study successful radio shows, especially *Amos 'n' Andy,* for techniques that worked in the new medium. She concluded that "intimacy was the keynote to radio acting" and that she could convey action and mood with her voice. "When I was supposed to be lifting a weight I learned to let the strain show in my voice. I would speak more loudly in an outdoor scene than I would in a fireside conversation at home."[12] These imaginative and subtle techniques, unnecessary in a visual medium, made Higby a great success in radio. She played in many shows and starred in *When a Girl Marries* for 19 years.

Many radio actors and actresses, in contrast to singers or comedians who appeared under their own names, were virtually unknown, even to the fans who absolutely would not miss the shows these performers starred in. Few listeners knew the names of the people who played Superman, Stella Dallas, Jack Armstrong, or Mr. District Attorney. The reasons lay in the nature of the medium. Radio audiences could identify actors only by their voices. But what listeners heard were the voices of the *characters,* not the natural voices of the performers. The actress who played a young boy at 9:00 a.m. might take the role of an old woman at 9:30, a lawyer at 10:00, and a seductress at 10:30. If she was good, listeners would have had no idea that one actress had played them all. This allowed skilled performers with adaptable voices to play an incredible range of parts. Actor Matt Crowley, for example, was the announcer for *Pretty Kitty Kelly,* John in *John's Other Wife,* Doctor Brent in *Road of Life,* and Jim in *Jungle Jim.* But the lack of public recognition for the actor also meant relatively low status and pay for radio stars compared with movie stars, which represented the great contrast between the two most popular entertainment machines of the period. Movie stars, working in a bigger-than-life, visual medium that commanded the audience's full attention, projected powerful personal images that overshadowed the roles they played. The personality of the movie star, not the character, held the central appeal. In contrast, radio actors, working in an intimate, aural medium that was part of the audience's home life, subordinated their personalities to the roles they played. The character, not the personality of the star, held the central appeal. People went to movies to see a Clark Gable or a Bette Davis picture, but they tuned in to radio shows to hear about the Lone Ranger or Helen Trent. Especially in radio's unique format, the daily serial, listeners believed in and cared about the characters as if they were real people, which further decreased interest in the actors and actresses.

Radio also developed its own unique specialist—the sound-effects man, who stimulated listeners' imagination with sounds. "This ability of the ear to convey a *picture* to the mind of a listener is one of the radio's most fortunate gifts," observed journalist John J. Floherty in describing how radio worked. Give listeners "the right sound effects and music," comedian Fred Allen explained, "and their imaginations will work for you. A man in his armchair can picture all kinds of fantastic scenes: a fly crawling up the Empire State Building, scenes in outer space or under the sea. These are things radio can do best—better than the movies."[13] The first problem the sound-effects man had was that he could not simply use recordings of actual sounds because microphones distorted them. On radio a record of a real automobile crash, for example, sounded like a battleship being torpedoed, so sound men had to find another way to re-create the familiar sound. They did it by dropping a stovepipe, a steel bar, and tin cans into a box of broken glass. As they mastered their new craft, sound-effects men stocked studios with the odd-looking tools of their trade—cellophane to crumple for a crackling fire, bird seed to spill onto stretched parchment for driving sleet, a shoe to tread in a box of gravel for footsteps on a path, a door to slam in a jamb, and coconut shells to thump for a horse galloping. Sound-effects men also faced some incredible challenges such as the scene in a *Lights Out* episode in which a man was turned inside out. After a great deal of experimentation, one sound-effects man slowly peeled off a tight-fitting rubber glove close to the microphone, while another crunched a strawberry box for the sound of breaking bones.

The same technological breakthroughs in electrical amplification that made possible radio's development also radically changed the record business. In the mid-1920s electrical microphones and amplifiers ended the era of direct acoustical recording. No longer was the quality of a record determined by a performer's volume, pitch, tone, and distance from a recording horn. With sensitive microphones to pick up all kinds of sounds and amplifiers to boost their intensity, soft-voiced crooners like Rudy Vallee and Whispering Jack Smith and sweet-sounding bands relying on strings and subtle arrangements could for the first time become recording stars. The new electrical equipment also allowed entertainers to perform naturally when recording. A full orchestra could now set up in its normal configuration, rather than being forced to eliminate instruments and to cram musicians together in front of the recording horn. A dynamic entertainer like Al Jolson could now prance around while he recorded rather than having two men hold him still so he would sing directly into the recording horn. The result of the new recording technology was a new diversity and quality of discs that the public loved.

But when the upbeat 1920s collapsed into the depressed 1930s, nonessentials became expensive luxuries just when radio began broadcasting top-notch, free entertainment. Like the stock market, record sales plummeted—from 100 million in 1927 to 6 million in 1932. As a result the other entertainment media began to absorb the weakened recording industry. In 1929 the Radio Corporation of America took over Victor, forming RCA-Victor; in 1930, Warner Brothers, the pioneer of talkies, took over Brunswick's record and phonograph division; and in an ironic reversal that indicated the shift of power, CBS in 1938 bought Columbia Records, which originally had kept the fledgling radio network alive and had given it its name. By the late 1930s, record sales had recovered, led by Jack Kapp's new Decca Record Company, which dropped prices from 75 cents to 35 cents, signed up top stars like Bing Crosby and Tommy and Jimmy Dorsey, and emphasized records' major advantage over radio. "Hear them *when* you want—as *often* as you want—right in your home," Decca advertised.[14] Unlike radio, phonographs put the home listener in charge of programming, which proved especially popular with music because people liked hearing hits over and over. Record sales also got a boost from a new public entertainment machine—the jukebox, which provided inexpensive, popular dance music for Depression America in places like diners, taverns, and soda fountains. Hot new swing bands which received little prime-time exposure on family-oriented network radio burned up records at the "juke joints." By 1939 there were some 225,000 jukeboxes using about 13 million records. Within three years, the number of jukeboxes nearly doubled. The record business was again thriving, having found a role which supplemented radio.

By the mid-1940s, as America emerged victorious from World War II and the second period in the development of entertainment machines in the home ended, show business was more varied and popular than ever before. Even in the worst economic depression in the nation's history the American people had found enough money and time to support entertainment machines in their theaters, their recreation centers, and their homes. The public's appetite for entertainment grew more voracious as technology produced an even more varied diet of enjoyable, inexpensive, or free entertainment. Once a major entertainment medium became popular, it never disappeared, though innovations often forced major changes in the content, format, and audience of existing entertainment machines. The greatest example of this process came after World War II when a new machine revolutionized entertainment in the home.

The third major phase of home entertainment began in the late 1940s and was dominated by television, which brought the sights as well as the sounds of show business into people's homes. Television technology had been developed by the 1930s. Regular, limited telecasting had begun at the New York World's Fair of 1939, and in 1940 there were twenty-three television stations and some 10,000 sets in operation. World War II postponed television's development, but in the upbeat, postwar economic boom when a great many working-class people were able to buy homes in the suburbs, new cars, and conveniences of all sorts, television spread quickly. For the new entertainment medium the years between 1946 and 1955 were years of expansion and experimentation, years in which television absorbed the structure, financing, and formats of radio and developed its own qualities. Like radio, early television broadcast live performances to audiences, but, unlike radio, television producers had to be concerned with visual as well as vocal impact. Centered in New York and totally boycotted by major motion picture studios, television, in this first phase, looked to radio and the theater for writers, directors, and performers.

By the late 1940s, drawing heavily on radio, television began to develop a broad range of programming. In 1947 *Howdy Doody* and *Kukla, Fran, and Ollie* established children's shows; *Charade Quiz* got viewers participating in game and quiz shows; and *Kraft Television Theatre* introduced well-financed, well-produced drama. In 1948 Milton Berle proved that comedians would be superstars in the new medium, and Ed Sullivan began his influential variety show. In 1949 Arthur Godfrey popularized the personality talk show; *The Lone Ranger* staked the western's claim to the new territory; *Martin Kane, Private Eye* began the fight against urban crime; and *Mama* and *The Goldbergs* set up housekeeping for domestic, situation comedy. These and many other stars and shows made television into a major entertainment machine in American homes. The number of television sets in the nation grew from about 3 million in 1950 to 21 million in 1953, a 700 percent increase in three years.

Television contained elements of radio, film, and the stage, but it was a distinctive new medium that required its own performance styles and techniques. Television producers used radio formats, programs, and stars and had to churn out shows at nearly the pace of radio producers. Like radio, early network television also broadcast its shows live, which was a far more formidable task for television than for radio directors. Television directors, like movie directors, had to worry about camera shots and angles, and, like stage directors, about live performances with no retakes and no editing. Early television's limited technology and resources made this a doubly difficult task. Cut off from Hollywood's film experts who knew how to produce inexpensive, enjoyable pictures at a rapid pace, television's pioneers worked with the make-do, ad-lib approach of early film-makers.

Prior to 1952 television networks were not truly national. Until the first coast-to-coast telecasts in 1951, television producers could reach national audiences with their live shows only by making movies of the images on television sets and sending these murky, poor-quality kinescopes to other stations for rebroadcast. "Watching a kinescope," recalled television writer Max Wilk, "was like looking at a bowl of gray pea soup. Here and there you could barely make out the croutons." But in spite, or perhaps because, of the hectic pace, the limitations of the technology, and the lack of precedents, working in the experimental phase of this complex, new medium was an exhilarating experience. "That was a very exciting period in my life," reminisced producer Mort Werner. "Television was such a brand-new medium. I don't really know how the Pilgrims felt when they landed in Massachusetts, but we were in somewhat the same position. We had to construct a whole new business, and we went ahead and did it, from the ground up."[15]

Getting a weekly show on the air was an enormous challenge. The Sid Caesar-Imogene Coca shows, which ran from 1949 to 1954, were live, ninety-minute revues, the kinds of shows that stage producers like Florenz Ziegfeld or Earl Carroll had worked months to create and then had refined on the road before opening night. But *Your Show of Shows* had to open a completely new show *every week* for five years. Working in this pressure cooker brought out the best in people, leaving them with a feeling of accomplishment and camaraderie that they never forgot. "I don't know whether there are any shows today in TV where producer, performers and writers were as tuned to each other's talents as we were then," observed Lucille Kallin about the staff of *Your Show of Shows* which included writers Mel Brooks, Carl Reiner, and Neil Simon. "Coming up with an idea in that group was like throwing a magnetized piece of a jigsaw puzzle into the middle of a room. All the other pieces would come racing toward it, each one adding another necessary part. Suddenly there was the whole picture!" There was no time for discord. In early television, the need to produce show after show, week after week meant abundant opportunities for creative talents and no long, drawn-out process for filtering and modifying them. "Television was brand new," observed Charlie Andrews, who wrote for Dave Garroway, "you could do any damn thing you wanted to, and nobody could tell you, 'No, don't do that, it won't work,' because nobody knew anything. So there was this burst of creativity around NBC because there was so much room to burst."[16]

The type of show that best represented the distinctive problems and achievements of live television was the weekly dramatic anthology, a series of independent productions presented under a common name, which began on television in 1947 with *Kraft Television Theatre*. Unlike other series, dramatic anthologies had no continuing characters, stars, or themes to carry the shows and sustain audience interest. Each production was a totally self-contained play that attracted and held viewers on its own. To accomplish these goals, producers of television drama turned to the American stage for help. Major Hollywood studios not only denied early television their films and expertise but also their stars and properties, which included most past and present Broadway hits and most popular novels. With few guaranteed attractions and little money to spend on scripts, producers of live television drama of necessity turned to classics, like Shakespeare, which were in the public domain, and to original plays by unknown writers, like Paddy Chayevsky and Rod Serling who wrote major television plays such as *Marty* and *Patterns*. With early television's hectic production pace, young actors, directors, and writers had a chance to learn their craft on the job and quickly evaluate the results, just as D. W. Griffith had done with his early films. "You could get an idea and write it, and a couple of weeks later, you could see it performed," explained Chayefsky. Between 1953 and 1955 there were as many as a dozen original dramatic productions on network television *every week*. The great number of scripts needed for these shows meant that writers did not have time to produce blockbuster scripts, but had to write "small stories about people," which Chayefsky astutely argued was just what television did best. "Movies need much broader scope—but as far as I'm concerned," he explained, "on the home screen you work best on a small canvas. You create character, and that becomes your plot."[17]

Creators of live television drama had to learn to work within the restrictions of the new medium's "small canvas," which was best suited to mid-range shots and closeups. Live television drama was largely confined to interior settings with few scene changes, few characters, and lots of dialogue. Early television camera work did little to enliven productions because studios generally used only one fixed-lens camera for long shots and another for closeups. The cumbersome cameras made fast takes, dolly shots, and quick cross-cutting virtually impossible. As a result television drama had a far slower pace and much less visual variety than contemporary movies had. In this sense early television reverted to the limited camera work of pre-Griffith, silent one-reelers. And there could, of course, be no editing of live telecasts to pick up the pace or add tension and excitement. With limited settings, movement, and camera work, directors focused on people, dialogue, psychological tension, and characterization. Live television drama was like live theater with closeups.

Early television was an actor's medium. Since the stories centered on characterization, not action, the performers had to create the mood, feelings, and intensity of the shows. Their problem was to develop the right acting style for the new medium. Television's heavy reliance on closeups magnified actors' gestures and movements and forced actors to move slowly and to use a wide range of subtle visual gestures, as well as subtle gradations in intonation and phrasing. The television actor had to have the theatrical performer's command of dialogue, the movie performer's mastery of closeups, and the radio performer's intimacy. These broad requirements, plus the absence of established movie stars, perhaps explains why early television produced so many new stars, many of them trained in theater but not yet experienced enough to have to unlearn the styles of other performing media, people such as Paul Newman, Estelle Parsons, Steve McQueen, Kim Stanley, Lee Marvin, Lee Remick, Rod Steiger, and Joanne Woodward.

Although live telecasts dominated network television programming prior to 1952, some television series were filmed. Frederick W. Ziv, a radio producer who had syndicated his shows directly to individual stations instead of to sponsors or networks, did the same thing in the new medium in the late-1940s with modestly produced filmed adventure series such as the *Cisco Kid.* In 1951 Lucille Ball and Desi Arnaz greatly influenced television programming with their situation comedy *I Love Lucy,* which was filmed by three cameras before a live audience. The three films were then edited like a movie before being broadcast which gave the programs the variety of camera angles and the rapid pace of films along with the spontaneity and immediacy of live performances. Because *I Love Lucy* quickly dominated the ratings, there were soon many other short, filmed television series, comedies like *The Life of Riley* or *Make Room for Daddy.* By 1954 film had just about replaced short, live episodic series.

ABC Television, with few top dramatic anthologies, few top comedians, and no shows in the top fifteen, decided to gamble on new programming in 1954. Its telecast of the U.S. Senate hearings investigating Senator Joseph McCarthy's charges of Communist infiltration of the army won high ratings and demonstrated the power of television to bring news events into people's homes and to influence politics and politicians. But since live events with such high tension and drama were rare, ABC had to look elsewhere for programming to improve the dismal ratings of the network. Using the movie studio contacts of ABC corporate president Leonard H. Goldenson, who had headed United Paramount Theaters before it merged with ABC, the network looked to Hollywood, not to Broadway.

Robert Kintner, then responsible for ABC programming, went to Hollywood in 1954 to persuade major movie studios, which had not yet sold their old pictures to television, to film programs for ABC's regular schedule. At first he got an even colder and more antagonistic response than he feared. "You dumb young son of a bitch, you won't get any of my stars, you won't get any people—*you* can't make films!" bellowed Harry Cohn of Columbia. "People . . . want their movies the way they *are*—not on TV!"[18] But Jack Warner, the man who in the 1920s gambled successfully on the new, sound technology, again took a major initiative by agreeing to film forty hour-long action-adventure episodes for the network. ABC paid $3.5 million for the programs and the right to rebroadcast twelve of them. Of the three alternating programs—two of them based on the hit movies *King's Row* and *Casablanca*—only the television original, *Cheyenne,* became a hit television series. It ran from 1955 to 1963 with its filmed western action and made a star of Clint Walker. Kintner also convinced Walt Disney to film television shows, which proved tremendously popular. By 1956 most major studios were filming episodic series for television and had sold the rights to telecast nearly two thousand pre-1948 feature films.

"Starting with Jack Warner and his film shows," television veteran Perry Lafferty observed, "the live TV shows were doomed." Lafferty felt that dramatic anthologies, which were basically limited to four-walled studios, simply could not compete with "guys running up and down the streets, in cars, with guns, shooting at each other, and chases."[19] Without action stories to fill program schedules and provide basic plots, the 11 or 12 live network anthologies needed 450 or so good dramatic scripts every season, enough material to last years on the stage, where shows played to new audiences every night, and even in Hollywood, where major movie studios in 1955 made only about 250 films. Besides demanding so many plays, television drama anthologies also had to satisfy the tastes of a changing audience. When the price of sets dropped and television reached a mass audience, the appeal of live drama's talky, introspective scripts declined. "Our total audience then was about 20 percent of today's audience," observed Worthington Miner of *Studio One*. "There's a law of diminishing return when you increase an audience. That 20 percent is now the expendable part of the audience."[20] The new, broader audience had more of a taste for movie action and adventure than for the best drama that live theater could produce. Live drama was also at a decided economic disadvantage. While inexperienced television producers fought a losing battle with cost control, movie studios adeptly turned out entertaining, low-budget programs. The series that Hollywood made for television took the place, the form, and much of the audience of "B" movies. Another major advantage of filmed shows over live shows was that after the broadcast the film could be rerun, which decreased the demand for new material. The filmed shows could also be sold to other stations, or dubbed and marketed abroad, which increased the profit per show. In the late 1950s Hollywood replaced Broadway as a major influence on television.

As films were replacing live performances on television, Ampex, in 1956, introduced videotape, a system of recording and reproducing high-quality pictures and sound magnetically on tape, which offered television many advantages over film. With videotape, stations could record network telecasts and with no loss of clarity rebroadcast them locally in better time slots. Using this technique networks overcame the three-hour time difference between East and West and could

schedule programs for the same hour throughout the country. Videotape, which was cheap, reusable, and could be replayed instantly, also
cut production time and costs. Mobile videotape cameras revolutionized television news by allowing cameras to range freely and to bring
breaking stories quickly into people's homes. The instant replay, stop-
action, slow motion, and quick cutting from long shots to closeups that
videotape made possible enabled football, with twenty-two people exploding in short spurts of violent action, to surpass baseball, with its
slower, more easily followed action, as television's most popular sport.
Videotape even influenced entertainment formats. Quick electronic
editing made possible rapid-fire, kaleidoscopic barrages of disjointed
images in such distinctive *television* programs as *Rowan and Martin's
Laugh-In* and *Sesame Street*.

Just as it did with programming, television adopted radio's system
of commercial sponsorship. But the uneven distribution of early television stations made national advertisers reluctant to shift their major
budgets from radio. As late as 1952 the nation had only 108 television
stations in operation. Cities such as Austin, Denver, Little Rock, and
Portland had none. In late 1951 AT&T cables and microwave relays
made coast-to-coast television networks a reality, and the number of
stations and sets increased every year, which lured big advertisers to
the tube. Sponsors were also attracted by the response some television
ads received. In 1950 Hazel Bishop lipstick, with sales of $50,000, be-
gan advertising exclusively on television. In 1953 it had sales of $4.5
million. By the 1956-57 season television was truly national. America
had over 500 stations, three major networks, and some 40 million
homes with television sets, which people watched about five hours a
day, making television an irresistible way for advertisers to reach national audiences. Following radio patterns, sponsors usually bought
shows and the time to broadcast them. In October 1955 the networks
controlled only half of the 844 hours of weekly network shows and
produced only half of the 20 new shows scheduled for 1957-58. Advertisers, rather than networks, were determining television schedules in
the late 1950s.

Network executives, long unhappy that sponsors' control often left
networks with poorly designed, non-competitive schedules, used a
1959 scandal about sponsors' rigging major quiz shows to seize control
of scheduling. Network control of programs and schedules fundamentally changed television as a business. Instead of selling blocks of time
to sponsors or advertising agencies to fill as they chose, *networks* se-

lected and scheduled the shows and then gave businesses a chance to sponsor them. In the 1960s sponsor influence on programming was further weakened when high production costs made it virtually impossible for one company to sponsor an entire program. By 1971 ninety-three out of every hundred network shows had more than one sponsor. No longer did networks sell time at flat rates for given time periods. Instead, they sold thirty-second or one-minute "spots" to sponsors at prices that varied with the show's rating and demographic analysis. Ratings took on a new meaning. In radio and early television, the *sponsor* used ratings to judge the size of the audience. After 1960, the *network* used ratings to decide how much to charge the sponsor for a spot; ratings determined network income. For *The Flip Wilson Show,* for instance, NBC began in September 1970 with a rate of $46,000 per commercial minute, but as the show's popularity climbed, so did the price, which reached $80,000 per minute only four months after the show's debut.

The selection and scheduling of shows, obviously, became a central concern of the television networks. By 1969-70, program proposals had to go through at least five major steps, each reviewed and scrutinized by network committees until a pilot was finally produced—at a cost of about $600,000 for a one-hour show. This slow process of decision-by-committee stood in great contrast to the early days of television when ideas were virtually tried out on the air. The stakes had become so high that risk-taking had to be minimized, which was done by putting the responsibility on committees, not on individuals. Like other large modern institutions, television networks suffered the problems of bureaucratic thinking and decision-making. Insecure executives tended to choose tried and true formats and formulas rather than risky innovations that might be either great successes or disastrous failures. "We don't pick the shows we think will have the best chance of becoming popular," a network executive admitted in 1970. "To be honest, we're attracted to those that seem to have the least chance of failing." A frustrated agent complained that whatever he proposed to the networks ended up as "something very reminiscent of one or two shows that have been seen before. Everything on television becomes a composition of stale ideas that once worked."[21]

By the early 1970s ABC, dead last in the ratings, was in a position to gamble. When it found a man who ignored the committee system and relied on the same personal sense of audience moods and tastes that had always characterized top showmen, the network rose to the top. That man was Fred Silverman, who at age twenty-five had become director of daytime programming for CBS in 1964, and who in 1970 had taken over all its programming. In 1975 he moved to ABC as chief of programming. ABC did not have a single show in the top ten in 1974-75, but the following season it had five of the top ten shows, and the year after that it could boast seven of the top ten. What thrust ABC from last to first was Silverman's blend of youth-oriented, situation comedies such as *Happy Days* and *Laverne & Shirley,* sexy shows such as *Rich Man, Poor Man* and *Charlie's Angels,* and violent action such as *The Six Million Dollar Man* and *Baretta,* a lineup promoted extensively during the ABC telecasts of the 1976 Olympic Games, which drew many new viewers to the network. In 1978 Silverman reached the top of the business when he moved to NBC as president of the entire network operation at a salary reported at a million dollars a year. Yet, in 1981 Silverman, who proved a better programmer than he did a network president, resigned from NBC.

For networks the race for ratings was a race for profits. Even when the ratings spreads seemed relatively slight, the stakes were incredibly high. In 1977-78, when first place ABC was watched by only an estimated 2.7 percent more homes than third place NBC, ABC reportedly outgrossed NBC by something like $65,000,000. Advertising revenues, not entertainment for its own sake, remained the basic goal of broadcasters. Shows did not just have to draw large audiences, they had to draw the *right* large audiences as determined by demographic analysis of viewers. In 1969-70 even though CBS shows starring Red Skelton and Jackie Gleason were the most popular programs in their time slots, sponsors shied away from them because their audiences were too old. As a result CBS made only a slight profit on Skelton and lost money on Gleason. Despite top ratings, both shows were cancelled. "Television is a medium not so much for entertainment as for selling products," reminded Screen Actors' Guild executive John L. Dales. "Actors and actresses are the frosting on the cake mix, the medicine show that comes with cough syrup."[22]

Television advertising began as basically radio with pictures, what people in news reporting called "the talking head"—Arthur Godfrey raving about the pleasures of Lipton tea or Bill the Bartender boasting about Pabst Blue Ribbon beer. Then advertising agencies began to make fuller use of television's visual dimension with eye-catching advertising symbols, like the Old Gold dancing cigarette pack, and appetite-whetting shots, like a beautiful slice of white meat rolling off a

Swift Butterball turkey—a shot that required two days of production time, sixty-one turkeys, and the services of a professional slicer. In the 1960s commercials became much more sophisticated as the price of advertising time mounted and as advertising agencies turned to complex technology to make commercials appealing enough to "stop the lady with the full bladder for one full minute."[23] Advertisers caught people's attention with spectacular scenes, like the beautiful woman in a chiffon dress and a shiny new convertible on a Colorado pinnacle 2000 feet above the desert; with special effects, like giant arms coming out of washing machines or carless drivers steering down the street; or with lavish production numbers such as a thirty-second canned soup ad featuring tap-dancer Ann Miller and a large cast directed by Busby Berkeley, which reportedly cost $250,000, or some $8300 a second.

Television viewers, like radio listeners, gladly accepted commercials. In a 1960 national poll designed by Gary A. Steiner, people were asked if they would "rather pay a small amount yearly if they could have television without commercials," and only one out of every four said yes, which was the same attitude expressed about radio commercials in the 1940s. The poll also asked if the people sampled would agree that "I would prefer TV without commercials," which was loaded in the affirmative since people are more inclined to agree than disagree. But only 43 percent agreed! Well over half the people sampled said they preferred TV *with* commercials.[24] Besides the unconscious association people probably made between commercials and entertaining programs, many people felt the commercials were informative and entertaining. Since television commercials were the most expensive and most carefully planned, researched, written, produced, and edited shows on television, it is no wonder people vividly and affectionately recalled masterful commercials.

The American public loved television. Extensive surveying in the 1960s revealed that over 60 percent of the public considered television the invention in the last 25 years that had done the most to make life more enjoyable. Steiner's 1960 poll showed more than three-quarters of the people happy with what was on television and unable to think of anything else they wanted. Even the 25 percent of the public that criticized television programming watched essentially, the same escapist shows as the general pro-television public.[25] Still, many of the criticisms of programming were well founded. Television does seem to have detrimental effects on children who are virtually raised and socialized by it. But even though television may contribute to deeply disturbing modern problems—parental irresponsibility, hedonism, low levels of literacy and culture, and increasing violence and inhumanity—it can not fairly be charged with creating these problems. If television fare often resembles cafeteria food, it should be no surprise. It is doing the equivalent of delivering meals every hour of every day and night to tens of millions of homes. For all its weaknesses and shortcomings, television has brought more entertainment to more people than ever before in history.

Television's enormous popularity forced radical changes in other entertainment media. Although movies changed markedly in the age of television, it was radio that underwent the most profound and pervasive changes. Radio emerged from World War II at the height of its popularity and with its form and content intact. In 1950 network radio broadcast over one hundred series that had been on the air at least ten years, and a dozen others, led by *Amos 'n' Andy,* that were nearly as old as network radio. The major impact of television on radio did not come until after 1954 when the new medium became truly national and siphoned off radio's national advertisers, forcing radio to make its most basic changes since the late 1920s. From national networks broadcasting a wide range of entertainment designed for the general public, radio increasingly specialized in attracting narrow, local audiences by broadcasting one particular style of recorded music, such as jazz, rock and roll, classical, rhythm and blues, traditional pop, Latin, or country and western. This approach attracted sponsors who wanted to target their commercials at specific groups, and radio prospered. For most people, radio became a supplement to television, by providing the music and news people wanted when they wanted them, at home, in cars, or almost anywhere else. Transistorized portable radios even allowed people to carry music with them wherever they went. For some groups, such as teenagers, minorities, and intellectuals, radio became a kind of in-group communication, a central part of group identity.

When radio switched to local programming and recorded music, radio and the record business dovetailed as never before. This relationship was symbolized by radio's new star, the disc jockey, the man who introduced and played the records. By the early 1950s the power of disc jockeys to make hits out of the records they played and plugged was clearly evident. Deejays, as they were often called, could even create new markets, as Alan Freed did when he got white teenagers to buy rhythm and blues records originally intended for black listeners. Even though radio stations were local, or at most regional, broadcasters, the key disc jockeys, like Alan Freed, became national hit-makers. Every week the major trade publications printed charts of the records big-city deejays played most often, charts that stations all over the country then used to decide what records to play. In the lucrative youth market, radio stations evolved a simple, reliable format—Top 40. Using national pop charts and local sales figures, the station drew up a list of only forty records, which it played over and over for a week, with the Top 10 being broadcast as many as thirty or forty times a day. For records on the play list, sales were almost assured. But in the highly competitive record business getting on the lists was as difficult as it was essential.

To get exposure for their new releases with important deejays, record companies used the tried and true American way. They bought it. Payola, giving money or valuables to disc jockeys to play records, became widespread in radio. "Nobody will admit to paying off, and nobody will admit to getting paid," a music business executive explained off-the-record in 1957. "But trying to plug a tune without putting your hand in your pocket would be like trying to bail out a leaky rowboat with a pair of chopsticks."[26] In 1959 the lid blew off undercover payola, exposing disc jockeys throughout the nation who took money, gifts, trips, and even part ownership of record companies or distributorships, in exchange for plugging records. Payola became a federal crime, but it did not disappear because the stakes and the competition were high and the number of major outlets was low.

The post-World War II explosion of modern technology that produced television and transformed radio also radically changed every facet of the phonograph and record businesses. In the late 1940s, the perfection of tape recording, converting sound into electrical impulses, magnetically encoding them on tape, and then decoding the impulses to reproduce sound, revolutionized recording. Besides providing excellent fidelity, tape—which could be cut and spliced back together— made it possible to record several versions of the same music and then combine the best segments of each into a final product that was better than any of the takes. Tape recording also made entry into the record business much easier by greatly reducing the equipment needed. Between 1949 and 1954 the number of recording companies exploded from eleven to two hundred. Records themselves also changed. In 1948 Columbia introduced a new 33⅓ rpm long-playing record (LP) by unveiling two stacks of records, each containing 325 selections. The pile of LPs stood about fifteen inches high, while the conventional 78 rpm records towered well over a man's head to a height of eight feet! RCA Victor responded with 45 rpm records that held no more music than 78s, but were lighter, smaller, more durable, easier to store, and more quickly and cheaply shipped. The 45s replaced 78s in the single song, pop record market, while LPs dominated the classical and traditional popular music markets. For the first time average Americans were also able to buy high fidelity phonographs and recordings.

In the late 1950s, with these technological developments, record sales grew rapidly—from $277 million in 1955 to $460 million in 1957. These were the years when radio converted to recorded music, and when huge sales of rhythm and blues and rock and roll records established that there were large markets for 45 rpm singles produced for minority groups and teenagers. With a few notable exceptions like RCA Victor, which had Elvis Presley, and Decca, which had Bill Haley and the Comets and Buddy Holly, major record companies tended to leave the rock and roll, 45 rpm market to new, independent companies specializing in this music. The major companies could afford to downplay the youth singles market because long-playing albums of traditional music—pop, classical, and musicals—were selling so well. In 1955 LPs accounted for over half the dollar value of record sales in America. By 1960 that figure was about 80 percent. Original cast albums of stage and screen musicals led the way, *The Sound of Music* topping the list with sales of 15 million albums.

But in the late-1960s youth music invaded the LP field in a big way, beginning with The Beatles' *Sgt. Pepper's Lonely Hearts Club Band* (1967), an LP which sold more than seven million copies. After that, major record companies moved into youth music. "When we saw the numbers that those records could sell in, we said 'Wow, there's something here,'" explained an executive of Warner Brothers Records. "You'd struggle with a middle-of-the-road artist to sell maybe 300,000 albums when you could sell two million Jimi Hendrix albums. Frank Sinatra never sold two million albums. Dean Martin never sold two million albums."[27] The reason for the great rise in sales of rock LPs was not just that young people had money to spend on records. That had been true for decades. In the late-1960s a new youth "counter-culture" emerged—the world of hippies, love-ins, and psychodelic drugs—with rock music at its core, music which was made possible by major technological innovations, especially stereophonic sound and complex recording techniques.

Stereophonic sound, put very simply, reproduces the way people actually hear, with fine distinctions made between the sounds reaching each ear which gives depth and complexity to recorded music. By the early 1960s stereo was widely accepted. By the mid-1960s youth music had grown very complex—rhythmically, melodically, and instrumentally—and could no longer be captured on short, monaural 45s as early rock and roll had been. Rock albums also grew increasingly dependent on studio engineers whose highly sophisticated electronic and taping equipment could isolate every instrument and voice, control its quality, add or delete elements of all sorts, and mix the sounds into any form or structure. The resulting music, in many cases, was not only impossible to reproduce in live performance, but could not have been produced at all without studio technology and technicians. *Sgt. Pepper's Lonely Hearts Club Band* reportedly took hundreds of hours to produce, blending the Beatles' instrumentals and voices with crowd noises, barking dogs, kazoos, calliopes, barnyard animals, and a full symphony orchestra. In one of the songs, "A Day in the Life," the music of a full orchestra was built up by laying track over track on the tape to achieve a feeling of waves of shining, soaring sound that climaxed in a crashing crescendo. This stunning effect was entirely the product of the modern recording industry's sophisticated technology.

In the late-1960s the structure of the recording industry changed in ways that paralleled the decline of major movie studios as production units and the rise of independent movie producers. Head-strong popular rock groups frequently clashed with major record companies over work schedules, life styles, and the large amount of time and money the groups spent perfecting their albums. As a result it became common for independent record producers, sometimes for the groups themselves, to create the albums and for major companies to market and distribute them. By the end of the 1960s as many as 80 percent of all records may have been the work of independent producers.

The final change in the record and phonograph industry in this period was the development of tape equipment and recordings with broad, mass appeal. Tape previously had been important only to the recording industry and to a relatively small number of "hifinatics" who used reel-to-reel tapes and equipment too costly and cumbersome for the general public. But in the late-1960s the industry introduced self-contained, stereo tape cartridges which just had to be popped into playback equipment and turned on. Though these eight-track cartridges were unable to record or to replay selections without going through the whole tape, they proved very popular, especially for cars. By 1975, sales of cartridges, used primarily in automobiles, reached nearly $600 million, a quarter of all recorded music sales. In 1969 the industry produced small, self-contained tape cassettes that could run backward or forward, record or replay, skip to specific selections, and hold as much as an LP. These mass-produced cassettes made all the advantages of tape—high-quality sound, long wear, and ease of storage—available, affordable, easy to use, and very popular. By 1970 cassettes accounted for nearly a third of recorded music sales, and in 1971 the value of tape players sold exceeded that of phonographs.

By the mid-1970s, the end of the third major period of entertainment machines in the home, average Americans took for granted an astonishing number and variety of entertainment machines—televisions, phonographs, radios, and tape machines. In the early years of the twentieth century, only dreamers or lunatics thought there were disembodied voices, music, and specters whirling about in the air. Now the overwhelming majority of Americans get their entertainment from voices, music, and specters whirling about in the air, which remain unseen and unheard until people turn on wonder-working machines that transform this cacophony into entertainment.

In the late-1970s a new phase in entertainment in the home seemed to be beginning. Television, the most popular entertainment machine, faced major new challenges. Videotape and equipment that previously had been the preserve of technicians within the industry was becoming available and affordable for the general public, just as audiotape had become in the late-1960s. Using videotape equipment, the public could record and replay free telecasts and could purchase or rent video recordings of major movies and other attractions. Pay television offered people a wide range of films, sports, and other attractions that they might otherwise have gone out to see. Telecasting via satellite made it possible to diversify broadcasting and to reach the entire nation inexpensively, so television channels began to specialize in one type of programming and to appeal to specific, not general, audiences, as radio had done in the 1950s. Even as the sociological, psychological, and spiritual costs of having technology do more and more things for more and more people become evident, there is no evidence that the American people want to rid themselves of their entertainment machines or to reverse the revolution that has made even the most modest American home an amusement palace.

Beginning in the 1820s, masses of ordinary Americans crammed into theaters to watch popular plays like this production of *Pocahontas* at New York City's immense Bowery Theatre. *Harvard Theatre Collection.*

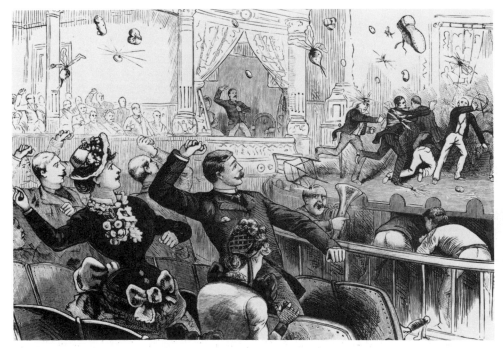

Interaction between boisterous nineteenth-century audiences and popular performers was at the heart of live show business. A White Plains, New York, audience routing an inferior minstrel troupe. *Harvard Theatre Collection.*

In the heyday of live show business, theaters of all sorts dotted the American countryside. Casino Theatre in Portland, Oregon. *Harvard Theatre Collection.*

Popular tastes for authentic-looking shows prompted producers to use realistic sets and live animals on stage. A 1901 production of *Uncle Tom's Cabin*. *Harvard Theatre Collection.*

Modern rock musicians recaptured the excitement of live performances for a new generation of audiences. The Rolling Stones from *Gimme Shelter* (1971). *Author's Collection.*

After film pre-empted most popular theatrical genres, stage musicals maintained their broad appeal by stressing the artifice and fantasy inherent in the genre and in the medium. The "Dream Ballet" from *Oklahoma!* (1943). *Vandamm photograph from The Billy Rose Theatre Collection, New York Public Library at Lincoln Center.*

Film closeups greatly intensified the emotional impact of acting, which helped compensate for the silent movie's lack of dialogue. Lillian Gish and Richard Barthelmess in D. W. Griffith's *Broken Blossom* (1919).

The colossal Babylon set built for D. W. Griffith's *Intolerance* (1916) demonstrated the spectacle that only film could capture.

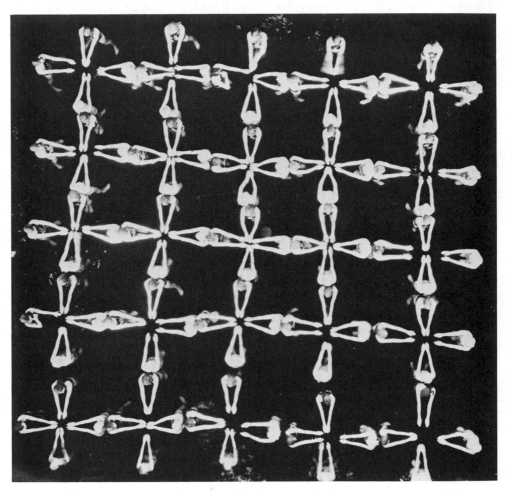

Using unusual camera placements, as in this overhead shot, director Busby Berkeley could transform 100 swimmers into an abstract kaleidoscopic pattern. *Footlight Parade* (1933).

Film's ability to capture the massive scale and grandeur of the West made the motion picture the most successful medium for westerns. John Ford's *Stagecoach* (1939). *Film Stills Archive, Museum of Modern Art.*

Orson Welles combined dramatic stage lighting with the art of film camera work to achieve powerful visual effects. Note the woman to the left of the fireplace who is dwarfed by the lighting and perspective. *Citizen Kane* (1941).

Space age special effects and fantasies play major roles in contemporary hit movies. *Close Encounters of the Third Kind* (1980). *Author's Collection.*

The phonograph first reached the general public in the early 1890s in penny arcades as an entertainment machine that could be enjoyed by only one person at a time. *Division of Musical Instruments, Smithsonian Institution.*

In the 1890s phonographs began the revolution in home entertainment. Before long the 1905 Columbia Gramophone's promise of "A Theatre in Your Home" became a reality. *Author's Collection.*

Before electrical microphones and amplifiers, orchestras had to set up in clumsy configurations and to use unorthodox instruments like the Stroh Violin—the stringed instrument with horn attached—in order to get their music to the recording horn. The Victor Salon Orchestra recording. *Clark Collection, Smithsonian Institution.*

The jukebox allowed people in public facilities as well as people at home to listen to the recorded music of their choice, which contributed to the development of specialized music markets. Wurlitzer Jukebox, 1946. *Division of Musical Instruments, Smithsonian Institution.*

The modern home music machine reproduces the high quality sound of performances of all sorts, whether recorded on 45 rpm singles, 33⅓ rpm albums, or tape. *Author's Collection.*

By the mid-1920s radios—in this case the horn on the shelf—were bringing popular entertainment into the homes of working Americans. *Clark Collection, Smithsonian Institution.*

Radio, with its evocative sound effects specialists and its performers with expressive voices, had horizons as wide as its listeners' imaginations. *Gangbusters'* cast and sound effects men in action. *The Billy Rose Theatre Collection, New York Public Library at Lincoln Center.*

N.B.C. sound effects man Ed Ludes beat coconut shells on gravel to make listeners "see" a galloping horse. *The Billy Rose Theatre Collection, New York Public Library at Lincoln Center.*

The sound effects man for *Dick Tracy* used elaborate equipment, including a wide range of recordings. *The Billy Rose Theatre Collection, New York Public Library at Lincoln Center.*

By the late 1940s television was bringing the sights as well as the sounds of show business into American homes. Note the ad's attempt to dignify the new medium by using formally dressed viewers. Ad for 1949 DuMont Bradford Television. *DuMont Collection, Smithsonian Institution.*

With his warm informality Arthur Godfrey made the celebrity "talk show" a basic staple of the intimate medium. Arthur Godfrey and The Chordettes on *Arthur Godfrey and Friends* in 1951. *The Billy Rose Theatre Collection, New York Public Library at Lincoln Center.*

Edward R. Murrow, more than anyone else, established the journalistic credibility of television news. *See It Now. The Billy Rose Theater Collection, New York Public Library at Lincoln Center.*

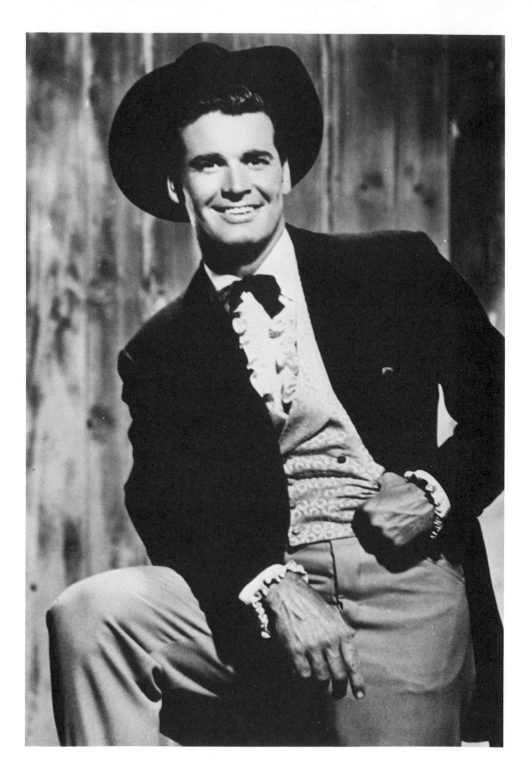

Live telecasts of sports—always popular television attractions—improved greatly because of modern video technology, including portable mini-cameras and long distance microphones. This technology also revolutionized news coverage, allowing it to broadcast events as they happened. *Monday Night Football. American Broadcasting Company.*

James Garner's expressive face and voice made him one of the greatest stars of the medium that emphasized closeups and characterization. *Maverick. The Billy Rose Theatre Collection, New York Public Library at Lincoln Center.*

Modern television has become so complex that even in a mobile control van at a live football broadcast the director must watch shots on some twenty monitors. *Monday Night Football. American Broadcasting Company.*

3

A Helluva Lot More American:
Westerns and the Media

The first white settlers on the Atlantic seaboard looked back over their shoulders, their eyes, minds, and hearts focused on Europe. But within a short time, European colonists became American settlers, and their focus shifted from the Old World to the New World, from east to west. From Puritan times on, West meant the frontier, where white people confronted the wilderness and the Indians, where European civilization clashed with what it called savagery, where America began to take shape. Since the Colonial period, the West, in this sense of an elemental environment where men and women fought against great odds to build a new society, has fascinated Americans and people all over the world in literature, legend, and entertainment. "Well, it's as classic as Italian opera," explained ex-cowboy turned movie actor Jack Montgomery of the enduring appeal of the western saga, "and it's a helluva lot more American!"[1]

Of all the major American entertainment genres only one—the western—took its name from a geographical region. Crime shows, for instance, were not called "easterns." The key to the western, then, was its setting, which was at once specific and mythic. Though much of America at one time had gone through a frontier stage, western lore by the early twentieth century centered on the vast, unsettled area between the Mississippi River and the West Coast, the area settled by whites after the Civil War, the area of cattle drives, Indians, outlaws, cavalry, and isolated settlements. Though this West had once actually existed, it became a symbol of the last, big American wilderness. While nominally set in the Great Plains, the western's most characteristic physical setting became the austere, inhospitable Southwest with its parched desert wastelands surrounded by soaring mountain peaks and punctuated with majestic, weatherworn buttes, like a vision of an alien planet. As commonly portrayed, then, the West was an exotic, timeless setting for American myths. This setting inspired spinners of tales—from dime novelists through Zane Grey to Louis Lamour—who created a wide variety of stories, ranging from simple, uncomplicated action adventures between the forces of good and evil to complex, sophisticated studies of psychological, social, and cultural issues. Westerns also became part of every major show business medium. The central themes, styles, heroes, and popularity patterns varied with changing times and tastes, but they also varied with the media.

The West had been part of American entertainment at least since the 1840s, when P. T. Barnum brought buffaloes, Indians, and other curiosities to the East. But the first big western star in American show business was William F. "Buffalo Bill" Cody, who gained fame as an actual buffalo hunter, cavalry scout, and Indian fighter in the late 1860s when he also became the hero of popular dime novels. In 1872 Cody entered show business by appearing in a Chicago theater in *Scouts of the Plains,* a show that featured Buffalo Bill swapping stories with his friend Texas Jack. Whenever the ad-libbed dialogue lagged, which was often, war-whooping Indians charged; the shooting started; and Buffalo Bill and his sidekicks "killed" the same Indians time after time. Though critics found little of merit in the show, audiences loved watching a genuine western hero fight real Indians. In the 1870s Buffalo Bill remained a bigger than life figure by periodically returning to the Indian Wars that raged in the northern plains. After General George Custer and his troops were annihilated at the Little Big Horn, Buffalo Bill, according to his effective publicity agent, was the first to gain revenge by taking "the first scalp for Custer." The bloody act was glamorized in inexpensive engravings of Cody standing over a scalped Indian and in his show, *Red Right Hand, or Buffalo Bill's First Scalp for Custer,* in which he re-created the great event every night along with his usual series of shoot-outs.

Buffalo Bill was a great attraction in the nation's theaters, especially in eastern cities. But he was an absolute knockout when promoters turned him loose in outdoor arenas. The confines of the stage simply could not capture the scale and spectacle of Cody's epic. The Wild West Show was born in 1883 in a large New York arena when Cody acted out his version of the history of the West—Indian villages, scouts, trappers, buffalo hunts, wagon trains, the Pony Express, Indian attacks, cavalry rescues, and the Black Hills wars. With huge casts, enormous amounts of equipment and livestock, and non-stop action, Cody's spectacles of the West were great successes. But they could not play year round in the harsh winters of the heavily populated East. After filling a Staten Island arena in good weather in 1886-87, Cody hoped to cash in on the show's popularity during the bad winter weather and moved into Madison Square Garden, which was large enough to house huge three-ring circuses. But when the Wild West Show moved indoors, it suffered. "Those who have seen the Wild West Show in an open field," a reviewer warned, "will not care for it at the Garden" because "its wildness and savagery" have been lost to "tame theatricality."[2] Once audiences glimpsed the possibilities of exciting, realistic-looking action, they wanted westerns to have the limitless scale of the great outdoors. Although western melodramas such as *The Girl of the Golden West* (1905) remained popular, the live stage could not hold the wide-open spaces and rip-roaring action audiences wanted to see in western epics. Cody took his Wild West Show back into the open air and toured with it almost until his death in 1917. By then he had become essentially a nostalgic relic. The western certainly had not faded in popularity. It had been taken over by a new entertainment machine.

Film was a perfect medium for the western for the most basic reason: moviemakers could take their cameras into the wilderness, record free-wheeling action, and bring the great outdoors into the smallest theaters. It is not surprising that the first story movie to score a great hit with the public was Edwin Porter's western, *The Great Train Robbery* (1903), a one-reel, eleven-minute film. Moviegoers loved Porter's combination of film technique and western action and filled theaters over and over again to see the exciting picture. In the wake of the *The Great Train Robbery*'s success came a flood of short, repetitive westerns that moviemakers shot as quickly as possible to meet the demands of the booming nickelodeon business. But by 1910 the novelty of westerns had worn off, and critics had begun to object to the lack of realism in many of the pictures made in the East by people who knew little if anything about the West. Reviews complained about the silly-looking "dude" clothing, the obviously painted backdrops, and other anachronisms like a cavalry troop galloping out of a frontier fort and onto a paved road with a sewer. By 1909 *Variety* was regularly ending its reviews of westerns with the observation that "it has all been done so often before, and usually better."[3] But at that time, moviemakers were on the eve of major developments that would produce the enduring features and techniques of film westerns.

By late 1908 Gilbert M. Anderson, who had played a small part in *The Great Train Robbery*, had become a moviemaker. His search for an area with authentic western settings and a climate that would allow more filming days took him to Niles Canyon, southeast of San Francisco. Besides seeking greater realism, Anderson concluded that westerns also needed a central character, a hero, which was an innovative idea in those pre-movie star days. Using his hefty frame and rugged looks, Anderson became his own star, creating the striking cowboy hero Broncho Billy in about 1910. Broncho Billy was so popular that Anderson played him in a series of short westerns with strong clear plots, effective action, realistic clothing, believable sets, and good camera work. Whether Broncho Billy began a picture as an outlaw, a lawman, or a doctor, whether he ended up fighting for religion, temperance, or justice, he was always on the side of goodness. By 1915 Anderson had made hundreds of short pictures, clearly establishing the appeal of the western hero who was tough with men, shy with women, and at home in the saddle.

With the appeal of outdoor action and of the individual hero well established, westerns were beginning to take the cinematic shape they would maintain. D. W. Griffith added his great technical artistry to the western by demonstrating the effectiveness of cross-cutting between parallel lines of action. In *Fighting Blood* (1911), for instance, Indians attack western settlers who cluster in a cabin to make their last stand while a boy rides off to get the cavalry. For most of the picture Griffith cut back and forth between the battling settlers, the attacking Indians, the hard-riding boy, the terrorized children in the cabin, and the cavalry racing to the rescue. The rapidly alternating images, which varied from long shots to closeups, relentlessly built tension and anticipation until finally the cavalry arrived. For the climactic battle Griffith pulled his camera back to a broad, panoramic shot that put together all the previously separated components in one grand, unifying shot. Such cross-cutting became a standard film technique in the action western, a technique made even more effective by continually decreasing the length of time each shot was held on screen, so the pace of the film accelerated with the pace of the action.

In 1911 Thomas H. Ince, in Los Angeles, added spectacle to the western film by hiring the Miller Brothers' 101 Ranch Wild West Show, one of the many spin-offs from Buffalo Bill's success. The Wild West Show gave Ince a huge Western stock company—longhorned cattle, buffalo, horses, prairie schooners, stagecoaches, cowboys, cowgirls, and Indians—which he used to make large-scale westerns centered on the wars between Indians and whites. By the end of 1912 Ince had produced a number of action-packed two-reelers on a massive scale, giving the war for the West the convincing look of an authentic saga. "The impression that it all leaves," *Moving Picture World* wrote of Ince's *War on the Plains* in January 1912, "is that we have looked upon a presentation of Western life that is real and that is true to life, and that we would like to see it again and again so as to observe more of the details."[4]

Western realism and the western hero took on new meaning in the work of William S. Hart. A veteran stage actor who had grown up in the West and had remained fascinated with western history, Hart was disgusted when he saw a sheriff in a movie western looking like "a cross between a Wisconsin woodchopper and a Gloucester fisherman."[5] In 1914, he made his first western two-reelers, which were popular enough that he expanded to feature-length films. The forty-four-year-old Hart was a great hit with his authentic western settings of dilapidated, frontier towns, his strong, believable action, his simple costumes that looked like outfits real cowboys would wear, and other down-to-earth details. With this stark realism, Hart blended Victorian morality and sentimentality, which he stressed by repeatedly playing a tough guy who was reformed by a good woman. *Hell's Hinges* (1916), one of his best films, demonstrated Hart's approach and appeal. The villainous boss of the tough town, Hell's Hinges, hires Hart to drive out a weak, young missionary and his sister, Faith, whose beauty, goodness, and piety convince Hart to change sides. But the missionary, corrupted by a dance-hall girl and by liquor, leads a drunken mob to burn the church while Hart is out of town. With the townspeople fleeing into the desert and a burning cross silhouetted against the sky, Hart returns, finds Faith alive, and in disgust burns the town down. Finally the couple walk off together to the mountains. The dramatically photographed melodramatic film was a great popular success. Its moralism and obvious religious symbolism had great appeal in the era of intense moral fervor surrounding World War I and the Prohibition movement. But Hart did so many similar pictures that even when the *Moving Picture World* praised *Hell's Hinges,* it also criticized Hart's "perpetual repetition of the Western badman reformed through the sweet and humanizing influence of a pure-minded-girl."[6] Yet, into the early 1920s, Hart continued with what he considered "the truth of the West" despite pressure from his studio and competition from a new type of hero.

   With breezy action-adventures that were just right for the light-hearted escapist 1920s, Tom Mix became a western star. If Hart represented the moralism of stage melodrama, Mix represented the showmanship of Wild West shows and rodeos, where he had worked as an entertainer. By 1917, having made some seventy to one hundred short movies featuring fast-riding, daredevil action, Mix signed with William Fox who added a dash of glamor to his new star by outfitting the tall, handsome Mix in fancy "dude" clothes and a white stetson hat. Mix generally played an invincible loner who singlehandedly fought weaker people's battles against outlaws or Indians. "I ride into a place owning my own horse, saddle, and bridle," Mix explained of his basic formula. "It isn't my quarrel, but I get into trouble doing the right thing for somebody else."[7] He was always pure of heart, never drank, swore, caroused, or used more force than necessary. He rarely killed villains, preferring to wound them, or better still to lasso them spectacularly. But no matter how ferocious the action, Mix never got dirt on his white hat—his symbol of goodness. As the Douglas Fairbanks of the western, Mix fixed the image of the pure, idealized, invincible western hero in the imagination of the American public.

   In the early 1920s, movie westerns added their last basic elements—vast panoramas of the American wilderness and monumental, epic themes. In 1923 director James Cruze filmed *The Covered Wagon,* the story of peaceful settlers crossing the Great Plains against the greatest human and natural adversities. Shot in primitive conditions in Nevada with a cast of thousands, the picture captured the sweep of the plains in shots of the wagon train struggling through roaring winds, scorching heat, parched desert, driving snow, and rampaging Indians, like a string of rowboats crossing a storm-tossed ocean full of pirates. Despite a trite romance, a heavy-handed villain, and unimaginative camera work, the colossal film captured the public's imagination and the critics' praise. Robert Sherwood called it "the one great American epic that the screen has produced."[8] Because of the film's popularity Hollywood produced three times as many westerns in 1924 as it had in 1923. One of these was John Ford's *Iron Horse*, the story of the men who built the first railroad to span the broad American continent. Ford had a monumental American theme: people from all over the world were forged together in the process of taming the wilderness with their sweat, determination, and lives. Though also shot on location in Nevada with a cast of nearly 5000 and a huge assortment of equipment, what most distinguished the film was Ford's film artistry. Besides dramatic panoramas of men and machines dwarfed by nature, or of Indians lining the crest of a hill, Ford filmed vast, carefully orchestrated, action scenes with as many as six cameras, some mounted on moving trucks and on the front of the train, so he could capture the action through the eyes of the attackers, the eyes of the attacked, and the eyes of neutral observers. With masterful editing, Ford moved viewers from the Indians attacking the railroad to the terrified passengers on the train, from the engineer pouring on the steam to the cavalry riding to the rescue. Epics like Cruze's and Ford's raised the stature, popularity, and artistry of westerns to new heights.

By the end of the silent film era the basic components of movie westerns were all well established—authentic, outdoor shoot-em-ups, vicious warfare between Indians and whites, rugged, realistic heroes, dashing western supermen, sweeping panoramas of the Great Plains, and epic struggles to establish civilization in the wilderness. Though sound could and did augment and amplify westerns, it did not fundamentally change the highly visual western genre as it did comedy, crime shows, and musicals.

The production and popularity of major movie westerns slumped during the 1930s, though Hollywood churned out a great many low-budget, action westerns during the Great Depression when the major action–adventure genre was crime. The public, concerned with law, order, and stability when the most basic American values and traditions seemed to be falling apart, looked to the government and President Franklin Delano Roosevelt to hold America together. In crime shows, as in the real world, government men solved the pressing problems of contemporary American cities, while in westerns, rootless individuals fought Indians and outlaws in distant times and places. The western and the crime genres seem to have had basically different

meanings and functions for the public, which meant that they had
their strongest appeal at different times. Westerns have tended to re-
tell myths about the heroic individuals produced by the American
land and have been most popular in stable, optimistic periods such as
1910-30 and 1950-65. Crime shows have tended to focus on immediate
concerns for law and order and have been most popular in unstable,
pessimistic periods such as 1930-50 and 1965-80. Obviously, these two
major action genres have overlapped, but the high points of one have
been the low points of the other. The thirties belonged to cops not to
cowboys.

The major new development in westerns during the Depression was
the emergence of the genre on radio. But the highly visual western,
which was so successful in silent pictures, was much less effective in
the new, sound-only medium. Even for inventive radio sound-effects
men, who could evoke a great many sights, there were no sounds for
an austere desert, a majestic mountain, a craggy butte, or a spiny cac-
tus. Settings, so central to westerns, were not one of radio's strengths.
Radio producers learned to concentrate on dialogue and on characterization in their series. The reliance on continuing characters was, in
itself, no problem for westerns, since stars like Hoot Gibson, Ken Maynard, and Tim McCoy made eight, low-budget "B" westerns a year, in
what amounted to episodic series. But because the motion picture industry refused to cooperate in any way with the potentially competitive new medium, radio was denied major movie studios' stars and
properties.

In 1933, Tom Mix, whose movie career was already finished, agreed
to let the Ralston Purina Company produce a radio show using his
name, though a radio actor played Mix. The Tom Mix Show was not
radio's first western, but it brought the glamor and familiarity of a famous movie star into people's homes. The show, which claimed to re-
count the adventurous past that movie publicists had created for Mix,
began as a serial with three installments a week and expanded to five
episodes a week in 1936. To make listeners feel the stories were true,
Mix and the other characters admitted that they were on the radio re-
creating their adventures. Designed for young listeners, the program
blended mystery, melodrama, action, adventure, and moralism. No
doubt to please parents, the show included a Ralston Straight Shooter
Pledge in which listeners took an oath to shoot straight with their par-

ents and friends by telling the truth, playing and working hard, and always trying to win but always being good losers. They also pledged to shoot straight with Tom Mix by eating the official Straight Shooter's cereal, because "I know Hot Ralston is just the kind of cereal that will help build a stronger America."[9] By the late 1930s, after exhausting the Mix legends, the show centered on the TM-Bar Ranch and on murders and other types of mystery stories that could have been plots for the detective-crime shows that were so popular on radio. The Mix show ran successfully on radio until 1950.

In 1934 WXYZ in Detroit believed that its successful year-old western would appeal to children all over the country, but it could not convince a network to carry it because programs about urban crime-fighters were the current rage. In fact George W. Trendle, owner of the independent station, had chosen to broadcast *The Lone Ranger* only because he wanted an inexpensive children's show and felt that parents would find a western more wholesome than a crime show. He also hoped to sell western gear if the show caught on. Uncertain about the appeal of a normal western, Trendle insisted on a strikingly different character. From Douglas Fairbanks's *Zorro* came the idea of a mask for the lone Texas Ranger who had survived an ambush and been nursed back to health by an Indian, Tonto, who called him "kemo sabe" and became his sidekick. Adding a white horse, Silver, and a mine that financed his crusade against evil and supplied him with his trademark, the silver bullet, Trendle produced an exciting hero who was introduced to listeners with the rousing sound of the William Tell Overture and by an announcer who set the mood with: "A fiery horse with the speed of light, a cloud of dust, and a hearty Hi-Yo Silver!— The Lone Ranger rides again!" Pure of heart and noble of purpose the Lone Ranger and Tonto rode the plains in the "thrilling days of yesteryear," fighting for law and order in stories that combined mystery, suspense, disguise, action, and the triumph of good over evil. The adventures commonly ended with the heroes riding off, leaving behind a silver bullet and thankful settlers wondering: "Say, who was that Masked Man anyway?" With its colorful characters and concept, the show was so popular that it gave birth to a radio network, the Mutual Broadcasting System, when WXYZ franchised the program to other stations. The *Lone Ranger* fought injustice three times every week for twenty-two years. But despite this and a few other exceptions, such as

Tom Mix, *Red Ryder*, and *The Cisco Kid*, westerns were not nearly as successful on radio as crime shows were. The western genre was simply too visual.

Ironically, the newest development in film westerns in the 1930s was vocal, not visual—the emergence of the singing cowboy. In 1935, in *In Old Santa Fe*, a typical "B" western starring Ken Maynard, a supporting player sang three songs, and a star was born. Gene Autry, a veteran of four years on the NBC country music radio show, *The National Barn Dance*, signed a movie contract in 1933 with Republic Pictures even though the studio realized Autry "knew nothing about acting, lacked poise, and was awkward."[10] Autry became a star in the late 1930s as a singing cowboy, an especially appealing image in an era when movie musicals were at their height and when crime was the dominant action genre. Autry, primarily a singer, built his pictures around music and light-hearted comedy instead of action and fighting, though the movies always had the requisite chases. Unlike typical western heroes, Autry played a fearless dude who strolled nonchalantly through villains and intrigues, strumming and singing his way to victories over evil, using his voice and songs as his basic arsenal. In *Red River Valley*, he calmed disgruntled dam workers by leading them in a song, conducting the chorus with his six-gun; in *Mexicali Rose* (1939), his song about Robin Hood persuaded a Mexican bandido to untie Autry and to go straight; in *South of the Border* (1939), he inspired terrified caballeros to join a cattle drive by singing to them. The singing cowboy movies were make-believe frolics, just as the non-western musicals of the period were.

Autry also crossed media lines. He and other singing cowboys, such as Tex Ritter and Roy Rogers, played a major role in giving popularized versions of country and western music a far wider audience than was reached by country and western radio shows such as *The National Barn Dance* and *Grand Ole Opry*. From "Tumbling Tumbleweeds" to "Rudolph the Red-nosed Reindeer," Autry had nine records that sold a million or more copies. Just as his music cultivated both the adult and children's markets, so did his radio program, which began in 1940 and ran for sixteen years. *Gene Autry's Melody Ranch* combined his typical movie plots with his songs and his "Ten Commandments of the Cowboy," a code that, like Mix's, stressed being patriotic, respectful, truthful, industrious, honest, and clean of mind and body. Though a popular part of the western genre, singing cowboys ultimately influenced popular music more than they did westerns, but they infused new vitality into the genre when its popularity was lagging. They also indicated that the children's market was becoming a major force in the movie, radio, and record businesses. But by the 1940s adults were turning back to westerns.

In 1939 director John Ford's first sound western, *Stagecoach,* reasserted the mythic qualities of the western and regained high status for the genre without losing its broad audience appeal. Beautifully photographed in Utah's dramatic Monument Valley with its tall, rugged rock formations towering over the stark, barren desert, the big-budget film captured the almost limitless scope, power, and grandeur of the inhospitable American wilderness. Into this menacing setting, which was also the home of hostile Indians, came a scattered assortment of whites riding in a lone stagecoach. In their battle for survival, the artificial distinctions of the East—manners, clothing, and pedigree—prove meaningless and useless. The people who emerge as natural leaders with real character and strength had been, in the past, a gambler, a prostitute, and an outlaw. Combining this theme of the West's producing natural aristocrats with fiery action, stunning settings, beautiful photography, fine direction, and excellent performances by Clair Trevor, Thomas Mitchell, John Carradine, Andy Devine, and John Wayne, the film was nominated for an Academy Award as best picture of the year and was also one of its most popular. *Stagecoach* triggered a new rage for major westerns, including William Wyler's *The Westerner* (1940), starring Gary Cooper; William Wellman's *The Ox-Bow Incident* (1943), with Dana Andrews, Francis Ford, and Anthony Quinn; and King Vidor's *Duel in the Sun* (1945), starring Gregory Peck and Jennifer Jones.

John Ford was the most powerful force shaping the modern western. Besides a keen eye for the right setting and the right shot that had made his visual artistry with the western evident as early as 1924 in the silent film, *The Iron Horse,* Ford also told western stories that had great appeal for Americans of the 1940s and 1950s. After making an outlaw the hero of *Stagecoach,* Ford found a new sort of hero in Monument Valley in 1946 in *My Darling Clementine,* which starred Henry Fonda as lawman Wyatt Earp in a story that symbolically reminded the public that World War II had been fought to preserve the democratic way of life the West had always stood for—the nobility, virtue, and freedom of the average American. The *New York Times* reviewer praised *My Darling Clementine* for showing audiences "the beauty of rugged people and a rugged world."[11] Despite its dramatic battle between good and evil at the O.K. Corral, the fine picture was far more than a well-directed action movie. The dedication of the town's church symbolized the planting of American civilization in the wilderness. With church bells tolling, American flags fluttering, towns-people frolicking, and fiddles playing, a gussied-up Wyatt Earp, the man who has used his gun to clear the way for settlement, uneasily, but gracefully swings into a square dance. But Earp finally rides off into the wilderness, even though "I wanted Wyatt to stay there and become a permanent marshall," Ford explained. "Instead of that, he had to ride away."[12] He had to ride away because of the myth he represented, the myth of the free, natural man who came out of the frontier, established order for a new society, and then restlessly returned to the freedom that spawned him. This myth was the heart of the classic, individual western hero.

In the wake of World War II Ford filmed another phase of the western myth—the war between white men and red men, between cavalry and Indians, for the territory of the West. In *Fort Apache* (1948), *She Wore a Yellow Ribbon* (1949), and *Rio Grande* (1950), Ford lionized the dedicated men of the U.S. Cavalry. Filmed in Monument Valley, *Fort Apache* co-starred Henry Fonda as an ambitious, unscrupulous, Indian-hating colonel who, like General Custer, wants to crush an Indian uprising to further his own career, and John Wayne as a cavalry veteran with respect for Indians, "the best light cavalry the world has ever known," a people he feels have been forced by white treachery to fight. But after Fonda is killed leading his troops into a foolish massacre and is falsely glorified as a martyr, Wayne takes over the command and participates in the hero worship because it is good for the army and for the country. In *She Wore a Yellow Ribbon*, Wayne played an aging cavalryman about to retire. The film begins after the destruction of Custer with Wayne and his small detachment trying to prevent the slaughter of all the scattered white settlers in the area. Ford masterfully creates the menacing mood with image after image of small groups of helpless whites dwarfed by the vast power of Monument Valley and hounded by large bands of vicious Indians. After trying unsuccessfully to make peace with an aging chief who complains that the young men cannot see beyond the glory of war to its anguish and will not listen to him, Wayne wins the battle if not the war with a night raid into the Indian camp to stampede their horses. The next day Wayne retires in an emotional ceremony that Ford filmed with Wayne's strong, weatherworn face in the foreground and the ageless enduring pillars of Monument Valley in the background. Ford ended the cavalry trilogy with *Rio Grande,* in which the thin, blue line again endured "all this danger to serve people as yet unborn."[13]

In *Wagonmaster* (1950), Ford returned to the epic struggle of settlers, in this case Mormons led by Ward Bond, who are seeking the promised land in the West where there is room for everyone to grow. The most striking feature of the film was the way Ford, like an abstract artist, used the wagontrain as a fine, moving line that weaved and bobbed across the fantastic shapes of the countryside. Such footage, which harked back to the silent classics that Cruze and Ford had made over a quarter of a century earlier, was a vivid reminder of the purely visual quality of the epic western, which made the western such an excellent genre for *film* whether silent or sound.

The 1950s—when large numbers of working Americans were moving into their own tract houses, filling their two-car garages, beginning to enjoy television broadcasts, and voting for Dwight Eisenhower—was a boom time for major western films with their hopeful, heroic visions of America. In this surge of production, the classic western reached its artistic and popular peak, one of the best examples being George Stevens's *Shane* (1953), which was nominated for six Academy Awards and was one of the year's box-office hits. The story begins with Shane, played by Alan Ladd, riding out of the soaring Grand Teton Mountains into a lush valley and going to work on a farm owned by homesteaders who are being intimidated by gunmen trying to drive off the settlers and return the land to open range. Shane, a soft-spoken gunslinger, refuses to fight when personally insulted, but does fight for the homesteaders. Ultimately, he destroys the villains, including an out-of-town gunfighter (Jack Palance) who wears the funereal black of the evil killer. The white-clad Shane then rides back to the mountains. Shane represented the classic western hero. With a mastery of violence, the freedom of the untamed, and a personal code of honor and morality, he was unable to turn his back on good people in need and unwilling to settle down, give up his independence, and live by society's rules. He stood for honor, courage, idealism, and freedom—traits many Americans wanted to believe all Americans possessed.

Westerns were also beginning to change in the early 1950s. In Fred

Zinnemann's *High Noon* (1952) hero Gary Cooper resigns as sheriff to settle down and marry Grace Kelly a Quaker schoolteacher who represents civilized eastern values. But when he learns that a killer he has sent to prison is being released and will arrive in town with his gang on the noon train, Cooper's honor compels him to face the killers, despite Kelly and his friends urging him to leave. The townspeople and his deputy refuse to stand with him, so he faces the four gunmen alone in a dramatic, mainstreet showdown. Finally, Kelly, choosing her man over her religion, picks up a gun and kills one of the outlaws. With her help, Cooper wins. Then, in disgust at the town he has made safe only to see it desert him, he throws his badge into the dirt and rides off with his wife. In contrast to *Shane*'s pure myth of the invincible western hero and the honorable settlers, *High Noon* depicted spineless townspeople and a vulnerable hero, who in director Howard Hawks's contemptuous terms, "runs around like a wet chicken trying to get people to help him" and "eventually his Quaker wife saves his guts."[14]

In 1956, the master of the genre, John Ford, returned the western to its mythic grandeur by focusing on a strong hero, again played by John Wayne, and on the elemental struggle of whites to survive in the alien environment that threatened their very existence. In *The Searchers*, when Wayne returns from chasing rustlers to find his brother's family massacred by Comanches who have carried off his two young nieces, Wayne and his adopted nephew begin a relentless quest to rescue the girls and avenge the killings. Year after year, he searches, enduring great suffering in the inhospitable beauty of the Southwest that Ford could photograph like no one else. In the search Wayne becomes a driven man with an unshakable Old Testament resolve and fanaticism that costs him his humanity. When he finally finds his surviving niece, a pretty young woman (Natalie Wood) who has been raised by and has chosen to live with Chief Scar, Wayne, like a tribal patriarch, almost kills her because she is a willing sexual partner of an Indian. In the end, he savagely scalps Chief Scar and takes his niece to live with a white family. Besides Wayne's powerful performance, the picture drew much of its overwhelming impact from Ford's masterful use of the landscape, which was made even grander by the vast, awe-inspiring images that were made possible by the era's huge movie screens. But, ironically, perhaps the single greatest impact on westerns after World War II came from the tiny screens of television.

In the late 1940s, when television emerged as a major entertainment medium and began to challenge movies for the general entertainment market, major motion picture studios refused to have anything to do with the new medium. But early television, which generally was performed and broadcast live, did air some old "B" pictures, the most important being the scores of popular Hopalong Cassidy movies that William Boyd had made in the late 1930s and early 1940s. With fine camera work, rapid-fire editing, and exciting background music, Boyd's films roared to thundering climaxes with posses riding hell-bent-for-leather to rescue Boyd or to help him capture outlaws. When the movie series ended in 1944, Boyd had become so identified with the role that he could get few other parts. After touring with a circus he and a partner in 1946 bought the rights to his movies and to the Hopalong Cassidy character and began to shoot new, low-budget pictures, which television stations snapped up. By 1950 some 60 stations around the country broadcast Hopalong Cassidy pictures. Boyd also filmed 52 half-hour Hopalong Cassidy programs, which made him television's first western star. More cowboys appeared on the tube when small financially pressured independent studios sold their backlogs of western films to television. In 1950 Republic sold its Gene Autry and Roy Rogers pictures for television broadcast, and Autry went into television production, making 91 half-hour Gene Autry shows, 78 half-hour episodes of *The Range Rider*, 81 of *Annie Oakley*, 42 of *Buffalo Bill, Jr.*, 26 of *Champion*, and the first 39 episodes of *Death Valley Days*. As usual, not far behind Autry came Roy Rogers, whose popular *The Roy Rogers Show* began in 1951. By the early 1950s, television programming included a number of old, "B" westerns and new, inexpensive, independently produced half-hour programs with very limited outdoor action.

Major movie studios still refused to provide television with any material. But the popularity of television caused movie attendance to drop sharply, from 90 million in 1946 to 60 million in 1950, 45 million in 1957, and less than 20 million in the late 1960s. Having lost much of the family market, moviemakers increasingly concentrated on blockbuster films that television could not equal, including wide-screen westerns like *Shane* and *The Searchers*. Hollywood needed spectacular attractions to pull adults and families out of their homes. The old double-bill, combining a big-budget "A" feature with a modest "B" movie, died because people stayed home for the "B" entertainment.

Major studios poured more and more money into fewer and fewer pictures. Though some production of "B"s with specialized appeal—rock 'n' roll, rebellious youth, car and motorcycle, horror, and sexy movies—continued, the producers were often independents with very limited resources. The decline of "B"s hurt the major studios much more than one might expect because the economic basis of the studios had been the mass production of a great many movies. In the early 1950s, many formerly bustling studio lots grew increasingly quiet as the motion picture industry paid the price for not expanding into the new medium that was bringing sound motion pictures into American homes.

The big break came in 1954 when Warner Brothers agreed to film a television series for ABC-TV. In 1955, the series alternated one-hour shows, one of which, *Cheyenne*, was so much more popular than the others that it became a weekly program in 1956. The Hollywood floodgate opened, and filmed western series poured into television. In 1956 there were four new western programs and in 1957 another nine. In 1958 there were at least twenty-five western series in prime time, and seven of the ten top-rated shows were westerns. Television featured western heroes of all sorts—sheriffs, outlaws, bounty hunters, cattlemen, Indians, and gamblers—in series that provided experience and exposure for some of the biggest stars of the next twenty years: Dale Robertson, James Arness, Gene Barry, James Garner, Richard Boone, Lorne Greene, Clint Eastwood, and Steve McQueen; and directors such as Robert Altman and Sam Peckinpaugh. A 1960 survey found that television viewers who liked action shows the best preferred westerns two to one over crime, a preference that seemed to reflect the hero worship of the era that saw the end of the Eisenhower years and the beginning of John F. Kennedy's brief reign in what was seen as an American Camelot. Westerns were right for the time, but they also had to be right for the medium, which was shifting production from New York to Southern California, from television studios to movie studios.

Television forced movie studios to make major changes in their western productions. The sheer number of shows needed was staggering. Each series consisted of at least thirteen episodes; those that lasted a full year needed thirty-nine shows every year. In 1959, producers had to create some 570 hours of new westerns in nine months, which was more than double the number of "B"s Hollywood had produced at its height. To meet this staggering demand for material, producers had to adopt radio's formats. Using the same core characters, same premises, and same motivations from week to week, each television western had its own formula into which new situations, problems, or characters could be inserted to produce different episodes without having to create entirely new ideas for each script. Unlike feature films, television shows were short, either twenty-six or fifty-two minutes, and required simple, direct stories. With some exceptions, the shows were fast-paced dramatic adventures that could be filmed quickly and simply.

Unlike moviemakers, television producers had to rely heavily on indoor sets, closeups, and limited action. After movie studios entered production, this stress on small-scale scenes certainly was not to avoid the costs of location shooting because studios had back lots and abundant stock footage at their disposal. Rather, it was a major adjustment to television as a medium. The television screen, especially in the early days, was very small, which meant that almost anything except midshots and closeups looked tiny and insignificant. Television could not capture the grandeur and scale of the western landscape. Even *Rawhide* (1959-66), a show based on a continuing cattle drive, concentrated on interaction between individuals in camp rather than on the action of the herd on the open range, which typically consisted of short pieces of stock footage of cattle herds, with quick cuts to the main characters surrounded by a few cattle. The medium dictated that television westerns would concentrate on human problems and small-scale action rather than on "B" movies' hard-riding chases or on "A" movies' themes of man against the overpowering environment. This gave the average television western a slow, talky feel when compared with movies. "The films we made had a good plot and a lot of action," observed "B" western star Johnny Mack Brown in comparing his sort of western with television's. "We had people tumbling over cliffs and swimming rivers. TV does the whole thing in a room, and they film it in two days. They just let their characters talk. We really showed them riding to the pass."[15]

In the late 1950s, the boom days of the television western, producers with far fewer options than moviemakers and the need to create far more shows grasped for gimmicks that would make each character distinctive and appealing. Unusual weapons, such as Yancy Derringer's miniature pistol, Josh Randall's sawed-off shotgun, Jim Bowie's huge knife, and Bat Masterson's cane, proved very popular in the man-to-man showdowns that were television's most common substitute for the massive action and free-wheeling chases of western action movies. But, in addition to action shows, television also produced its own version of the classic western.

Gunsmoke, one of the most popular and longest-running westerns in television history, premiered in 1955. It had been created in 1952 as an adult radio western with a fallible hero, U.S. Marshal Matt Dillon, who fought for law and order, but who was no superman. Like many other ex-radio shows, *Gunsmoke* kept its basic format, characters, and tone when it changed media. From the beginning of its first episode it was clear that this was a far different western than audiences were used to seeing in shows like *Hopalong Cassidy* or *The Lone Ranger*. When a killer challenged Dillon, he stepped dramatically into the dirt street and went for his gun—all according to the stereotyped script. But then Dillon was shot down, though he later killed the gunman. The central cast of this show with its flawed, human hero included an old doctor (Milburn Stone), a woman who ran a saloon (Amanda Blake), and a limping sidekick (Dennis Weaver). *Gunsmoke* was far different from most of its gun-slinging contemporaries even though its plots typically focused on conflicts between individuals in the one-street town of Dodge City and rarely moved into the expansive countryside surrounding it.

Played by tall, ruggedly handsome James Arness, Matt Dillon was tough when facing danger, but compassionate with starving homesteaders, families plagued by disease, and other people in trouble. With his fatherly image and deep local roots, Dillon definitely had a place in his society. He was a man of the town in a medium that devoted little attention to the great outdoors. He was also a believable human being viewers could identify with. "Matt Dillon is still making mistakes. He's still human," observed Norman MacDonnell, one of the originators of the show on radio. "And that's why people believe in him and keep tuning in. In this age of computers, mechanization, and pollution, man feels less and less important. But as long as Matt Dillon is there, and doing all right, the average man feels that he too still has a chance."[16] He was there for a long time. *Gunsmoke* was the first half-hour western to break into the top ten in the ratings, and in 1957 it became the most popular show on television, a position it held until late 1961. In the late 1960s, when television action westerns faded in popularity, *Gunsmoke* placed much more emphasis on social issues like prejudice and mob behavior and played up Dillon's counseling while playing down his fighting. The show ran until 1975, a full twenty years.

Gunsmoke showed the western hero as a lawman with a stake in his town; its only long-term rival, *Bonanza*, featured a western hero with an even more important domestic role as the ruler of an empire and a patriarch of an all-male family. Premiering in 1959, *Bonanza* was the story of Ben Cartwright (Lorne Greene) and his grown sons, Hoss (Dan Blocker), Adam (Pernell Roberts), and Little Joe (Michael Landon), who lived on the lushly wooded Ponderosa Ranch in the mountains of Nevada. Essentially a family show set in the West, a domesticated version of the cattle empire story, *Bonanza's* central appeal was the warm, familial relationship between father and sons. This kind of relationship was made possible within the rigid traditional roles of the western by making the father a widower who had to perform some of the duties women usually did. The three sons, each with a different mother, had totally different personalities: Adam, the oldest, was level-headed and cool; Hoss was burly, rather dull, and lovable; Little Joe was handsome, hot-headed, and violent. None was a complete person, but, with the direction, example, and guidance of their smart, strong, caring father, the four men became a model of a unified family. As a man who had carved out an empire with his own hands, Ben Cartwright had the heroic qualities of the western hero. But when the show began he was already settled down and teaching his sons to combine the strength of pioneering westerners with the values of civilized society. In many ways *Bonanza* represented a resolution of the long-standing conflict between the independent western hero with his own code of honor and the society that demanded that individuals submit to the group's values. Ben Cartwright, a strong-willed empire builder, was to an extent reversing that process by civilizing the society that grew up around him, shaping *it* as well as his family in his own image. *Bonanza* became the top ranked television show in the 1964-65 season and rode until 1973. But *Bonanza* and *Gunsmoke* were becoming the exceptions.

The boom in television westerns had collapsed by the mid-1960s. The action slots on television were increasingly filled with war and then crime shows, a reflection of the changing mood of society in the era of the assassination of President Kennedy, the escalation of the Vietnam War, the burning of American cities in violent race riots, and the exposure of corruption and immorality in the highest level of government. It is no wonder that people found it difficult to believe in a hero in a white hat who could solve all problems and destroy all evil. The focus of television action in these years changed from westerns to crime, from the frontier of the past to the cities of the present. In 1960 there had been some twenty-three western series on television; in 1970 there were only three or four.

In the violence-racked late 1960s, film westerns did not disappear but they were transformed. Free from network and sponsor censorship, moviemakers increasingly appealed to a youth market growing restive, rebellious, and cynical. As part of that appeal, many westerns centered on ruthless, professional killers who did what they did for money or the joy of fighting, not because it was right or because people needed help. In *The Professionals* (1966), *The Wild Bunch* (1969), and other such films, the stories involved settlers or townspeople hiring professional fighters to battle another gang of professionals. The two gangs often had more in common with each other than the heroes had with the people who hired them. At times the pictures looked like war movies set in the early West. The shootouts that had once climaxed westerns now dominated them. Skirmish followed skirmish, building to a final battle that ended the war with the villains defeated and perhaps, also with the death of the heroes. These western heroes could die because they no longer stood for the moral and spiritual virtue of America.

The Wild Bunch, directed by Sam Peckinpaugh, was a financially and artistically successful example of the changes in the western. It opens with William Holden, Ernest Borgnine, and their gang riding into a town dressed as cavalrymen and then robbing a bank. Hidden on the town's rooftops lying in ambush are a railroad official (Robert Ryan) and a group of vicious bounty hunters he has hired. Holden's gang spots the trap, waits until a temperance parade reaches them, and then callously races out into the parade. In the ensuing gunfight, innocent men, women, and children are slaughtered in bloody gore that is even more gruesome because of the visual artistry with which it is portrayed. While the bounty hunters plunder the dead bodies of the townspeople, Holden and the wild bunch flee, discovering later that they have stolen lead washers, not gold. With Ryan and his men hot on their trail, the wild bunch is hired by a Mexican revolutionary who betrays them. After a long battle in which the four whites kill hundreds of Mexicans, the wild bunch lies dead. The bounty hunters descend like vultures, pick the dead bodies clean, and then ride off to collect their rewards. The beautifully filmed, well-constructed picture, which features bloodbath after bloodbath, has no admirable heroes. It portrays a world on the edge of anarchy, a world where organized society is so weak that when it is plagued by amoral, violent gangs, its only response is to hire another of the amoral, violent gangs to fight for it, a world-view that reflected the despair of the late sixties.

The roles played by the most popular new western movie star of the late 1960s and early 1970s, Clint Eastwood, also represented the same trend toward the anti-hero. In 1964, while playing the second lead on *Rawhide,* he made an inexpensive western in Italy, which was released in America in 1967 as *A Fistful of Dollars.* Eastwood played a nameless, cigar-chewing gunslinger who rides into a town where two families are warring for control, kills four members of one family, goes to work for the other, and then gets them to murder each other. After being beaten up and nearly killed, he hides out, recovers, returns to town, kills five men in one fight, and rides off with the gold the two families were fighting over. Eastwood's character, a self-serving, emotionless killer he described as "a gunman out for his own well-being, placed himself first, and didn't get involved in other people's problems unless it was to his benefit," was an almost total reversal of the classic western hero.[17] The picture was an enormous success, and Eastwood followed with picture after picture in which he played a brutal, amoral, money-hungry killer in a corrupt, exploitive world, an expression of the general perspective of many moviegoers in the chaotic violence of the late 1960s and early 1970s.

In 1969 the Academy Award for best actor of the year went to the star of a hit western that combined elements of the mercenary and of the classic hero. The actor was John Wayne, who had been making westerns for over thirty years and was both a man of the time and a man of the tradition. Wayne's career in many ways summed up the evolution of the western film. In 1930 he broke into movies in low-budget, high-action westerns, where he stayed for nearly ten years. But even in the "B"s, he insisted on making westerns on his own terms, rejecting the pristine white hat, chaps, shirts, and boots of a romanticized Tom Mix character and insisting on wearing a sweat-stained Stetson, dirty kerchief and shirt, rumpled pants, and old boots. "I felt many of the Western stars of the twenties and thirties were too goddamn perfect," he explained. "I was trying to play a man who gets dirty, who sweats sometimes, who enjoys really kissing a gal he likes, who gets angry, who fights clean whenever possible but will fight dirty if he has to. You could say, I made the Western hero a roughneck."[18] He also made himself a star of the "B" western, but he wanted to move up to movies with bigger budgets, salaries, and status.

Wayne's big break came in 1939 when John Ford gave him the chance to play the Ringo Kid in *Stagecoach*, the film that triggered the resurgence of big-budget westerns and made a major star of Wayne, who had already appeared in about 130 films. During World War II, while many romantic actors were in the military, Wayne became a leading man as well as a hero of war movies. But in the late 1940s he returned to westerns and started to shape the character that would make him a towering figure in modern American life. For many people Wayne came to symbolize the best in American patriotic manhood. As he aged Wayne began to play older men who were models of strength, conviction, honor, and guts, men who threw themselves into their causes with total commitment and no regard for their own safety or comfort, but men who were at the same time humanized by the limitations and perspectives that came with age.

In director Howard Hawks's first western, *Red River* (1948), Wayne played an aging cattleman who becomes so brutal and tyrannical in his obsession with completing a 1000-mile cattle drive that his own son takes the herd away from him. When Hawks wanted Wayne to cringe as he lost the herd, he refused. "Howard, a guy can kill," Wayne explained, "he can be mean and vicious—and he could still hold an audience. But let him show a yellow streak and he will lose them. I'm not about to cringe."[19] Instead, "standin' tall" he mounts his horse and rides off vowing to revenge himself by killing his son, the person he loves most. When the two meet again, Wayne taunts and shoots at his son in an attempt to make him draw his gun. When he refuses to draw, the two beat each other up in a brutal fistfight. The following year Wayne broadened his treatment of powerful, older men in John Ford's *She Wore a Yellow Ribbon*, playing the sixty-year-old cavalry captain who fights Indians right up to the day of his retirement. In the sensitively handled, emotional retirement ceremony, tears well in the tough old soldier's eyes, and in an especially touching scene, he stands at his wife's grave and talks aloud of the past. By 1949 Wayne had become a major star with his portrayals of strong-willed, hard-hitting he-men who were growing older, more humane, but no less committed to fighting for what was right.

But by the late-1960s even Wayne's characters began to reflect the mood of the times and the trends in westerns. In 1969 Wayne, who was over sixty, starred in *True Grit* as Rooster Cogburn, a drunken, swaggering, old ex-U.S. Marshal who wears an eye-patch, is reluctant to get into anything more challenging than a whisky bottle, and will do anything to win if forced to fight. "In Rooster's world," Wayne observed, "a kick in the face was clean fighting, especially if it was a struggle for life."[20] The role was, in one sense, a culmination of Wayne's past portrayals of westerners. Rooster Cogburn could have been Wayne's hard-drinking, hard-fighting, woman-loving, sweaty, "roughneck" "B" movie cowboy who had aged thirty-five years and had acquired some of the human foibles and sentimentality that Wayne developed in his older characters. But Cogburn was also a mercenary. When a desperate, idealistic fourteen-year-old girl (Kim Darby) wants him to catch her father's murderer, Cogburn, like other hired professional gunfighters of the period, agrees to the mission only for money. But unlike the mercenaries who care nothing about the people they fight for, he develops a warm, personal relationship with the spunky girl. In a moving scene, he tells her about his wife and the life he left to maintain his independence. The girl, Cogburn, and a Texas Ranger (Glenn Campbell) eventually get the gang, though on the way the girl is captured, and Cogburn gets drunk and falls off his horse. But he also gallantly fights a joust-like battle, riding with a gun in each hand and the reins in his teeth as he charges three men, though he is eventually pinned under his horse and has to be saved by the Ranger. In contrast to many of the violent, mercenary westerns, which ended in bloodbaths, *True Grit* had an upbeat conclusion. When the girl offers Cogburn a gravesite next to hers because he has no family, he refuses to think of death. Instead, he mounts his horse, jumps a fence, and rides off, calling out for her to come and visit a fat, old man sometime.

Wayne made a film in 1972 that in many ways is the proper conclusion to the story of the western at the close of the third-quarter of the twentieth century. *The Cowboys* opens with Wayne, a cattleman, in trouble because there are no more cowboys, his wranglers having run off to hunt for gold. With a black cook (an untraditional ally), Wayne finally hires and trains fourteen young boys to herd his cattle. He is trying to pass on the old ways to a new generation at a time when there are no more cowboys to be found. He is also raising the boys to be men by taking them out on the range. In traditional mythic westerns, it is the experience in the American wilderness that shapes the character of young growing Americans. But in this case it is human, not natural, forces that do the shaping. On the cattle drive the boys have their first experiences with whisky and women. They also have to face a gang of vicious killers, a group of rustlers who, like wolves waiting for the right time to strike, track the herd. When the rustlers strike, Wayne beats the leader badly in a fight, but one good man can no longer defeat an entire gang of outlaws. The fight ends with Wayne dead, the gang riding off with the herd, and the boys burying Wayne and vowing to recover the cattle and complete the drive. Led by the cook, they succeed, killing most of the gang in the process. In a sense one group of professionals has destroyed another. But the boys do it for traditional reasons—honor, revenge, and to finish what they set out to do, not strictly for money. After they finish the drive, they have a tombstone made for Wayne and ride back to the scene of the fight. But unable to find the grave, they can create no memorial to their roots. In *The Cowboys,* as in the best tradition of the western, life on the land has made men of boys, men who finish what they set out to do and do what is right. But in 1972 the heroic individual dies at the hands of an immoral gang of thieves and lies in an unmarked grave, which represented both a symbolic end of a tradition and a symbolic statement that the tradition resided in the open land.

By the late 1970s and early 1980s, westerns, like Wayne's cowboys, had just about disappeared from the nation's movie and television screens, except for reshowings of earlier films and shows. This disappearance coincided with the general despair of the era when inflation, unemployment, and violent crime all grew rapidly, when America seemed to have lost its power and sense of purpose, and when it seemed that no one could do anything about it. In such times the western has little appeal because it represents much more than just good action entertainment. Underlying all the hard riding and fast shooting, all the magnificent scenery and dramatic showdowns, and all the noble deeds and heroic sacrifices, at the heart of the classic western stands the belief that one person can make a difference, that the heroic natural man spawned by the rugged, American wilderness can, in a time of crisis, put the country back on the right track. But on the nation's two hundredth birthday, the optimistic vision of the western did not even seem a plausible fantasy. On the eve of the 1980s many people feel the western is dead. But there is nothing in American history to suggest that the nation will not again bounce back, take pride in itself, look optimistically toward the future, and once again thrill to the sight of a lone figure emerging out of the immense western landscape with hope in his saddlebags and fire in his eyes.

4

Everybody's Doin' It:
Popular Music and the Media

They came from England and the Orient, from Germany and Russia, from Spain and Senegal, from Italy and Mexico. They came from almost everywhere to settle in America, bringing their traditional music, playing instruments of all sizes and shapes, and singing in all tempos and tongues. America became the home of the world's music. It also became the home of new blends of musical traditions that had originated worlds apart. Some of these were the unconscious products of people living and working and playing side by side. Others were the conscious work of professional entertainers and songwriters who tried to appeal to the widest possible range of Americans by finding common denominators in the country's rich musical diversity and by using them as the sources of new popular songs. American popular music grew up with the nation and with show business. At first, the folk music of traditional groups and the popular music of the general public existed side by side, influencing each other. But as professional show business took over more and more of the entertainment functions that people had once performed for themselves, popular music pushed folk music into increasingly smaller and more isolated pockets. This chapter briefly discusses some of the major trends in mainstream popular music since the 1890s, but it is principally concerned with the effects of the entertainment media on American popular music.[1]

Until the 1890s, popular music for most Americans consisted of a combination of traditional folk songs, old show-business favorites such as the songs of Stephen Foster, and new songs. Outside the major cities, new songs spread slowly. Though show business did popularize new tunes, the bulk of entertainment in smaller cities and towns was provided by traveling performers who often used the same old reliable songs and shows year after year, rather than continually updating their repertoires as big city showmen had to do. Besides live performances, the other major medium for popularizing new songs was sheet music, which was in great demand because people all over the country were playing music at home on the pianos that mass production put within the reach of average citizens. But during most of the nineteenth century music publishers seemed content just to print a range of popular and classical music and to promote neither. The publishers viewed themselves as members of the gentlemanly cultural establishment rather than as merchants in the popular entertainment business. "These old timers of the game," observed young music publisher Edward B. Marks of his predecessors, "maintained the same Dickensian dignity as the book publishers of their era."[2]

The modern, popular music business began to emerge by the turn of the twentieth century. Music publishing changed radically and reshaped popular music. In the 1890s ambitious, young entrepreneurs, many of them songwriters frustrated by the current practice of publishers buying songs outright and paying no royalties, became music publishers. M. Witmark and Sons, Will Rossiter, Leo Feist, Edward B. Marks, and other new publishers concentrated on printing popular songs and on aggressively promoting and marketing them to the general public. By the early twentieth century, these aggressive music merchants had clustered in New York, many of them on 28th Street, which was nicknamed Tin Pan Alley, reportedly because of the rinky-tinky pianos being played in offices up and down the street. These popular music factories cranked out new songs as fast as possible while continually fine-tuning them to capture shifts in public interest and to capitalize on other companies' successes. Any new topic or fad, be it bicycles, airplanes, women's names, or black dialect, almost immediately appeared in scores of songs. In the highly competitive music business Tin Pan Alley became adept at producing sheet music that the public would buy to play and sing at home. Between 1900 and 1910, there were nearly 100 songs that each sold over a million copies of sheet music.

Tin Pan Alley hit songs of the 1890s were not merely updated versions of the sorts of songs that had been popular for decades. Because they were published to sell to a mass audience, they were simplified in both form and style. Instead of emphasizing numerous verses that told a long and complicated story, new songs stressed a short catchy chorus with simple lyrics and a punchy message. The chorus was repeated over and over, making the songs easy to learn and remember. "My Wild Irish Rose" (1899), "In the Good Old Summer Time" (1902), or "Wait 'til the Sun Shines, Nellie" (1905) did have verses, but it was the choruses that made these and other early Tin Pan Alley songs enduring standards. Many of these early popular songs, such as "After the Ball" (1892), "The Band Played On" (1895), "Meet Me in St. Louis" (1904), and "In the Shade of the Old Apple Tree" (1905), were also written in familiar, easy-to-follow waltz time. All were easy to sing and easy to play, and America's parlors rang with the sounds of Tin Pan Alley songs.

The new music merchants realized that in a highly competitive business producing an appealing product was only the first step to success. The product also had to be distributed and promoted effectively. Besides selling their sheet music in music stores as traditionally had been done, publishers used the new mass-marketing techniques of the period. They placed their sheet music in department stores and five-and-ten cent stores which drew large crowds of people, and they sent along song-pluggers to perform the new music for shoppers. But, even though the business of music publishers was selling sheet music, not entertainment, they found that their most effective promotional vehicle was show business, which at first meant the live stage. The lesson was made clear in 1892, when Charles K. Harris, a young songwriter in Milwaukee, wrote "After the Ball," which was a flop in local vaudeville. But after Harris paid the star of Charles Hoyt's traveling musical *A Trip to Chinatown* to add the song to the show, it proved as great a hit as did the show's "The Bowery" and "Reuben, Reuben." *A Trip to Chinatown* demonstrated that book musicals would be a major source of popular music. Harris refused to sell the rights to his song, published it himself, and had the first piece of sheet music to sell millions of copies. He moved to New York and became one of the new breed of music writers, publishers, promoters, and merchandisers who looked to show business to create demand for their sheet music.

In the 1890s as transportation became less expensive and more efficient, show business began to become a well-organized, truly national business. Central booking agencies sent musicals, burlesque shows, vaudeville bills, minstrel troupes, and popular plays on regular theatrical circuits around the country. The great many productions on the live stage created an enormous demand for music. "With 1200 vaudeville acts routed all over the country, a thousand dramatic and musical shows on the road, more than a hundred burlesque troupes, and dozens of circuses, each carrying a band, these were boom days for publishers," Marks recalled.[3] Since the inclusion of a song in a big-time show was the most direct road to sheet-music sales, by the early years of the twentieth century publishers were bidding against each other to have their songs played by top performers or used in hit shows.

When entertainment machines developed, music publishers at first used them in the same way they had used live shows. In the 1890s phonographs and records, which were still little more than crude novelties, did not seem a threat to sheet-music sales, even though records brought professionally performed music into the home. "The recording of a number was considered something of a plug," Marks recalled, because people "might hear your song and then buy the sheet music."[4] When coin-in-the-slot phonographs with earphones—the forerunners of the jukebox—became popular in penny arcades, music publishers tried to convince arcade operators to use recordings of their songs and to put the title pages of the sheet music on top of the machines as further plugs. Silent movie nickelodeons also attracted song-pluggers who provided entertainment between the short movies with slides that showed the lyrics and illustrated the story while the plugger played the piano and the audience sang along. In this early period music publishers received no royalties. But the sheet music business was lucrative as long as the majority of people produced most of the music in their homes. That soon changed.

Early in the twentieth century, the American public began to buy more and more phonographs and recordings. Given the opportunity, most people chose to be entertained in their homes rather than to entertain themselves. The limited range and quality of early recording technology forced record makers to concentrate initially on brass bands and booming voices, which made recording stars of performers such as operatic tenor Enrico Caruso, whose highly successful 1902-03 recordings gave great status and great popularity to the new entertainment machine. But even with their narrow limitations and poor fidelity, early recordings still featured a wide range of popular entertainers, from old minstrel man Lew Dockstader to young Al Jolson, from Nora Bayes to Sophie Tucker, from John Philip Sousa to George M. Cohan. Recordings also had a powerful influence on popular music, which became much more complex because it was again written to be performed primarily by professionals, not by amateurs. Since recordings could be mass produced and distributed throughout the country, they were also the first step toward creating a truly mass market in which new music and new entertainers could reach national audiences within a matter of weeks, not the years it sometimes had taken on the stage.

The powerful effects of recordings on popular music became clear in the first two decades of the twentieth century with the rapid spread of complex music based on Afro-American ragtime and jazz. "A wave of vulgar, filthy and suggestive music has inundated the land," complained the *Musical Courier* in 1899. "Nothing but ragtime prevails and the cakewalk with its obscene posturings, its lewd gestures. It is artistically and morally depressing and should be suppressed by press and pulpit." Press and pulpit may have denounced ragtime, but the public loved the catchy, upbeat music that W. C. Handy described as "rhythm without much melody."[5] Combinations of Afro-American rhythms and Euro-American melodies were almost as old as the country, but in the 1890s foot-tapping ragtime with its pulsating, syncopated rhythms struck just the right chord for a country emerging from the economic depression of the early 1890s to the heady optimism of the Spanish-American War, the political leadership of Teddy Roosevelt, and what seemed to be the dawning of an American age. Ragtime was the tonic the public needed to lift its spirits and get it up on its feet dancing to a bouncy beat.

Ragtime, which at its simplest put the accent on the weak beat and called for the piano player to play a steady, march-like rhythm with the left hand and complex syncopated rhythms with the right, was an Afro-American performance style alien to the many people accustomed to traditional American popular music. Black entertainer and composer Ernest Hogan, for instance, seemed to white writer Robert Hughes to have "an impudent determination to keep out of key and out of time."[6] Even with manuals like ragtime innovator Ben Harney's *Rag Time Instructor* (1897), conventional piano players found it very difficult to play all the notes in the sheet music and to put the accents in the right places. But these difficulties did not kill ragtime or even inhibit its popularization. Besides anybody being able to listen to it on records, the songwriters of Tin Pan Alley were about to absorb the rather peculiar sounding Afro-American music into the mainstream of American popular music.

After 1910 Tin Pan Alley's music writing factories retooled and began to mass produce ragtime songs, or at least upbeat songs called ragtime. In 1911 Tin Pan Alley's versions of ragtime became America's most popular music. Besides such novelties as "When Ragtime Rosie Ragged the Rosary," Irving Berlin's "Alexander's Ragtime Band" helped make ragtime a household word and helped make Berlin in the general public's eyes the "King of Ragtime"—even though "Alexander's Ragtime Band" was more of a march than a ragtime tune. The new rage included "Ragtime Soldier Man," "Ragtime Goblin Man," "Ragtime Cowboy Joe," and even a song about a ragtime suffragette. Through broad exposure in theaters and especially on nationally distributed records, Tin Pan Alley's rags swept the nation. In 1911 Irving Berlin, who would later give America its most popular Christmas song ("White Christmas"), its most popular Easter song ("Easter Parade"), its most popular patriotic song ("God Bless America"), and its entertainment anthem ("No Business Like Show Business"), prophetically wrote "Everybody's Doin' It." What everybody was doin' was dancin', dancin' to ragtime.

"The public of the nineties had asked for tunes to sing," observed music composer and publisher Edward B. Marks. "The public of the turn of the century had been content to whistle. But the public from 1910 on demanded tunes to dance to."[7] Marks was right. After 1910 every generation would seek its own dances as well as its own music. In the age of entertainment machines, the new dance music could be complicated, but the new mass dances could not be. Almost anyone could learn to do the Turkey Trot, Bunny Hug, Grizzly Bear, Monkey Glide, Kangeroo Dip, Camel Walk, and the other "animal dances" that spread with ragtime and created a sensation with their close body contact. In 1913 Americans were also introduced to the first of what would be many Latin fads in American music and dance, the Tango, which sparked great excitement and controversy with its exotic rhythms and erotic movements. As popular as these new dances were, they were widely accepted only when they were adapted to middle-class American tastes and sensibilities, as had happened earlier with the new music. The leading figures in this adaptation were Vernon and Irene Castle, a husband and wife dance team who became stars in vaudeville and musicals by translating the blatant eroticism of Afro-American and Latin dances into graceful, refined forms. "When the Tango degenerates into an acrobatic display or into a salacious sensation," the Castles wrote reassuringly in 1914, "it is the fault of the dancers and not of the dance. The Castle Tango is courtly and artistic."[8]

Tin Pan Alley songwriters and dancers like the Castles were essentially popularizers who translated the unique innovations of America's sub-cultures—Afro-American, Latin-American, country folk, and others—into material with great appeal for the American mass market. The original creators were rarely the ones who gained the greatest fame and wealth. This was partially because of prejudice, discrimination, and exploitation, but also because the innovators appealed to limited groups, did things that were not generally accepted, and sometimes consciously challenged popular trends and tastes. But it should not be forgotten that people like Berlin, the Castles, and other popularizers, who had the opportunity, sensitivity, and talent to reach across the bounds of race, age, region, sex, and background to entertain Americans of all sorts, were also innovators who made great contributions. Their adaptations and amalgamations gave popular music and dance much of its unique blend of creative vitality and broad appeal. Entertainment machines gave them the exposure to make the adaptations and amalgamations national, even international sensations.

After 1911 the record business boomed because of the great demand for danceable rags and tangos that people could play in their homes. In 1913-14 Victor and Columbia turned out dance records as fast as they could, each claiming to have the most danceable music. Columbia advertised that its dance series was under the direction of dancing authority G. Hepburn Wilson, "who dances while the band make the record."[9] Victor countered by hiring the Castles to supervise their dance records. The Castles must have been in step with popular tastes. Victor's assets jumped from under $14 million in 1913 to nearly $22 million in 1915. As demand for phonographs and recordings grew so did competition in the business. When the founding companies' original patents expired, the number of phonograph businesses exploded, from three in 1912 to forty-six in 1916. Records and record players were becoming big businesses that greatly influenced popular music and popular tastes.

Because of records, Dixieland jazz, which had been born and bred in southern black bars and bordellos, got broad national exposure in a very short time. In 1917 the Original Dixieland Jass Band, a white group without the credentials to justify its name, made the first jazz recordings. They were followed by a number of innovative black bands, such as those led by Edward "Kid" Ory and Joe "King" Oliver, who first featured the soaring trumpet work of Louis Armstrong. Around the country young musicians, such as Bing Crosby in Spokane, Washington, and Jimmy McPartland in Chicago, learned to play jazz by imitating the new sounds they heard on records. "We'd have to tune our instruments up to the record machine, to the pitch, and go ahead with a few notes," McPartland explained. "Then, stop! A few more bars of the record, each guy would pick out his notes and boom! We would go on and play it."[10] With its strong rhythm and brassy sound, Dixieland jazz came through loud and clear on the period's fuzzy records. Dixieland also gave people a good, happy feeling, which was what the public needed after the suffering of World War I. Afro-American music once again lifted the public's spirit, provided the creative spark for a new trend in general popular music, and brought with it new dances. While the new generation could not generally play Dixieland music, it could participate in the jazz age by doing the Charleston, Black Bottom, and other popular dances of the 1920s, when the word "jazz" became nearly synonymous with bouncy, danceable, popular music. But while historic musical innovations took place in jazz circles in the 1920s as great creative artists shaped an American art form, for the general public the jazz popularizers, such as bandleaders Fred Waring, Vincent Lopez, Ted Lewis, and Paul Whiteman—all of whom became top recording stars—were most important, none more so than Whiteman.

Paul Whiteman popularized jazz by purging it of what he called its "raucous," "crude" qualities and by using his training in classical music to produce what singing star Rudy Vallee called "symphonized syncopation."[11] After hiring classically trained Ferde Grofe as pianist and arranger in 1919, bandleader Paul Whiteman began to play and record meticulously orchestrated, well-rehearsed harmonious arrangements of jazz numbers. The national audience Whiteman gained through sales of his recordings made him a star. His 1920 recording of "Whispering" and "Japanese Sandman" sold over a million and a half records. Such exposure and popularity earned Whiteman the title "King of Jazz," though he deserved the title only in the way that

Irving Berlin deserved to be called the "King of Ragtime." Each man
reached mass audiences with popularized versions of Afro-American
musical innovations.

In the mid-1920s, when records had already become a major force
in popular music, recording technology was greatly improved by electrical microphones and amplifiers that eliminated all restrictions on
the types of instruments, arrangements, orchestras, and voices that
could be recorded effectively. Recording bands grew larger, because
it was no longer necessary to cram musicians together in front of the
recording horn so they could be heard on the record. Orchestras added
strings, used subtle arrangements, played in normal configurations,
and produced full, rich sounds. These technical improvements made
the big bands that played sweet refined melodies as effective as the
small combos that played hot snappy tunes. Electrical amplifiers also
enabled soft-voiced singers like Rudy Vallee and Bing Crosby to challenge belters like Sophie Tucker and Al Jolson as recording stars. With
its new diversity the record business continued to expand. In 1927,
record sales reached 100 million. But a new entertainment machine,
radio, was beginning to challenge records for the home music market.

Radio became an important popular entertainment medium in the
1920s. Before commercial sponsors produced a broad range of shows,
radio programming relied heavily on music—records, performers in the
studios, and remote broadcasts from hotels, ballrooms, and nightclubs.
In 1930, when dance music filled an estimated three-quarters of radio
time, national radio networks gave entertainers a larger audience with
one broadcast than they could have reached in a lifetime of touring.
No longer was there a big time lag between the music heard in New
York City and Walla Walla. From coast to coast, from border to border, from big city to isolated farm, all of America could listen to the
debut of a new performer or a new song. Radio created the first truly
mass audience.

The career of Rudy Vallee illustrated the enormous impact of radio
on performers, popular music, and public opinion. After leaving Yale,
Vallee, a saxophonist, formed his own band in 1928 and began to sing
with it, using a megaphone to project his weak voice. Remote broadcasts of Vallee and his band performing in a New York City nightclub
created a great many fans who wanted to see as well as to hear the
band. When Vallee and his Connecticut Yankees appeared for three
days at Keith's vaudeville house in New York they were greeted by an

excited crowd that had to be subdued by mounted policemen, a turn-out that earned Vallee and his band a major vaudeville tour, including a date at the Palace Theater in New York. In 1929, only one year after his band had opened in a New York club, Vallee played in nightclubs and theaters, made his first records, appeared in his first movie, and starred in his first sponsored network radio show. His success in one entertainment medium led to success in others, a clear example of the instant multi-media stardom that would become increasingly common as national entertainment and communication media developed. Though successful in film, his greatest triumphs came in radio and recordings, where his relaxed, collegiate image, his "radiophonic" voice, and his soft crooning style were welcome changes from the loud, blaring styles of the recent past. His radio show, the Fleischman Hour, a hit almost from its inception, initially concentrated on his band and his singing. But in 1932 as well-produced radio programming became common, Vallee broadened the show into a model of radio variety, mixing music and singing with comedy, drama, novelties, and guest stars. With the national recognition gained from his radio show Vallee had a long string of hit records, from "I'm a Vagabond Lover" (1929) to "The Whiffenpoof Song" (1936).

The changes in the popular music business that began in the mid-1920s rapidly accelerated in the early 1930s because major changes in entertainment media coincided with the shock of the Great Depression, which struck not only at America's pocketbook but also at its morale, making the escapism of popular entertainment grow more necessary even as ticket money grew more scarce. Radio proved a great hit when it began regular broadcasts of free, well-produced, professional programs, including musical variety shows like Rudy Vallee's and the *Kraft Music Hall* that broadcast all the new songs of the period. Inexpensive sound motion pictures also dazzled the public with lavishly produced musicals. Although many hit songs were written for and introduced in stage and film musicals, the major media for popularizing songs were radio and recordings, which offered an immediate national market and made the individual song their basic unit. Though musicals often provided an important initial showcase, radio and recordings provided the repeated performances that fixed the songs in people's minds and memories. No program had more impact than Lucky Strike cigarettes' *Your Hit Parade*. Every week from 1935 to 1959 regular cast members and guest stars, who included many top singers, performed what the show claimed were the nation's most popular songs. Announcement of the top three songs built to a climactic finish that drew large, curious audiences and gave those songs unprecedented publicity, guaranteeing that they would be major hits.

In the early 1930s free radio music seemed about to destroy the sheet music and record businesses and to dominate the home music market. "Today, songs are made hits in a week, and killed off in sixty days," Edward B. Marks complained in 1933. "Before a person decides to buy a piece of sheet music, it has been succeeded in broadcasting favor by six others."[12] Sheet-music publishers, who once had used local radio to plug their songs, saw their sales collapse as network radio ran rapidly through hit after hit. The publishers had received royalties from record companies since the early 1920s, but they received none from radio until a long struggle by the American Society of Composers, Authors, and Publishers (ASCAP) forced broadcasters in 1932 to pay ASCAP a percentage of gross income for the use of its music. By the 1930s, sheet music, no longer the major medium shaping popular musical tastes, had become dependent on other entertainment media. The combination of free music on radio and the scarce money of the Depression also caused record sales to plummet from 100 million in 1927 to six million in 1932. But as early as 1933 record sales began to recover as record companies, led by Decca, cut their prices, increased their advertising, and featured major stars like Bing Crosby.

Crosby was a product of the age of entertainment machines. Growing up in the small, out-of-the-way city of Spokane, Washington, he could still listen to and learn the latest popular songs and the newest jazz because of radio and records. In 1925, at age twenty-one, he and Al Rinker set out for Los Angeles where they performed in clubs and vaudeville and then signed with the famous Paul Whiteman band as vocalists in 1926. On tour with Whiteman, Crosby and Ringer were successes in small midwestern theaters, but they flopped in New York at the Paramount because they did not have the booming voices needed to fill large houses in those pre-microphone, pre-amplification days. Joined by Harry Barris with his loud, hot piano style, Crosby and Rinker became the Rhythm Boys. They recorded a hit disc on the new phonograph technology in 1927 and toured with Whiteman until 1930 when Crosby became a single act. His success at the Coconut Grove in Los Angeles led him into many forms of show business, first with local radio broadcasts, then with a hit record of his own, a movie short, and finally a network radio show.

Crosby became a star in all entertainment media. His major movie career began with *The Big Broadcast* (1932) in which he sang "Where the Blue of the Night Meets the Gold of the Day." In 1934 he signed with Decca, playing a major role in that company's successful revival of the record business. He hosted *Kraft Music Hall* on radio from 1935 to 1946. Over the years, he starred in movie after movie, ranging from his light-hearted, comic sparring with Bob Hope in the Road pictures to his serious, Academy Award winning acting in *Going My Way* (1944); he recorded hit after hit, including many of America's greatest all-time favorites, such as "Silent Night" and "White Christmas"; he delighted live audiences for decades; and he proved just as popular on television as he had been in other media. Whether in the 1930s or the 1960s, whether in radio, records, theater, movies, or television, Crosby sang in the same relaxed, lightly jazzy, crooning style and projected the same warm, easy-going personality. He seemed to be a fun-loving golfer and fisherman who was taking a little time out from his life of leisure to entertain his friends. "They feel I'm more like one of them, rather than a professional," Crosby reflected. "My singing is sort of natural and I don't suppose its stylistic. It doesn't sound like a trained voice and most of them think: 'Well he sings like I do, you know, when I'm in the bathroom, or in the shower, and feel good and wake-up with a gay feeling.' Why they think I'm one of the fellas."[13] Yet, as popular as Crosby was, he probably could not have become a national star with his distinctive style in the days before entertainment machines and amplification, the days when a singer could count on only the power of his own voice to entertain in huge theaters that held thousands of people. The new media provided the technology that made it possible for a Bing Crosby to reach the public. But it was Crosby's talent, style, and personality that made him one of America's and the world's most beloved stars.

By the 1930s, when radio, talkies, and records all had to compete for the general entertainment audience, pressure mounted for some media to tailor their material to limited special-interest audiences. Live show business had always been able to adjust to specific audience tastes, either by modifying a touring show or by creating special shows for special audiences. The flexibility inherent in the great many productions of the live stage made it feasible for highly specialized regional or ethnic shows and circuits to develop, such as foreign-language entertainment in big cities, white country music shows, and Afro-American theatrical circuits. But when records, movies, and radio took the general audience away from the live stage, which played to increasingly high-brow audiences, popular entertainment lost much of its flexibility and adaptability. Mass-produced motion pictures had to be designed to entertain the maximum number of people and were, of course, totally inflexible once edited and reproduced. National network radio programming was performed live, but the performance was broadcast to everyone, so it, too, had to appeal to the widest possible audience.

The record business was the first of the new media to target its entertainment to specific groups. Records combined the economy of mass production and national distribution with great flexibility because they were designed to be bought and played by *individuals*. Like sheet music but unlike stage, radio, or movies, recordings were essentially consumer goods that could be produced in great variety and marketed selectively to people who controlled their use. Unlike movies and network radio, then, the record business could continue to appeal to the general pop audience as its major market while at the same time producing entertainment for limited special-interest groups. In the 1920s record companies discovered the great profits they could make selling Afro-American blues by performers like Bessie Smith to black people and country music by entertainers like Jimmie Rodgers to rural whites. Each of these creative musical subcultures strongly influenced pop music, but each also remained separate music markets that grew larger and more lucrative as prosperity returned in the 1940s. In the long run, though, the special interest group with the greatest impact on popular music was the general, white, youth market that began to surface in the mid-1930s with swing music.

The beginning of the swing era is usually dated in 1935 in Los Angeles when Benny Goodman's big band jolted a young audience with music that recaptured some of the exciting, hot rhythms of small Dixieland jazz bands, rhythms that had been largely lost in the soft, sweet sound popularized by Paul Whiteman. Goodman did not create swing music, but he popularized it with white audiences. Born in 1909, he grew up listening to recorded jazz music and began to tour as a young professional musician in the 1920s and early 1930s, the era dominated by the Whiteman sound. But Goodman found his inspiration in the pioneering work of black musicians and arrangers Don Redman and Fletcher Henderson, who had solved the problem of how to swing a big band, which needed written arrangements because the band was too large to improvise like a small, freewheeling combo. Put very simply Redman and Fletcher used a group of instruments playing in harmony as if it were a single voice and alternated back and forth between groups in call-and-response patterns, leaving time for some improvisational solos. That concept, developed and played in the 1920s in Harlem, became the basis of Goodman's success in the mid-1930s.

Before it could become popular music, swing had to buck current trends and find its audience. By late 1934, Goodman had his own band and had purchased arrangements from Henderson, which Goodman adapted to white tastes. To many white ears, the black big bands, which played in Afro-American styles, sounded out-of-tune and ragged, so Goodman smoothed out the sound without sacrificing the beat. With that preparation Goodman's refined, rhythmic sound began attracting attention through records and a three-hour, late Saturday night radio show, *Let's Dance,* on which his band alternated with Xavier Cugat's rhumba band and Kel Murray's sweet dance music. The show, which began at 11:00 p.m. in New York but at 8:00 p.m. on the West Coast, built up a large following among western young people because of the time difference. When the Goodman band set out on a national tour in 1935, it was booked into places where conventional bands had played to conventional adult audiences. At the Hotel Roosevelt in New York, the home of Guy Lombardo, the staff, Goodman remembered, kept "motioning to us not to play so loud." Such negative responses during the tour convinced Goodman to switch to stock arrangements. But on the last date at the Palomar Ballroom in Los Angeles, he decided that "if we had to flop, at least I'd do it my own way, playing the kind of music I wanted to."[14] When the band burst out with the Fletcher Henderson swing arrangements, the young crowd, primed by the radio broadcasts, went crazy, roared its approval, and began to dance wildly. Like ragtime and Dixieland, swing, too, had its own distinctive dance borrowed from Afro-American cultures. The Lindy or jitterbug, an energetic dance in which the partners could break apart and improvise steps with gliding feet, twisting pelvises, and gyrating bodies, became very popular with young people.

After that night at the Palomar, Goodman quickly built a huge following of teenage fans who embraced swing and the jitterbug as their music and dance, crowned Goodman "The King of Swing," and clamored to see and hear Goodman's and the many other swing bands that emerged. Live performances and records were the major media of this blossoming youth culture.

Record sales boomed in the late 1930s, partially because of a new entertainment machine—the jukebox, an updated version of the coin-in-the-slot phonograph of the 1890s which had entertained only one person at a time listening through earphones. But the jukebox played its music for *groups,* especially groups of teenagers who wanted to do their jitterbugging away from home and found little of the new swing music they liked on radio, which catered primarily to a general family audience. By 1942 there were some 400,000 jukeboxes around the country in malt shops, bars, restaurants, and drugstores. "One tremendous hit on a jukebox, most bandleaders now agree," critic Francis Chase wrote in 1941, "will do as much for a dance band as six solid weeks of broadcasting, and many of the great dance bands which have come to the front in recent years have done so on the basis of a jukebox hit."[15] Between 1937 and 1941 big band music, played by the likes of Count Basie, Glenn Miller, Jimmie Lunceford, Benny Goodman, Artie Shaw, Jimmy and Tommy Dorsey, and Harry James, accounted for nearly 70 percent of the records that sold over a million copies. Swing music was not exclusively or even distinctively teenage music, but there were clear signs of the emergence of a large youth market by the early 1940s, a trend that became much clearer as adolescents reacted to Frank Sinatra.

Born in 1915, Frank Sinatra grew up in the era of big bands, radio, and records. After hearing Bing Crosby in person in 1932, Sinatra decided to become a singer. In 1935 he and the Hoboken Four won a prize on the Major Bowes Amateur Hour on the radio. In 1939 a radio broadcast of one of his live performances brought Sinatra, now a single act, a job singing and recording with trumpeter Harry James's new swing band. "Already the kids were hanging around the stage door screaming for Frank," singer Connie Haines recalled. Sinatra then became the vocalist with Tommy Dorsey. Generally in the swing era, the band, not the singer, was the major attraction, but soon the people who had been coming to Dorsey concerts to dance began to cluster around the bandstand to listen to Sinatra. After learning phrasing from Dorsey's trombone work and making records with the band, Sinatra again became a single in 1942. His rise to fame was greatly aided by the well-publicized hysteria of the swooning, screaming, teenage bobbysoxers who idolized "The Voice." "Not since the days of Rudolph Valentino," observed *Time* magazine, "has American womanhood made such unabashed love to an entertainer."[16] In October 1944, when Sinatra was booked into New York's Paramount Theater, young women began to line up to buy tickets at 3:00 a.m.; by 6:00 a.m. an estimated one thousand people stood in line; at 8:00 a.m. the theater opened and was filled with kids ignoring the movie and chanting "We want Frankie, We want Frankie." When Sinatra appeared, the crowd went berserk, screaming, moaning, and swooning. The next day was even wilder. Some 10,000 fans lined up to buy 3600 tickets, and another 20,000 overran Times Square. When 200 police were sent in to establish order, the crowd panicked, destroyed the ticket booth, and broke windows while screams of "Frankie," "Frankie" echoed through streets.

Though Sinatra's publicist, George Evans, later admitted hiring and coaching screaming, swooning teenage fans in the beginning of Sinatra's career, there was much more to Sinatra's success than that. A press agent, even one as skilled as Evans, who was given an award by *Billboard* in 1943 for "the most effective promotion of a single personality," had to have the right product for the time. Sinatra, a young, blue-eyed, tousled-haired man nicknamed "Swoonatra," gave young women an emotional outlet for the anxiety and anguish they felt in the early years of World War II when a great many young American men were off fighting and dying in a bloody war. "I get an audience involved because I'm involved myself—if the song is a lament at the loss of love, I get an ache in my gut," he explained. "I cry out the loneliness."[17] Throughout his career he has remained a master of lyrics, singing songs as if they reflected his own personal feelings. After dipping in popularity in the late 1940s, Sinatra bounced back stronger than ever with a dramatic role in the film *From Here to Eternity* (1953) and with record albums arranged and conducted by Nelson Riddle, albums featuring music that traced the joy, frustration, agony, and loneliness of searching for meaning and love through young adulthood and middle age. Sinatra kept alive accomplished singing of traditional popular music in an era of profound changes.

After World War II the music business changed radically in ways that rapidly accelerated the development of specialized music markets. The record industry was the first medium to be transformed. Besides the development of 45 rpm singles and 33⅓ rpm long-playing albums, portable magnetic tape equipment allowed small companies to enter the business, travel to regional musical centers, and inexpensively record and edit songs. Between 1949 and 1954 the number of record companies mushroomed from eleven to nearly two hundred, and the industry, no longer New York based, was now dispersed around the country—in Chicago, Cincinnati, Houston, Memphis, and Los Angeles. Many of these new small independent record companies specialized in the growing black rhythm and blues or white country and western markets that major record companies had tended to ignore since World War II had forced a decrease in record production. As competition mounted, record companies had to find the right singer and arrangement for each song in order to produce records that would stand out from the hundreds of others issued every week. Rather than just recording the material entertainers had already worked out in their performances, record companies were trying to manufacture original hits.

Creating hits became the job of the Artists and Repertory (A&R) man, essentially a producer who selected material and arrangements for his company's performers. An astute A&R man, which Columbia Records president Goddard Lieberson described as "a combination of musician, creative man, businessman with a flair for all these," could be as valuable as top stars.[18] Using unusual instrumentation—a harpsichord, a single guitar, or French horns—and adapting country and western songs like "Jambalaya," "This Ole House," and "Cold, Cold Heart" to the general public's taste, Mitch Miller, who joined Columbia Records in 1948, produced 22 hits by 1952 when record companies were flooding America with a variety of new releases.

While the record business was being transformed, so was radio. As television became the general entertainment machine in the home, radio networks gave way to independent local stations that increasingly concentrated on recorded music and on the disc jockeys who played the records rather than on a wide variety of genres, shows, and stars. By supplementing television, radio drew large audiences which attracted sponsors, often local businesses, who found radio very effective as an advertising medium. As a result of the emphasis on recordings, radio stations and record companies in the 1950s became closely intertwined, especially after it was clear that repeated exposure on radio produced hit records. In Cleveland in 1951, for instance, disc jockey Bill Randle made hits of Mantovani's "Charmaine" and Johnny Ray's "Cry" by playing and plugging them over and over. Such results made record companies, from the largest majors to the smallest independents, anxious to get their new releases on the air. Ultimately the "payola" scandals of the 1950s exposed the bribes record companies paid to get their songs played on radio. The competition was intense, but the opportunities were broad because the many local radio stations around the nation tended to appeal to specific segments of the population by playing only one type of music. The radio dial was filled with all sorts of music, which was being written, published, and recorded faster than ever before. In 1941 after ASCAP had withdrawn its music from radio because of a conflict over use fees, Broadcast Music, Inc. (BMI) was created to provide music for radio. BMI attracted new and inexperienced songwriters and gave a boost to minority music, which greatly diversified music publication just as the record and radio businesses were catering to the tastes of America's ethnic, regional, and age groups as never before.

The general white youth market came into its own after World War II when "teenage" became a widely accepted status between childhood and adulthood. In the past, the vast majority of people between fifteen and twenty had been considered adults, old enough to go to work, support themselves, marry, and begin families. But, increasingly, teenagers were encouraged to remain students, getting the educations that their parents had been denied, a luxury made possible by the postwar economic boom that brought affluence to more American families than ever before. With time and money to spend, teenagers became major consumers of clothing, cars, food, movies, and records. Like past generations of whites, they found their own music and dance in Afro-American culture—not in jazz, which had become an essentially undanceable musical art form, but in black dance music called "rhythm and blues."

White youths of the 1950s discovered rhythm and blues because radio disc jockeys, such as Alan Freed who began in Cleveland and then moved to New York in 1954, got fantastic responses by playing the black music on stations with white audiences. In the mid-1950s, rhythm and blues records created by independents for black Americans began to appear on general (white) pop music charts, which prompted major record companies to respond. After "Sh-Boom," recorded by the black singing group The Chords on Cat Records, made the breakthrough in 1954, a white group, The Crew Cuts, recorded an almost identical version of the song for Mercury, a process called "covering." Again and again in 1954 and 1955 major record companies' white pop singing groups "covered" independent companies' black groups' rhythm and blues records that broke into the pop charts. The covered versions tended to outsell the originals, partly because major record companies had superior promotion and distribution, partly, perhaps, because of racial discrimination by white disc jockeys and record stores, and partly because the black musicians' records had a somewhat foreign sound to white ears. White singers *adapted* the appealing new Afro-American music to the ears of white audiences who were getting their first exposure to rhythm and blues, just as white popularizers had earlier done with ragtime, jazz, and swing.

A new popular music evolved to suit the tastes of white teenagers in the early 1950s. The new music combined the rhythm of rhythm and blues, the twanging guitar of country and western, and the sentimental lyrics of general pop into rock and roll. The first band to popularize the new music, Bill Haley and the Comets, surfaced in 1953 with "Crazy Man Crazy" and reached the Top Ten in 1954 with "Shake, Rattle, and Roll," a cover of a recording by black singer Joe Turner. When Haley's "Rock Around the Clock" was included on the soundtrack of *Blackboard Jungle*, a movie about rebellious high school kids, it became the nation's top hit, selling some three million records and remaining in the Top Ten for nineteen weeks. Movie makers as well as record companies then cashed in on the youth market with a series of rock and roll, "B" movies, including Bill Haley and the Comets in *Rock Around the Clock* (1956) and *Don't Knock the Rock* (1957). Radio stations and disc jockeys around the country began to specialize in rock and roll and to evolve the Top Forty format. Rock and roll was becoming a big business. The career of Elvis Presley demonstrated just how big it could become.

Born to poor, white parents in Mississippi in 1935, Elvis Presley learned his first music in fundamentalist churches where preachers jumped around, screaming, shaking, and shouting to make congregations feel the spirit of the Lord. As he was growing up, Presley also absorbed the styles of country and western and black music. Ultimately he merged these three strains into his own distinctive style. In 1954 Presley made his first record, a cover of black singer Arthur

Crudup's "That's All Right," and began touring in the South, developing his wiggling hip movements and sounding like a black man crooning country songs. His style created a rage among white, southern teenagers, especially young women. "The girls just went crazy for him when he was up there on stage," his pal Red West recalled of Presley's tours in 1955. "Suddenly, to these young chicks Elvis was Marlon Brando and James Dean all rolled into one."[19] By the end of 1955 Presley used his undulations and sultry expressions to provoke his female fans into jumping up on stage and tearing off his clothes. Such wild responses attracted the attention of promoter Colonel Tom Parker, who had managed top country music stars and saw the potential of Presley's combination of a black sound, a white face, a sexy look, and a humble, off-stage manner. Parker set out to make Presley a national star, using radio stations to test the reactions to Presley's records. "I don't know what those Presley records have," Cleveland disc jockey Bill Randle observed, "but I put them on yesterday, and . . . the switchboard lit up like Glitter Gulch in Las Vegas. He hits them [kids] like a bolt of electricity."[20]

Presley was on his way. RCA Victor bought his contract and recordings from Sun, a small, southern independent, and in early 1956 released "Heartbreak Hotel," which sold over two million single records and gained Presley national television exposure. As if to symbolize the revolutionary changes that were about to rock pop music, Presley's first television appearance came on Tommy and Jimmy Dorsey's *Stage Show*. After the Dorseys' smooth big-band sound, Presley leapt on stage wearing an off-white sport coat with huge draped shoulders. He grabbed the mike, jerked it across his body, crouched into the tense stance of a streetfighter, and then erupted. With his legs shaking, his hips swiveling, his lips sneering, and his rich, lush voice dripping emotion, he sang the love-hungry lament of "Heartbreak Hotel." The twanging guitars and pulsating drum riffs seemed to possess Presley's pliant body and make it throb with the beat. In the days of the sedate styles of Snooky Lanson and Dorothy Collins on *Your Hit Parade*, Presley was an explosive, television performer, whose gyrations were condemned as scandalous and immoral. The controversy only made him a more desirable attraction for television and for kids looking for ways to defy their elders. Presley appeared on some of television's best variety shows. An estimated 54 million people watched the first of Presley's three appearances on *The Ed Sullivan Show*. The young people in the studio audience screamed and howled every time Presley moved, but the viewers at home did not see his undulations because Sullivan's cameras photographed Presley only from the waist up. In 1956, after appearances on television, in *Life* and *Time* magazines, on radio stations keyed to the youth market, and in movies, Presley's records sold so fast that Victor reportedly had to use the pressing plants of its rivals—Decca, Capitol, and MGM—to keep up with demand. After his 1956 sale of ten million records, the largest total sales for one performer in one year, Presley was widely acclaimed as the king of rock and roll.

Beginning in 1956 with *Love Me Tender* and continuing for fifteen years, Presley starred in a series of low-budget motion pictures, which served primarily as vehicles to publicize his records and to give his fans a chance to see "The King" in action. By using films, which could be made in a short time and widely circulated throughout the country, Colonel Parker kept Presley before his public. By allowing him to make only one or two movies a year and by severely limiting Presley's personal appearances, Parker also kept him in demand year after year. But there was much, much more to Presley's appeal than expert management and media manipulation. Besides combining the most exciting features of rhythm and blues and country and western music into rock and roll that white teenagers all over the country could call their own, he gave the youth culture its own sex symbol. Even more important than his attention-getting, exotic hip movements was his lush, sensual voice, which explained why Presley, unlike most other rock and roll stars, made sentimental love songs without a prominent beat a basic part of his repertoire.

There were many rock and roll performers who had long, successful careers, most notably perhaps Chuck Berry, who crossed over from rhythm and blues and wrote songs that openly rejected traditional music ("Roll Over Beethoven"), traditional values of work and marriage ("Too Much Monkey Business"), and traditional education ("School Days"). With song after song, Berry glorified the world of fast souped-up cars ("Maybellene"), of pretty young women ("Sweet Little Sixteen") and good-looking young men ("Brown-Eyed Handsome Man"), of hot rock and roll ("Rock and Roll Music"), and of dancing wildly all night long ("Reelin' and Rockin'"). While Berry's lyrics expressed teenagers' feelings, his infectious, pulsating melodies gave the young their dance music. In "School Days," which contrasted the boredom of a classroom to the joys of a "juke joint," Berry produced the song that might be considered the anthem of the youth culture of the 1950s. If Elvis Presley was the king of rock and roll, Chuck Berry was its poet laureate.

As "Elvis the Pelvis" Presley's controversial hip shaking and Chuck Berry's bouncy tunes indicated, rock and roll was dance music. While the primary media for the youth music were records and radio, the primary media for the youth dances were movies and television, which gave young people twisting, bopping models to emulate. Blending bits of the Shimmy, Lindy, Charleston, Eagle Rock, Camel Walk, and other Afro-American-based dance fads of the past, America's teenagers—in little towns as well as in big cities—stomped their feet and swung their bodies to the pulsating beat of rock and roll. They copied the movements and steps they saw in rock and roll movies and on Dick Clark's *American Bandstand* television show, which, after local success in Philadelphia, became a daily late afternoon ABC network show in 1957. *American Bandstand* featured rock and roll records, performers "lip-synching" their latest releases, and typical teenagers from the audience doing new dance routines. In a real sense the dance masters of the rock and roll generation were the Philadelphia amateurs on *American Bandstand,* who created national dance crazes overnight, just as the show created hit records and new stars.

By the late-1950s, popular music had clearly fragmented into two different music markets, which were to a great extent concentrated in different media. Youth music, dominated by white rock and roll singers such as Presley, Jerry Lee Lewis, and Buddy Holly and by black rhythm and blues singers such as Chuck Berry, Fats Domino, and Little Richard, tended to be recorded by independent companies on 45 rpm singles and promoted on radio. The adult market, dominated by traditional pop singers such as Frank Sinatra, Dinah Shore, and Nat Cole, bands such as Mantovani's and Mitch Miller's, and original Broadway cast albums from musicals such as *South Pacific* and *West Side Story,* tended to be recorded by major companies on long-playing albums and promoted on television. In the mid and late 1950s, the stars of long-running musical-variety shows on television were traditional, non-rock and roll performers such as Lawrence Welk, Liberace, and Perry Como. There were a few notable exceptions, principally *American Bandstand,* its imitators, and occasional guest appearances by headline grabbing rock and roll stars, but prime-time television music remained overwhelmingly mainstream Tin Pan Alley songs which appealed to the adults national advertisers wanted to reach. Major record companies were also generally content to leave the risky rock and roll singles market basically to independents because traditional popular music dominated the more predictable and more lucrative long-playing record market. Between 1960 and 1965 the list of the Top Ten LPs contained twice as many Tin Pan Alley albums as the total of all the folk, rock, rhythm and blues, soul, and country and western albums combined. But pop music changed radically in 1964 when a new, musical force burst into mainstream American music. This time the force came from England.

In the late 1950s and early 1960s the singing group, The Beatles, emerged out of the English rock and roll scene which had preserved the vitality and spirit of early American rock and roll and rhythm and blues. By 1963 The Beatles' joyous, upbeat sound, with its blend of driving rhythms and soft harmonies, put their records at the top of the English pop charts, and their distinctive image—especially their collarless, four-button coats and their long hair—put the group in the spotlight. With some 15 million people watching on television, a huge crowd of young fans at the London Palladium mobbed John Lennon, Paul McCartney, George Harrison, and Ringo Starr, making the group great celebrities on both sides of the Atlantic. Arriving in America in early 1964, they were greeted by thousands of screaming teenagers. Their first appearance on *The Ed Sullivan Show* drew 50,000 requests for the 700 seats and the largest viewing audience in the popular show's history. An estimated 75 million Americans tuned in to see and hear the controversial, long-haired English rock and rollers. The boost from this instant, national publicity kicked off a well-orchestrated multi-media blitz, including records, radio, and their first movie, *A Hard Day's Night*. In April 1964, only a few months after their arrival, The Beatles had the five best-selling American singles, twelve singles in the top one hundred, and the two top-selling LPs. There was no precedent in American musical history for such success, which came in part from their blend of early rock and roll and rhythm and blues. But they also arrived in America not long after the assassination of President John F. Kennedy, when their boyish charm, upbeat escapist music, and simple message that love was the answer to all problems were right for the time. The Beatles also appealed to a new group of teenagers who wanted their own music and stars.

The Beatles signaled the emergence of the second generation of the post World War II youth culture, a generation that, in less than a decade, lived through a lifetime of jarring changes, a generation that sought to make its own counter-culture a reality. In the age of instantaneous mass-communication and crisis after crisis, young teenagers had to decide where they stood on such profound and perplexing issues as sexuality, war, racism, and drugs in the decade of birth-control pills, Vietnam, assassinations, race riots, and LSD. The Beatles' music in many ways reflected the experiences of their generation. The Beatles' music grew increasingly complex and experimental. From a simple, four-man rock and roll band, the group explored every potential of modern recording technology, ultimately producing albums that could only be created in the recording studio. Their lyrics moved from simple songs about individual romance to explorations of mind-altering drugs, the search for meaning in a world of chaos, and the quest for personal fulfillment. For their answers they looked to love, drugs, religion, and mysticism, as did many of their fans. In The Beatles' large and varied body of music, which included a number of songs like "Yesterday" and "Michelle" that were destined to become standards, they wrote and sang about many themes. But their principal theme was the individual's search for meaning and belonging. Though they grew very sophisticated in every way, the power of love remained at the core of their music. The Beatles represented the introspective, apolitical, personal quests of the 1960s and triggered a great outburst of musical innovation in rock music.

Another influential English rock group of the period, the Rolling Stones, who also arrived in America in 1964, represented the other side of the youth of the 1960s, the side that openly rebelled against authority, fought the black revolution, struggled against the Vietnam War, and mocked conventional values and morality. While The Beatles featured light bouncy beats and smooth harmonies, the Rolling Stones stressed the heavy, pounding rhythms and raw energy of Afro-American urban blues. While the early Beatles dressed neatly, had hair that barely covered their ears, and sang innocently, "I Want To Hold Your Hand," the early Stones looked scruffy, had shoulder-length hair, and sang bluntly, "I Just Want To Make Love to You." While the mature Beatles sang "All You Need Is Love," the mature Stones lionized the "Street Fighting Man." While The Beatles reassured people that in times of trouble "Mother Mary" would comfort them, the Stones expressed their "Sympathy for the Devil." While The Beatles experimented musically, the Stones preserved their gutsy, blues style. While The Beatles basically stood still as they performed, Mick Jagger, the lead singer of the Stones, wore androgynous makeup and clothing and threw himself totally into taunting, teasing sexual gyrations that provoked *Time* magazine to call him "the king bitch of rock."[21]

Though The Beatles and the Rolling Stones tapped many of the emotions, longings, and frustrations of the sixties and stimulated the growth of rock music, an indigenous American musical development was at the heart of an attempt to develop a separate, youth counterculture which began in the mid-1960s in the San Francisco Bay Area. A great many young people left their middle-class homes and universities for a far different life. Rejecting what they felt was a materialistic, intolerant, unjust, meaningless society, they "dropped out," wore old clothes, begged spare change, preached non-violence, communal sharing, and free love, experimented with hallucination-inducing drugs, slept wherever they could, and ate whatever they found. Perhaps even more than ever before, dance was at the center of the new generation's music. In fact, the Fillmore Auditorium, the Avalon Ballroom, and a number of smaller clubs and halls that housed live, rock dance-concerts, provided some of the only common denominators and communal meeting places for the people often called "hippies," "streetpeople," or "flower children." In these dancehalls a great many electric rock bands, such as the Jefferson Airplane, the Grateful Dead, Big Brother and the Holding Company with Janis Joplin, and Country Joe and the Fish developed the "San Francisco sound," a blend of blues and country styles refracted through the intricate prisms of modern electronic wizardry. As elaborate and sophisticated as the best of the music was, in live performances played at deafening volumes, the complex, throbbing beat of the bass, rhythm guitar, and drums, the intricate, soaring melody lines played by lead guitars, often with counterpoint from an organ, and the frequently unintelligible lyrics shouted over the screaming music, all combined to create an overpowering emotional experience, which often was augmented by psychedelic light shows that simulated the visual effects of drug "trips." In this atmosphere of supercharged, sensory overload, groups of dancers who were "doing their own thing" surrendered themselves to the pounding music, letting their bodies undulate with the shifting rhythms. Though individual, the dance took on the aura of a group ritual. Even though rock music could not have been produced without elaborate and expensive electronic technology, the principal medium of the early San Francisco sound was the live performance, which restored the intimate interaction between audiences and entertainers that was absent from most other forms of modern show business. But live performances also meant limited, local audiences until the music was recorded and nationally distributed.

After The Beatles' *Sgt. Pepper's Lonely Hearts Club Band* (1967) sold over seven million albums, major record companies quickly signed the promising San Francisco groups. RCA got the Jefferson Airplane, Columbia, Big Brother and the Holding Company with Janis Joplin, and Warner Brothers, the Grateful Dead. At first the groups, accustomed to controlling their own volume and sound mix with their own technicians, had great problems with their recordings because major record companies' sound men, accustomed to general popular music, toned down the instruments and made the vocals more prominent than they were in live performances. The rock groups, who often considered themselves members of the youth counter-culture, frequently disregarded costs and insisted on perfecting their music on the complex, modern technology that allowed almost limitless opportunities for refinement. Warner Brothers, for instance, reportedly considered dropping its contract with the Grateful Dead when the band spent $120,000 on recording without producing a single album. But because of the great potential profit from music that could sell millions of albums, major companies generally reached compromises with the rock groups in which independent producers, often the groups, created the albums and the companies marketed them. This method represented a major institutional change in the record industry, which sold more rock albums between 1966 and 1971 than all other major categories of music combined. Rock music continued to dominate LP sales in the 1970s.

Radio even changed to accommodate the rock albums that featured long, complicated cuts, rather than the three-minute songs that Top Forty A.M. stations continued to use for their tightly scheduled time slots. In San Francisco a new sort of radio station emerged. F.M. stations, high fidelity radio without the static of A.M. stations but with a limited broadcast range, had been the preserve of classical music, jazz, light classics, and intellectual programming. But San Francisco disc jockey Tom Donahue, frustrated with Top Forty radio, bought failing F.M. station KMPX and made it an "underground" radio station. Playing long rock album cuts, tape recordings, and test records, the station was almost like a broadcast extension of the local dance-concerts. Following KMPX's success, commercially sponsored counter-culture radio stations emerged across the country, providing important exposure for rock groups who were not suited to Top Forty radio. But as lucrative and important as rock albums and underground radio were, the most distinctive facet of rock music and the youth culture was the huge live concert.

In San Francisco in January 1967, rock bands, including the Jefferson Airplane and the Grateful Dead, gave a free dance-concert in Golden Gate Park. Called the "Gathering of the Tribes" and a "Human Be-in," the free performance, which attracted some 20,000, became common in San Francisco and spread to other cities as the youth culture seemed to many to be emerging as a true counter-culture, a true alternative way of life with music and dance as its central rallying points. In the summer of 1969 an estimated half-million people gathered at the Woodstock Music and Art Fair, near Bethel, New York, for three solid days of rock music and living on the land, a demonstration that the counter-culture could work. It did—at least in the sense that hundreds of thousands of strangers, many high on drugs, lived peacefully together, singing, dancing, and sharing. Woodstock seemed to be a culmination of the forces of love that The Beatles had set in motion five years earlier. Even though it was a commercial concert that was filmed for a commercial movie, Woodstock became a catchword for a dream, a dream that was shattered shortly after it was born.

In 1969, at the end of a coast-to-coast tour, the Rolling Stones gave a free concert at Altamont Race Track east of San Francisco. It was to be the climax of the 1960s, the ultimate love-in. To police the event the Rolling Stones hired the Hell's Angels, an Oakland-based motorcycle club with a reputation for orgies and violence. After a long day of heavy alcohol and drug use, the crowd of some 300,000 grew restless and frustrated as it had to sit waiting for hours after the last warmup band had finished until the sun went down because Mick Jagger's makeup and costume would look better under the lights. When the Rolling Stones finally appeared, the crowd surged forward, egged on by Jagger's prancing, strutting, and teasing, but it was beaten back by club-swinging Hell's Angels guarding the stage. In a horrible irony too bizarre and grotesque for fiction, as Jagger spat out the words to "Sympathy for the Devil," the Hell's Angels jumped on an eighteen-year-old teenager, pummelled him with their boots, stabbed him with their knives, and left him lying dead in a pool of blood. That night all over the country television news broadcast the scene of surrealistic horror.

By the end of 1970 the euphoria of the early years of rock music and the counter-culture was dead, the victim of Altamont, the overdose drug deaths of young rock stars, and the disbanding of The Beatles. If rock music was no longer seen as a foundation for a new society, it was still seen as a foundation for big business. In the affluent 1970s rock albums sold even better than before, and independent producer-promoters like Robert Stigwood learned to make full use of all media, coordinating rock movie musicals, sound-track albums, and single records with expensive and sophisticated multi-media advertising and promotional campaigns. At their most effective these rock–movie-record projects could reap incredible profits. In mid-1978, for instance, the soundtrack recording of the popular film *Saturday Night Fever* (1977) reportedly had sold 12 million albums.

In the age of mass communication, multi-media successes linking live performances, records, television, radio, and movies became the common pattern. Though rock music dominated popular music in the 1970s, America was filled with music of all sorts, which appealed to the many specialized markets that the general prosperity and diversified media of modern show business made possible. But on the eve of the 1980s it had been decades since the last major musical development. Popular music seemed due for a new outburst of creativity. Where it might come from was, of course, uncertain, but judging from the past the most likely source would be one of the nation's largest, most dynamic minorities, perhaps the growing, generally ignored Spanish-speaking population with its rich variety of Caribbean, Central, and South American musical traditions. But whatever the new trends and directions in popular music, it was clear that the diversity of the nation and of its entertainment media would keep America the home of the world's music.

5

American Popular Opera: Musicals and the Media

In 1866 two New Yorkers, hoping to cash in on the public's desire for escapist entertainment, pooled their money and imported a French ballet troupe with beautiful sets and sexy costumes. Before the show could open the Academy of Music in which the troupe was to perform burned down. Niblo's Garden, the only other suitable house, was already committed to an untried melodrama, *The Black Crook*, a story of a man's receiving magical powers in exchange for delivering a soul to the devil every year. The promoters convinced Niblo's manager to combine the ballet and the Faustian melodrama. He added lavish production numbers and presented a five-and-half-hour hodge-podge of dance, drama, music, variety acts, and special effects that the public loved. The show's most striking quality, other than the legs of the female ballet dancers, was its spectacle. Beautiful sets magically rose out of the floor; people popped in and out of trapdoors at unexpected times and places; a hurricane of gauze swept through a mountain pass; and Satan dramatically appeared and disappeared. The "lavish richness and barbaric splendor," climaxed in a spectacular scene: "One by one curtains of mist ascend and drift away," wrote the dazzled *New York Tribune* critic. "Silver couches, on which the fairies loll in negligent grace, ascend and descend amid a silver rain. Columns of living splendor whirl, and dazzle as they whirl. From the clouds droop gilded chariots and the white forms of angels. It is a very beautiful pageant." This "beautiful pageant" ran for a totally unprecedented 475 performances in its initial New York booking. During the long run producers added an opulent ballroom scene, two new ballets, a military march, 150 children in a baby ballet, and an "original and wonderful mechanical donkey."[1] The popular extravaganza was revived in New York eight times between 1868 and 1892 and was performed in many other cities.

In the late nineteenth century when a number of distinctive entertainment forms were developing, popular musical entertainment tended to fall into two broad categories—the variety show, with no attempt at continuity, and the book show, with a story, characters that carried throughout the production, and music and songs that expressed the story. Variety shows were structurally simple and matured quickly, but book shows were complex and took much longer to mature into truly integrated musical plays and to be naturalized from European imports into an American performing art. This chapter focuses on the evolution of the book musical during the entertainment revolution.

The astounding success of *The Black Crook* taught stage producers that the American public loved opulent, musical extravaganzas crammed full of all sorts of attractions. *Humpty Dumpty*, which opened in New York in 1868 and ran longer than *The Black Crook*, for instance, featured the first American roller-skating troupe, bicyclists, a drill team, circus acts, a panorama of Naples, underground grottoes, and a steamboat explosion and fire. All these were included in a show which starred the greatest American pantomimist of the century, George L. Fox, in a pantomime extravaganza, a theatrical form imported from England. In 1874 *Evangeline*, another lavishly produced extravaganza, proved a great hit with settings ranging from Africa to the Wild West and with such gimmicks as a spouting whale, a dancing cow played by two men in costume, a woman in tights playing the male lead, and a 300-pound man in a dress playing a female role.

In the late 1870s as American extravaganzas were packed full of more and more unrelated attractions and the line between book and variety shows blurred, the European operetta, or light opera, became a popular musical form in America. The impetus for the new imports came from the great American success of Gilbert and Sullivan's *H.M.S. Pinafore* with the witty lyrics of W. S. Gilbert and the catchy melodies of Arthur Sullivan creating unified musical theater. After *Pinafore*'s popular acclaim, sumptuously produced English, French, and Viennese comic operas became the rage in America. In 1880 ten comic operas were produced in New York; in 1883 there were thirteen. With scores by such first-rate composers as Gilbert and Sullivan, Jacques Offenbach, and Johann Strauss, comic operas remained a staple of the American musical stage. Set in Europe with sentimental stories of upper-class life, often a romance between a dashing, young, military officer and a lovely young woman, the operettas gave the public beautiful music performed by formally trained voices in gorgeous productions that often included lovely ballroom scenes and graceful dances, especially waltzes, which became fashionable after the success of Viennese composer Franz Lehar's stylish *Merry Widow* (1907), with its lilting waltz.

Operettas written in America long remained only poor imitations of the European originals. But in the early twentieth century the American operetta, while still derivative, reached a new level of artistry in the hands of Irish-born, European-educated Victor Herbert. His finest show, *Naughty Marietta* (1910), represented the form at its best. The story, far removed from the contemporary world of ragtime and vaudeville, was set in Spanish-ruled New Orleans in 1780, a typically exotic comic opera setting, and centered on aristocratic ladies, men in uniforms, grand ballrooms, courtly flirtations, complicated intrigue, rocky romances, and happy endings. In the complex but unimportant plot: Captain Richard chases a pirate; Marietta, an Italian noblewoman masquerading as a commoner, chases Captain Richard; Etienne, the Lt. Governor's son, who turns out to be the pirate, chases Marietta; and Adah, a light-skinned slave, whom Richard buys and frees, chases her master, Etienne. In the end Captain Richard captures Etienne; Marietta captures Richard; and Herbert's beautiful music, including "I'm Falling in Love with Someone" and "Ah, Sweet Mystery of Life," captures the public's fancy. In the next twenty years, Victor Herbert, Rudolf Friml, Sigmund Romberg, and others dominated the American musical stage with beautiful operettas featuring exotic settings, lovely scores, and aristocratic characters.

Operettas in many ways resembled adult fairy tales—idealized versions of the way the world ought to be—a world of beauty, grace, manners, nobility, and gentility. Operettas seemed to have a universal quality that transcended time. Franz Lehar's *The Merry Widow*, for instance, had great appeal in the Hollywood films of 1934 and 1952 as it did on the stage in Vienna in 1905, in New York in 1907, and in its other major revivals. Though operetta remained popular in America, it was essentially a European musical form.

By the 1880s producers were experimenting with musical comedies about everyday Americans, using popular language, songs, comedy, and dances. The variety stage, traditionally as lowbrow as book musicals had been highbrow, provided much of the vitality, material, and personnel. Beginning in the 1840s blackface minstrel shows perfected fast-paced performances of earthy humor, eyecatching ethnic characters, production numbers, lively dances, and foot-tapping popular songs that audiences loved. These performances led directly to burlesque and vaudeville and indirectly to distinctively American book musicals. The first big step in that direction was taken in the 1870s when minstrel man Edward Harrigan traded his burnt cork makeup for his natural Irish brogue, teamed up with performer Tony Hart, composer David Braham, and a talented cast, settled in New York City, and produced a series of musical plays centering on the city's minorities— blacks, Germans, Jews, and especially the Irish. Harrigan starred as Dan Mulligan, a leader of Irish immigrants in a tenement neighborhood bristling with the richly varied sights and sounds of lower-class New York. Harrigan and Hart's popular shows had a startling realism and vitality because they drew material—slang, dialects, costumes, and mannerisms—from the streets, not the drawing rooms. "Polite society, wealth, and culture possess little or no color or picturesqueness," Harrigan observed. "The chief use I make of them is as a foil to the poor, the workers, the great middle class."[2] The richly praised shows, which drew huge followings of working-class New Yorkers, were primarily innovative blends of dramatic sketches and popular music, rather than fully integrated book musicals, but they clearly demonstrated the great potential of using variety entertainment as the basis of musicals.

In the early twentieth century the first true master of the American musical emerged—George M. Cohan, who grew up on stage as part of a vaudeville family. Accustomed to success in vaudeville in the hinterlands, Cohan set out to create a hit Broadway musical. His first two efforts—overblown expansions of vaudeville skits—flopped in New York in 1901 and 1902, yet succeeded on the road where competition was less intense. But in 1904 Cohan gained a foothold on Broadway with *Little Johnny Jones*, which included "Give My Regards to Broadway" and "Yankee Doodle Boy," and demonstrated that he could write full-length shows without losing the rapid-fire pace, catchy songs, breezy dialogue, and snappy delivery of vaudeville. "At times," a critic wrote of one of his shows, "it goes so fast that it almost bewilders and gives the impression of a great machine shooting out characters, choruses, songs, dances with rapid-fire quickness and precision." Besides that, he had the perfect star for this sort of show—himself. Bursting with brash self-confidence, Cohan shot out slang and wisecracks with the staccato pace and force of a jackhammer. One critic denounced him as a "vulgar, cheap, blatant, ill-mannered, flashily-dressed, insolent, smart aleck," but he also had to admit that Cohan "appeals to the imagination and apparent approval of large American audiences."[3] What the critics disliked about Cohan, the public loved.

Cohan boasted of bringing "actual living characters from the street to the stage."[4] What he really brought was an idealized version of the cocky, young city boy of the early twentieth century. During the era of Teddy Roosevelt when the Panama Canal was being built and America was emerging as a world power, Cohan's swaggering strut, his emotional sentimentalism, and his flag-waving patriotism were just what the American public wanted. In place of comic opera's refined elegance, genteel leisure, and European glamor, Cohan brought to the musical stage the raw vitality of a new Yankee Doodle dandy from the sidewalks of New York, who could not stand still for an instant, did not know a waltz from a quadrille, but *did* know that Broadway was a better place to be than London. Almost every year for a decade after *George Washington, Jr.* (1906), Cohan produced a bouncy, new musical, which earned him the title "Mr. Broadway." His shows, so well suited to the optimism and self-confidence of the early part of the century, proved less appealing to Americans after the disillusionment of World War I. But Cohan had made a major step in establishing musical comedy that was distinctively American.

Like America itself, musical comedy was a blend. From extravaganza it got lavish costumes and production numbers; from burlesque it took satire and chorus girls; from popular plays it absorbed melodramatic, romantic plots; from operettas it drew beautiful melodies and glamor; and from vaudeville it borrowed popular dance, music, comedy, and stars, along with a breakneck performance speed. But the full integration of these diverse elements into cohesive shows in which all the components fit together like pieces in a jigsaw puzzle took decades of experimentation on the nation's stages. Since silent movies could not effectively do musicals, the stage remained the only medium for this experimentation until the late 1920s. No one played a greater role in transforming musical comedy from disjointed conglomerations to integrated wholes than Jerome Kern.

After studying music in Europe and writing popular songs for London musicals, Kern returned to America in 1904 at age nineteen. Doing everything from plugging songs to playing as a rehearsal pianist, he worked his way up in American musical theater in an age dominated by operettas, which Kern worked on as a "score doctor," helping to adapt European shows for American tastes. In 1912 after contributing a number of individual songs to typical musicals of the period, which had scores made up of many composers' work, he began writing his own full musicals. His first success came in 1915 when he collaborated with librettist Guy Bolton on *Very Good Eddie,* a show about everyday people in believable if far-fetched situations. Fourteen-year-old Richard Rodgers saw the show a dozen times, absorbing the sparkling music that he later described as blending European operettas "with every thing that was fresh in the American scene to give us something wonderfully new and clear in music writing." In the next few years Kern and Bolton, joined by P. G. Wodehouse, created a series of musical comedies about middle-class people for the 299-seat Princess Theatre whose limited resources meant the shows could not compete with the grand spectacles of the period. Rather, they were models of modest, fast-moving, fully integrated musical plays. "Every song and lyric contributed to the action," Bolton observed of their hit *Oh Boy!* (1917). "The humor was based on situation, not interjected by the comedians." In 1917 at the height of the Princess shows' success, Kern argued that "the musical numbers should carry the action of the play and should be representative of the personalities of the characters who sing them."[5] When the songs in many other current musicals had little to do with the story or characters, the Princess shows took another step toward the perfection of musical comedies. But the Princess shows did not immediately revolutionize commercial musical theater.

In the 1920s Kern and such other great American composers and lyricists as George and Ira Gershwin, Vincent Youmans, Irving Berlin, Cole Porter, Richard Rodgers, and Lorenz Hart wrote excellent music for conventional, frothy musicals such as *Sally* (1920), *Lady Be Good* (1924), *No! No! Nanette!* (1925), *The Girl Friend* (1926), and *Good*

News (1927). The upbeat musicals of the 1920s are remembered more for dances like the Charleston, the Black Bottom, and the Varsity Drag, for songs that became standards such as "Look for the Silver Lining," "Fascinating Rhythm," "Tea for Two," "Blue Skies," "The Best Things in Life Are Free," and "Thou Swell," and for stars such as Al Jolson, Marilyn Miller, Fred and Adele Astaire, Eddie Cantor, and Beatrice Lillie, than for their unity of score and story. But near the end of the decade, Kern set a new standard for the American musical.

In the jazz age, Edna Ferber's best-selling novel *Show Boat,* which included the harsh realities of black life, racial prejudice, and broken romances, seemed a most unlikely prospect for adaptation to the musical stage. But Jerome Kern and Oscar Hammerstein II were enthralled with it, convinced Florenz Ziegfeld to finance it, and threw themselves into the project. "We couldn't keep our hands off it," Hammerstein recalled of their exhilarating creative process. "We acted out scenes together and planned the actual direction. We sang to each other. We had ourselves swooning."[6] As soon as it opened in 1927 *Show Boat* had audiences and critics swooning and has kept them swooning ever since. The story, set on a Mississippi River showboat, centers on the rocky marriage of Magnolia, the Captain's daughter, and the unhappy fate of Julie, whose marriage is broken because she has a black ancestor. The plot, which ends happily for Magnolia, was unusually serious for the musical stage of the day. But what drew the greatest accolades from critics and audiences were Kern's marvelous melodies and Hammerstein's great lyrics, which included "Bill," "Can't Help Lovin' Dat Man," "Why Do I Love You?," "Make Believe," and "Ol' Man River." The emotional power of the music more than made up for the contrivances and other weaknesses in the story. The score was truly the heart of the show. From the unconventional opening scene, which substituted black wharf hands for the perfunctory chorus girls and the sad lament of "Ol' Man River" for the normally upbeat song and dance, *Show Boat* integrated its music into the story so that the songs expressed the deepest feelings of the characters. The musical was also a visual delight. Produced by Florenz Ziegfeld, known for his tasteful, expensively-mounted productions, and designed by Joseph Urban, known for his artistic innovation, the show's fine sets took the audience from a Mississippi River levee and the excitement of the showboat's arrival, to the ship's theater for a show–within–a–show, back to the river, to the Chicago World's Fair of 1893, into a Chicago night club, and back to the showboat.

Show Boat was truly a landmark musical—much more than just the best of its year or even its decade. It was something new. Ziegfeld realized that and billed it "an American musical play." Critics at the time also saw its distinctiveness. "Some of its best numbers are so successful in their combination of the theatrical elements, music, acting, scene," critic Stark Young perceptively wrote in his review of the show, "as to suggest openings for the development not of mere musical comedy, but of popular opera."[7] With this show, the European operetta had been naturalized. Kern and Hammerstein had taken a characteristic American theme—the interaction of blacks and whites in the heartland of the country—had drawn on Afro American spirituals, American popular songs, and European music, had used common Americans as heroes and heroines, had made the story an epic romance, and had produced a distinctive American show with much of the grandeur and beauty of the operetta and with a form and style that had the mass appeal of the popular stage. Though the phrase is too aristocratic sounding to please a great many people, *Show Boat,* and other notable musicals that followed it, deserved to be considered *American* "popular opera."

The popular show ran on Broadway for over 570 performances, but even in a 2400-seat theater, Ziegfeld claimed that *Show Boat* netted only about $2000 a week, which underscored the major financial problems stage producers faced. Besides initial production costs, high operating expenses had to be paid every week, and no matter how popular the show, the number of people who could buy tickets to see it was strictly limited to the number of seats in one theater. Even hit shows did not make enough profits to compensate for the flops that even the best producers had in the uncertain live entertainment business. Unlike movie producers who worked within the financially solid structure of the studio, producers of stage shows, with only their own resources to draw on, faced an increasingly difficult dilemma. The public wanted lavish, expensive shows, but there was no way to make those shows available to masses of people, which would have allowed both low prices and the high profits necessary to finance other shows. Taking shows on tour did not solve the problem because costs were high and the number of tickets was still limited by the house size. Raising ticket prices or cutting the scale of the productions or the size of the casts would have made the shows less appealing. By the late 1920s producers of live musicals had to watch helplessly as costs rose faster than revenues. Things got worse—much worse—when sound motion pictures began to bring lavishly produced musicals to masses of people at cheap prices at the same time that the Great Depression made money for productions and for tickets scarcer than ever before.

By the mid-1920s people all over the country were used to watching famous actors, actresses, and comedians like Douglas Fairbanks, Mary Pickford, and Charlie Chaplin. But most people were denied the opportunity to see and hear Broadway musical stars such as Al Jolson, Marilyn Miller, and Fred and Adele Astaire and dazzling productions like Sigmund Romberg's *Student Prince* and Jerome Kern's *Show Boat.* Some major stars and productions did not tour at all, and even when they did travel, they generally reached relatively few people in a few big eastern and midwestern cities. Because few people could afford to make the trip to New York City to see America's most famous musical productions and stars, Broadway musicals took on an aura of alluring mystery and enchantment. "Times Square," "Forty-second Street," "Ziegfeld," "Shubert Alley"—the very words became almost magical incantations to summon up the spirits of big-time show business. The word "Broadway" became synonymous with musicals and with glamor and excitement.

Early sound pictures understandably drew heavily on stage musicals for new, crowd-drawing attractions. It was, of course, the 1927 musical *The Jazz Singer,* starring Al Jolson, that sparked the rage for sound motion pictures. Between 1928 and 1930 Hollywood studios cashed in on the allure of Broadway by turning out musicals as quickly as possible. From classic operettas such as *Vagabond King, Viennese Nights,* and *The Desert Song* to distinctively American musicals such as *Show Boat, Whoopee,* and *Sally,* Broadway shows proved a great asset to moviemakers because the musicals were ready made, consumer-tested shows that could be quickly and easily filmed as they had been done on stage. But film was a different medium and had to evolve its own style of musicals.

When MGM finally made its first sound motion picture in 1929, it was a musical, *Broadway Melody.* But unlike most others, it was an *original* musical written for film. Besides capitalizing on the mystique and glamor of Broadway with its title, the film's story followed the rise of two sisters from small-time vaudeville to stardom in a major Ziegfeld-like show. Blending theater and romance, laughter and tears, *Broadway Melody* capitalized on public curiosity about live show business by taking viewers behind the scenes. "The microphone and its twin camera," enthused *Photoplay* in 1929, "poke themselves into backstage corners, into dressing rooms, into rich parties, and hotel bedrooms."[8] Besides letting audiences peek into the personal lives of performers and into the work of preparing and performing a musical, films about producing a stage show also allowed moviemakers to insert songs and dances whenever the pace lagged by showing the production in rehearsal. *Broadway Melody* was a great hit, grossing far more than ten times its cost, and earning its star, Bessie Love, an Academy Award as best actress. It was also the first talkie to win an Academy Award as best picture.

During Hollywood's pre-1930 rush to turn out as many musicals as possible, the vast majority were typically static, early talkies. But in such early musicals as *The Love Parade* (1929), *Monte Carlo* (1930), and *Applause* (1929), directors Ernst Lubitsch and Rouben Mamoulian demonstrated that sound films could have the visual artistry of silent pictures. Lubitsch used mobile cameras and tracking shots and subtly blended sound and music as in *Monte Carlo*, when the driving tempo of a train's wheels became the rhythm of "Beyond the Blue Horizon." Mamoulian recorded two sound tracks at once to capture the vocal complexities of dialogue and used vocal "flashbacks" to complement screen images with reminders of what had gone before. These innovations in early sound films were not all strictly *musical*, but they came in musical pictures, perhaps because working with the relationship between the rhythms of music and the movements of visual imagery stimulated creative directors to new heights of integrating sight and sound.

By 1930 film musicals had declined in popularity, perhaps because the glut of poorly made musicals had satisfied the public's appetite, but more likely because the upbeat, happy-go-lucky films of the 1920s no longer appealed to a public faced with the worst economic depression in American history. By 1930 it was distressingly clear that the economic slump had become a nosedive, that life was not going to be the romp that many musicals of the late 1920s had suggested. As the economy and the public mood changed radically, so did the movies. Audiences laughed as the Marx Brothers and Mae West ridiculed social, political, and moral values; they cheered as James Cagney, Ed-

ward G. Robinson, and Paul Muni shot their ways from poverty to
prosperity; and in 1933 they found musicals they liked in *42nd Street*
and *Gold Diggers of 1933*, which reportedly were the second and third
best moneymakers of the year.

Like *Broadway Melody* and many of its predecessors, *42nd Street*
took the audiences backstage at the creation of a musical. But in this
picture on opening day the star breaks her leg, which threatens to kill
the show, throw the cast out of work, and destroy the director, who
is facing bankruptcy because of the stock market crash. At the urging
of cast members the lead goes to an unheralded chorus girl, Ruby
Keeler. All afternoon, Keeler rehearses, with the cast helping and root-
ing for her. That night as the show is to open, desperate director Warner
Baxter gives the spunky, talented unknown from the back row of the
chorus a rousing pep talk. "You're going out a chorus girl," he tells
her, "but you're coming back a star."[9] She does, which saves the jobs
of everyone in the show. The popular Cinderella story was just right
for the Depression. *Gold Diggers of 1933*, Warner Brothers' second hit
musical of the year, which also offered hope to little people, opened
with a lavishly costumed production number, "We're in the Money."
Just as the chorus girls are belting out a line about no more headlines
about breadlines, the sheriff forecloses the show. The desperate chorus
girls, gold diggers who survive by getting everything they can from
lecherous old sugar daddies, help raise the money for a musical that
hits hard at the nightmare of the thirties. In "Remember My Forgotten
Man," its unusually tough closing number, a woman sings a lament
about America cheering the World War I soldier as he marched off to
fight, but then neglecting him when he is in need, making him a forgotten man. As she sings, the camera cuts to boys enlisting, fighting,
returning, being refused jobs, and forming a breadline. Then it zooms
in to show the men's grim, desperate eyes.

Besides appealing to audiences with stories about unknowns rising
to stardom against great odds and about the injustice of the Depression, these Warner Brothers' musicals also featured stunning production numbers created by Busby Berkeley, a veteran stage dancer,
choreographer, and director, whose cinematic effects made his movie
musicals far more than just filmed stage shows. For *Footlight Parade*
(1933), the story of a theatrical producer on the skids, for instance,
Berkeley created the first film aqua-ballet, "By the Waterfall," which
began with scores of scantily-clad women on a high waterfall with

20,000 gallons of water flowing over it every minute. When the women slide down the waterfall into a forest lake, it turns into a swimming pool in which the women move rhythmically as a group, flowing from one intricate, geometric formation to another, which the movie audience saw from a wide range of camera angles. "With technicians I designed the pool and made caverns underneath it with thick plates of glass that I could shoot the camera through," Berkeley recalled. "It was my toughest number to film because of the camera set-ups underwater, abovewater and for the high sets. . . . The set underneath the stage looked like the hold of some enormous ocean liner."[10] Such elaborate productions became Berkeley's trademark.

Berkeley was essentially an abstract artist with the movie camera, working on a large scale with people as well as things. He became a designer, not a choreographer, and he designed for *film.* "If you go through all of my pictures you will see very little actual dancing," he reflected. "It wasn't because I didn't know how to create it and do it, but I wanted to do something *new and different.* Something that had never been seen before. Had they ever seen seventy or a hundred pianos waltzing? Had they ever seen lighted violins before? The same goes for all my various formations. I wanted to do something unusual and entertain an audience."[11] In many of his extravaganzas the *camera* was the major actor. Berkeley frequently opened with closeups that looked ordinary and then pulled the camera back and up, revealing people and props arranged in complicated patterns in which people often became indistinguishable from props. Many of these long shots taken from unusual perspectives resembled the intricate variations of a kaleidoscope. Besides providing audiences with beautiful and elaborate visual novelties, Berkeley's human kaleidoscopes may also have had an unconscious appeal to Depression audiences. Beneath their glittering, escapist surfaces, his elaborate numbers, like the casts of the shows within his films, were smoothly functioning models of people working together, people who made something of themselves only by working within a group. Berkeley, who had to create ever more spectacular productions, had carried his approach to its limit in the matter of a few years. But by then the nature of film musicals had changed.

In the mid-1930s the focus of movie musicals shifted from directors to stars, from down-and-out show people struggling to survive to fantasies of glamorous people in carefree romances. In a series of beautifully produced, idealized film operettas, Jeanette MacDonald and

Nelson Eddy endeared themselves to the public and infused new life into operettas, which had declined in popularity on the stage. But the most important new development in film musicals was not the popularity of trained voices but the popularity of trained feet. Dancing became a major force in movie musicals because of the graceful, popular artistry of Fred Astaire and Ginger Rogers.

Fred Astaire became a headliner in vaudeville and stage musicals dancing with his sister Adele. After she retired in 1932, he established himself in movies with a major supporting role in *Flying Down to Rio* (1933) in which he danced with Ginger Rogers. The pert freshness and emotional spontaneity of Rogers added warmth and spark to Astaire's suave, sophisticated but cold perfectionism, which critic Pauline Kael later called "almost a dance version of Buster Keaton."[12] It was Rogers who supplemented that style with impulsive outbursts and with sensuality. He had the magic in his feet, but she had the twinkle in her eyes. Rogers and Astaire complemented each other so beautifully that in 1935 and 1936, when they made four films including two of their greatest pictures, *Top Hat* (1935) and *Swing Time* (1936), Astaire and Rogers were Hollywood's top box office attractions. The eight musicals they made together between 1934 and 1939 made them the most celebrated dance team in film.

Astaire and Rogers gave movie fans a welcome escape into a world of grace, romance, and beauty, a world of elegant hotels, luxurious ocean liners, refined nightclubs, and palatial mansions, a world of elegant manners and dress, of gentlemen in top hats, white ties, and tails and ladies in long gloves and lovely evening gowns. Unlike typical operettas, the settings and characters were contemporary American, and the scores, composed by the likes of Irving Berlin, Jerome Kern, Cole Porter, and George and Ira Gershwin, were fine, popular music that did not require trained, classical voices, as Astaire proved with his charming but high, thin voice. But what most distinguished these musical films was that dance was their most important feature. Though the dances usually ran just a few minutes each and totaled far less than a quarter of each film, they were the emotional cores of the pictures, not just added attractions as dance production numbers usually had been.

Typically, Astaire, playing a debonaire dancer, falls immediately in love with temperamental, headstrong Rogers, who plays hard to get through a squabbling romance until their emotions burst out in dance.

Astaire usually begins to sing and then entices Rogers into dancing with him. During the dance, he courts her, wearing down her resistance with graceful, alluring movements that express his feelings more effectively than words. Just when she seems won over, she pulls away. But he pulls her back into his arms for the romantic climax when the two merge in a lovely, sweeping dance. Astaire and Rogers danced out an idealized version of the American rites of romantic courtship, like two gorgeous birds doing a splendid mating dance.

Besides their complementary screen personalities and their lovely courtship rituals, the other major reason for the great popularity of the Astaire-Rogers films was the artistry of Fred Astaire, a masterful choreographer and director who made dance the center of movie musicals. "Music isn't necessary to him in creating a dance," a *Photoplay* reporter observed during rehearsals for *Top Hat*. "The dances for *Roberta* were rehearsed for two weeks before Jerome Kern's score arrived. Astaire adapts the music to his steps, not his steps to the music. Kern's music has been re-arranged to suit Fred's rhythm." Unlike Busby Berkeley, Astaire subordinated the camera to the dance, but he used film effectively, if unobtrusively. "I always try to run a dance straight through in the movies," Astaire explained in 1937, "keeping in view the full length of the dancer or dancers, and retaining the flow of the movement intact." Unlike the stage, he observed, film allowed the director to concentrate "attention directly on the dancer so that the audience is able to follow intricate steps that would be all but lost behind the footlights. Each person in the audience sees the dance from the same perspective and, I think, gets a bigger reaction. He has a larger, clearer, better-focused view."[13] Concentration on the full figure of the performer made Astaire's dances look natural and human, which was essential because they expressed the films' emotional messages. In 1939, an era in the movie musical ended when Ginger Rogers and Fred Astaire made an affectionate film tribute to the greatest dance team of an earlier age, *The Story of Vernon and Irene Castle*, after which Astaire and Rogers were no longer cast as a screen dancing team. Both had long, distinguished careers after that and did team up again for *The Barkleys of Broadway* (1949). But it was the Astaire-Rogers pictures of the 1930s that made dancing a central feature of film musicals and left the lasting impression on the public of the man about town and the girl next door dancing through lively, playful courtships.

In the 1930s Hollywood musicals, with their high entertainment value and low ticket prices, cut sharply into audiences for live musicals. The Depression also made it difficult for stage producers to finance their expensive shows. In 1929-30 the number of new Broadway musicals dropped to its lowest point in eleven years. For the next few years as many stage directors, performers, and composers left New York for Hollywood, production of live musicals continued to slump. In the 1933-34 season, for the first time in the twentieth century, there were fewer than twenty new Broadway musicals. Because of the loss of their mass appeal, Broadway musicals tended to be modestly produced and to focus on the topical events, witty word play, biting satire, and sophisticated music that appealed to New York's culturati. The Broadway shows of the period featured some truly great scores written by a virtual honor roll of American popular composers and lyricists, including George and Ira Gershwin, Cole Porter, Harold Arlen, E. Y. Harburg, Vincent Youmans, Arthur Schwartz and Howard Dietz, Jerome Kern, Irving Berlin, and Richard Rodgers and Lorenz Hart. But it produced few musicals that captured the broad public imagination as film did.

In the 1930s success on Broadway seemed to require glib, sophisticated shows, which at their best reached the heights of *Anything Goes* (1934). Set on an ocean liner, the wacky story focused on the romantic entanglements of an evangelist turned nightclub singer (Ethel Merman). She has a crush on a Wall Street businessman (William Gaxton) who has stowed away on the ship at the last minute to be near the pretty socialite (Bettina Hall) he loves. While Gaxton goes from disguise to disguise and from romance to romance, the lovers also have to deal with a revival meeting staged by the ship's captain and with Public Enemy No. 13 (Victor Moore), who masquerades as a clergyman but carries a tommy gun instead of a Bible. The greatest appeal of the funny hit show, which made Merman a major star, was the suave, witty score by Cole Porter, including "I Get a Kick out of You," "Blow, Gabriel, Blow," "You're the Top," and "Anything Goes."

In the context of tight money and urbane, contemporary shows, it is no wonder that Richard Rodgers, working for the first time with Oscar Hammerstein II instead of his long-time partner, Lorenz Hart, found it extremely difficult to finance a musical version of a twelve-year-old play set in the rustic West during the innocent days of the early twentieth century, a play about cowboys, farmers' daughters, and box lunch socials. But Rodgers raised the money, and the show opened

in March 1943. With unsold seats in the audience, the curtain at the
St. James Theater in New York rose on a simple, stylized backdrop of
a farm and cornfield, where a lone woman churned butter. From the
wings came a baritone voice singing a cappela, "Oh, What a Beautiful
Morning." This unprecedented, understated opening was in sharp contrast to the realism of film and to the rousing production number that
normally opened a stage show. "By opening the show with the woman
alone onstage and the cowboy beginning his song offstage," Richard
Rodgers later wrote, "we did more than set a mood; we were, in effect,
warning the audience, 'Watch Out!' This is a different kind of musical."[14] It certainly was different. Instead of witty word play and caustic
commentary on current events, *Oklahoma!* gave audiences the homey
charm of a romanticized past. Richard Rodgers's pretty melodies found
a warm, humane voice in the lyrics of Oscar Hammerstein, producing
a score that was thoroughly integrated with the story and thoroughly
delightful to hear. Though the songs sounded perfectly natural when
sung by farm people and cowboys in Indian Territory, they were far
from simple. "Surrey with the Fringe on Top" bounced along to the
beat of horses' hooves; the words and music of "People Will Say We're
in Love" melted together in a beautiful love duet; and the long first
note of "Oklahoma," like a cowboy's "whoopee," captured the building
excitement of settlers learning that their territory had become a state
and then exploding into the joyous rhythm of a rousing celebration.

The score was just one part of the show's great appeal and importance. Blending square dances, western steps, and ballet techniques,
choreographer Agnes De Mille's dances artistically captured the tone
and feel of the show, dramatically advanced the story, and entertained
the audience. To end the first act, she staged a full ballet. Using the
device of a dream, she substituted trained ballet dancers for the lead
actors and singers and had them dance out the heroine's dream about
a violent conflict between her two lovers. The dramatic dream ballet
was such a hit in *Oklahoma!* that it later became a common feature in
stage and film musicals. Director Rouben Mamoulian, a pioneer of
both film and stage, masterfully integrated music, dance, and story to
create a cohesive, joyous experience. Designer Miles White created
bright costumes based on a turn-of-the-century Sears Roebuck cata-
logue, and set designer Lemuel Ayers used poster styles and lively
colors for background drops that *suggested*, rather than realistically
depicted, the settings. Ayers's sets represented a major change in stage

design, from authentic realism to abstract fantasy, a change that occurred for complex artistic and technical reasons but also meant that
stage shows had made one of their weaknesses in the age of motion
pictures into a strength.

As *Oklahoma!* demonstrated, stage musicals could compete with
films for the public's interest and dollars by emphasizing, rather than
trying to conceal, the artificiality of the musical. *All* musicals, film and
stage, are inherently fantasies. In real life unseen orchestras do not
suddenly strike up, and otherwise ordinary people do not suddenly
break out in song or burst into dance to express their innermost feelings in ryhmed lyrics and choreographed movements, with no explana-
tion and no reaction from other people. The stage certainly cannot
match film in realism, but musicals do not require realism and, in fact,
can be more effective without it. Musicals' blend of color, music, singing, dance, and spectacle is essentially an evocative emotional experience that can be intensified by live performances, but not necessarily
by realism. The sheer theatricality of *Oklahoma!*'s stylized sets, bright
costumes, imaginative ballets, and unconventional staging greatly enhanced the inherent fantasy of musical comedy. When combined with
a story and score like *Oklahoma!*'s, the stage could and did hold its
own against movies as a medium for musicals with broad popular
appeal.

Oklahoma! ran on Broadway for over five years and a national company toured for ten years. It was the first musical whose original cast,
conductor, and orchestra recorded the entire show on 78 rpm discs,
an album which became a national best seller. For all its outstanding
features, *Oklahoma!* was such a great hit because it was almost perfect
for its time. In 1943, well over a year into World War II, the economy
was stronger, making ticket or record money easier to find. Though the
Allied armed forces had begun to win some major victories, the nation
and all it stood for in human dignity, liberty, and democracy was still
seriously threatened. While not overly patriotic or directly addressed
to the war, *Oklahoma!* reaffirmed that America's pioneering, frontier
past had produced a people with strong, simple values and an unshakable spirit. The show, which toured the country throughout World
War II and the onset of the Cold War with the Soviet Union, seemed
to be saying that America, not just Oklahoma, was O.K. In the wake
of *Oklahoma!*, the stage blossomed with such great musicals as Irving
Berlin's *Annie Get Your Gun* (1946), Alan Jay Lerner and Frederick

Loewe's *Brigadoon* (1946), Rodgers and Hammerstein's *South Pacific* (1949) and *The King and I* (1951), and Frank Loesser's *Guys and Dolls* (1950).

While *Oklahoma!* was reminding Broadway of the great appeal of nostalgic musicals about traditional American values, MGM was pointing Hollywood in the same direction. In 1942, after his successes with such movie musicals as *The Wizard of Oz* (1939), *Babes in Arms* (1939), *Lady Be Good* (1941), and *For Me and My Gal* (1942), songwriter turned producer Arthur Freed had emerged as MGM's leading musical producer and had begun planning *Meet Me in St. Louis.* "What I wanted to make was a simple story," Freed explained, "a story that basically says, 'There's no place like home'." Set in St. Louis in 1903 before that city's World's Fair, the picture tells the story of a close-knit happy family with deep local roots suddenly facing a move to New York so the father can take a better job. But he finally decides to stay in St. Louis because there are things more important than money. With no film script, cast, or score, only the idea, Freed set out to make the movie adaptation of the original short story "the most delightful piece of Americana ever."[15] The way he did it demonstrated the major difference between stage and screen.

Freed had to convince only one man, studio boss Louis B. Mayer, not a group of investors, to make the film and to make it Freed's way. With that accomplished Freed had the nearly limitless financial, artistic, and technical resources of MGM at his disposal. When the studio art department decided to film the exteriors on the dignified, tree-lined street that it had used for the Andy Hardy pictures, Freed insisted on construction of a new St. Louis street and brought in designer Lemuel Ayers fresh from his success with *Oklahoma!*, to give the picture a new look. Adjusting to the different medium, Ayers produced richly detailed interior and exterior sets by meticulously researching and selecting everything from period wallpaper and lamps to ornamentation and grill work so that moviegoers would feel they were really seeing St. Louis in 1903. MGM spent $1.7 million on the film, while only one year before, *Oklahoma!* had been put on stage for about $75,000.[16] With superb direction by Vincente Minnelli, a fine, beautifully integrated score, including "The Trolley Song," "Have Yourself a Merry Christmas," "Meet Me in St. Louis," and "The Boy Next Door," and a fine cast headed by Judy Garland, Mary Astor, Leon Ames, and Margaret O'Brien, the warm, homey picture with the overstuffed, gaslight look of a simpler America, was a great hit. "The real love story is between a happy family and a way of living," observed *Time*'s reviewer.[17] It was a way of living that for a great many Americans was as much a fantasy as Oz had been, but, like *Oklahoma!*, it was a fantasy that masses of people wanted to believe in, a fantasy of tightly knit communities, secure, loving families, and old-fashioned values. The picture grossed over $7.5 million, reportedly more than any previous MGM picture except *Gone with the Wind*, another romanticized American fantasy.

With his string of successful musicals capped by *Meet Me in St. Louis*, Arthur Freed demanded and got his own autonomous musical production unit at MGM. With a small core of close associates, Freed built a large, talented repertory company that was to produce many of America's greatest film musicals, including, among many others, *Ziegfeld Follies* (1946), *Easter Parade* (1948), *On The Town* (1949), *Annie Get Your Gun* (1950), *An American in Paris* (1951), *Singin' in the Rain* (1952), *The Band Wagon* (1953), *Kismet* (1955), *Silk Stockings* (1957), and *Gigi* (1958). The Freed Unit was feasible only because of the vast resources, production facilities, and national distribution system of a major Hollywood studio, which could finance, film, edit, market, and promote scores of major films every year. No producer of live shows, not even Ziegfeld at the height of his career, could have built and maintained such a vast production company. If it had been simply a matter of money, other studios could have duplicated the Freed Unit. But it had no equal. MGM made it possible; Arthur Freed made it a reality.

Freed was determined to be innovative. "I brought in a whole new crowd of people," he recalled. "I wanted a fresh start from what had been before, a combination of the new ideas that had been happening on the stage and what could be done with film. The early musicals were novelties, but few of them were *real* musicals." While hiring stage innovators, Freed fully understood that even the most successful live musical had to be adapted substantially if it were to be a successful film because of the basic differences between the media, principally that "a movie is a story told by a camera." To create innovative adaptations and originals that were "real musicals," Freed chose talented people and had the strength to delegate authority and creative freedom to them. "Nearly all the best people were working at MGM in those days," choreographer and director Charles Waters reflected. "We'd get wild ideas and say 'Let's do it!'" Gene Kelly later called the Freed Unit "a unique repertory company, in which all boosted one another's egos and worked together as a really inspired team. It was no accident that MGM musicals were the best in the world."[18]

Some of the best and the most important of these pictures, especially for understanding the relationship between film and live musicals, were the work of Gene Kelly, one of the many extraordinary talents Freed brought to MGM. After starring in the original stage production of *Pal Joey* in 1940, Kelly became a major force in film musicals, acting, choreographing, writing, dancing, and directing. Kelly brought a style of dance to films different from Fred Astaire's. Where Astaire floated with effortless elegance, Kelly exploded with athletic power. Where Astaire seemed part ice-skater, part ballroom dancer, Kelly seemed part gymnast, part ballet dancer. "Fred's steps were small, neat, graceful, and intimate," Kelly observed of their different styles. "Mine were ballet-oriented and very athletic." Astaire's dancing style led him to play sophisticated gentlemen; Kelly's led him to his shirt-sleeved he-men. While Kelly explored new characters, Astaire refined his basic role to the nth degree. "I was the Marlon Brando of dancers," Kelly observed, "and he the Cary Grant."[19]

Kelly had to make major adjustments when he moved from stage to screen because of the differences between the two media. He discovered that the camera tended to diminish the action and movement in dance, which worked fine for Astaire's smooth style, but not for Kelly's athleticism. On the two-dimensional screen, there was a loss of depth, so Kelly had dancers race directly toward the camera from great distances. Because panning cameras, which moved with the performers and gave moviegoers a consistent view of the dance, decreased the sense of lateral motion, Kelly put vertical props behind the dancers to accentuate their movement, as telephone poles did with speeding trains. Perhaps most importantly, Kelly insisted that performers move in character throughout the film, so that when they began to dance, it would look natural. "I realized that there was no character—whether a sailor, or a truck driver, or a gangster—that couldn't be interpreted through dancing, if one found the correct choreographic language," Kelly explained. "There was a way of getting that truck driver to dance that would *not* be incongruous."[20] Out of Kelly's understanding of film, characterization, and dance came a series of great film musicals.

By the late 1940s Kelly had mastered the film medium, which he clearly demonstrated in *On the Town* (1949). Following three sailors (Kelly, Jules Munchin, and Frank Sinatra) on a twenty-four-hour pass in New York City, where many of the exteriors were filmed, the innovative picture bristled with energy and excitement. It opens as the sun rises on a New York wharf, where a single longshoreman is singing "I Feel Like I'm Not Awake Yet" as a slow solo. Then, a steam whistle blows, upbeat music begins, and sailors come racing off their ship on a one-day pass. To the bouncy beat of "New York, New York—It's a Wonderful Town," the screen pulsates with five-second shots of Manhattan—the Brooklyn Bridge, Central Park, Wall Street, The Bowery, Fifth Avenue, the Empire State Building. Capturing the verve and vitality of the nation's most famous city, the beautifully choreographed cinematic effect, set the film's tone. "It was only in *On the Town* that we tried something entirely new in the musical film," Kelly recalled. "We did a lot of quick cutting—we'd be on the top of Radio City and then on the bottom—we'd cut from Mulberry Street to Third Avenue— and so the dissolve went out of style. This was one of the things that changed the history of musicals more than anything." The entire well-integrated film throbbed with the frenetic intensity of New York and of people living life to the hilt. Kelly, who made it seem perfectly natural for a sailor to dance out his emotions, made ballet acceptable to many men for the first time. As choreographer Bob Fosse put it, Kelly looked "like a guy on their bowling team—only classier."[21] The musical, which grossed more than double its cost, was clearly a dance *film*.

Flushed with success and anxious to explore the new and innovative in film musicals, Freed in late 1949 persuaded Ira Gershwin to sell him George Gershwin's tone poem "An American in Paris" to use uncut for a ballet to end an all-Gershwin musical about an ex-GI who stayed in Paris after the war to become a painter. Besides Vincente Minnelli directing, Alan J. Lerner writing the book, and Leslie Caron, chosen from a magazine cover, co-starring with Gene Kelly, *An American in Paris* (1951) had a Gershwin score that included "I Got Rhythm," "Our Love Is Here To Stay," "Embraceable You," and "Nice Work If You Can Get It." But it was the seventeen-minute, half-million-dollar ballet, containing no dialogue and no singing, that most distinguished the film. For the ballet Irene Sharaff designed six backdrops in the styles of six major French painters, and Kelly carefully planned a ballet that reflected the mood and style of each painting and of the music.

"We really tried to make a *ballet*," he recalled, "not just merely a dance, not a series of beautiful, moving tableaux, but an emotional whole, consisting of the combined arts which spell ballet whether on the screen or the stage."[22] The film was as successful financially as it was artistically. It earned nearly three times its cost.

MGM and Kelly turned next to a light-hearted, affectionate spoof of the transition to sound movies, a spoof that was one of the Freed Unit's and Hollywood's greatest musicals. *Singin' in the Rain* harkened back to the early years of film musicals in more than subject matter. The title song and the score were drawn from music created by Nacio Herb Brown and Arthur Freed, who had written the title song for MGM's first musical, *Broadway Melody,* long before Freed became a powerful producer. *Singin' in the Rain* featured fine performances by Jean Hagen as the lovely silent movie star whose piercing, cracking voice and Brooklynese dialect doomed her career, Debbie Reynolds as the hoofer who filled in and became a star, Donald O'Connor as the male star's ex-vaudeville partner whose "Make 'Em Laugh" was a model of hilarious pantomime-clowning song-and-dance numbers, and Kelly, whose joyous dancing, laughing, and singing in the rain produced one of the most memorable and beloved musical sequences in the history of film. These two 1951 musicals, *American in Paris* and *Singin' in the Rain,* represented the range, artistry, and talent of Gene Kelly and of a major Hollywood studio at their peaks.

The Freed Unit sailed into the 1950s full speed ahead, but by mid-decade changes in movie audiences, popular music, and the movie business were threatening Freed's and other major Hollywood musicals. It was the era of rock and roll, Elvis Presley, and television, the era when movies lost the family entertainment market that had been Freed's stock in trade since *Wizard of Oz* and *Meet Me in St. Louis,* the era of the new youth culture that had little interest in traditional musicals, and the era of studios' being forced to sell their theater chains and to end block booking. Movie production dropped, and the studio system collapsed. By the mid-1950s MGM had fewer than a dozen stars under contract. Such cuts destroyed the possibility of training new stars. No longer would MGM be able to develop young Judy Garlands, Mickey Rooneys, Leslie Carons, and Gene Kellys. The Freed Unit could not survive in that atmosphere. Freed remained at MGM until 1970, but he produced no musicals after 1961.

In the mid-1950s television made rather substantial experiments with full-length book musicals. In 1955 NBC broadcast the Broadway musical *Peter Pan,* starring Mary Martin and Cyril Ritchard, to an estimated audience of 65 million people, and in 1957 Rodgers and Hammerstein's hour-and-half-long television adaptation of *Cinderella,* starring Julie Andrews, was seen by as many as 107 million Americans. But despite, or even because of, these gigantic audiences, television could not afford to do many expensive, full-length musicals. Unlike stage or film, which could assume a different audience for every performance, television had to assume the same audience every night, so it had to provide new shows for every hour of every day. Television stations also wanted to create regular viewers, so they scheduled shows at the same time every week and used the series format with continuing characters. Besides being very expensive, book musicals did not fit this pattern. But television did broadcast a good deal of music and dance. Variety shows, such as Ed Sullivan's, often included songs and stars from hit musicals; others, like *Kraft Music Hall,* mounted their own production numbers; and major musical stars, such as Judy Garland and Fred Astaire, either hosted their own musical variety series or starred in their own special broadcasts. Though television did few original book musicals, it cut into the general audience for both stage and film musicals by presenting a wide range of singing and dancing to people at home.

Stage musicals, after thriving in the post-*Oklahoma!* days of the 1940s, slumped badly in the early 1950s as television became a major attraction, and movie musicals were at their peak. In the 1951-52 season the number of Broadway musicals fell to a new twentieth-century low of five new book shows. In the early 1950s as the cost of live productions shot up, even stage musicals with good runs had a hard time breaking even. In 1951-52 *Top Banana* ran for 350 performances and *Paint Your Wagon* for 289, yet both lost money. Faced with competition from lavish film musicals, some stage producers felt that to succeed with the public they had to equal the grandeur of major movies. *Wish You Were Here* (1952), a story centered in Catskill Mountains resorts, for instance, had a real swimming pool on stage—a very costly gimmick that kept the show from touring. The stage simply could not compete with film for spectacular staging. Even if stage producers found the financial and physical resources to create eye-catching effects, they had to reproduce them for every performance and in every place they played. The answer for Broadway was not to imitate

Hollywood but to return to the convincing musical fantasies that had made Broadway musicals a success.

In 1956 Alan Jay Lerner and Frederick Loewe proved that adapting a literary classic into a musical with a catchy score, appealing characters, and a strong cast could still produce a great stage success. *My Fair Lady,* adapted from George Bernard Shaw's *Pygmalion,* told the story of the transformation of a young Cockney woman, Liza Doolittle, from a dirty-faced flower-seller into a refined lady at the hands of Professor Henry Higgins, who accomplished the transformation by teaching her to speak English correctly. As in all the best modern musicals, the songs grew out of the situations and the characters. "When we felt we really knew them," Lerner explained, "then we began to work on the score. We try to find some thought of a character that motivates him and, in turn, the story."[23] With witty, urbane lyrics, lovely melodies, a fine cast led by sophisticated Rex Harrison and sprightly Julie Andrews, the deft direction of Moss Hart, the beautiful sets of Oliver Smith, and the delightful period costumes of Cecil Beaton, the charming show was a fine example of a stage musical comedy. It ran for a record 2717 performances—over six years. Revealing the growing interdependence of different entertainment media, CBS-Columbia records invested heavily in the original stage production in exchange for the recording rights. It proved a wise investment. The long-playing cast album ultimately sold over six million copies.

In 1957 a different sort of musical adaptation of a classic opened in New York. The choice of Shakespeare's *Romeo and Juliet* may not have been novel, but the decision of creators Jerome Robbins and Leonard Bernstein to place the tragic story of lovers destroyed by the senseless prejudices and violent hatreds of their families in the tenements of the West Side of Manhattan, where Puerto Rican immigrants clashed with white New Yorkers, was very daring. The Capulets and Montagues became rival gangs, the Puerto Rican Sharks and the white Jets, whose vicious rivalries flared into killings that destroyed the romance of Maria, a Shark, and Tony, a Jet. For many contemporary theatergoers, the powerful show gave new meaning and emotional impact to Shakespeare's story. But *West Side Story,* though far from realistic, also shocked some people with its street slang and its glimpse of the harsh, brutal, frustration that fed prejudice, despair, and violence. The score by Leonard Bernstein and Stephen Sondheim fit the story beautifully. While melodic songs, like "Maria" and "There's a Place for Us," expressed the lovers' tender feelings and hopeful dreams, hard-driving songs, like "Something's Coming," underscored the mounting violence, and "America" and "Officer Krupke" voiced protests coated with humor. Choreographer Jerome Robbins's exciting dances used ballet to capture the bravado, power, pride, and explosive energy of knife-wielding, finger-snapping street gangs that moved like graceful athletes playing a life-or-death game. The controversial show, which ran for 981 performances, seemed to suggest an artistic way for musicals to deal with serious, modern issues and still entertain audiences. But the biggest hit and biggest award winner of 1957, *The Music Man*, a well-crafted piece of sentimental nostalgia about an America that never existed, indicated the direction live musicals would take.

By the mid-1950s, while stage musicals rebounded, film musicals suffered a relapse, except for the highly profitable, low-budget rock-and-roll movies aimed at the new youth market, especially the many Elvis Presley pictures. But apart from such special interest features, the movie industry, suffering from the breakup of the studio system and from competition from television, cut back on production of costly musicals. The major exceptions were biographies of famous musical performers and composers, such as Helen Morgan, Eddie Foy, and Sigmund Romberg, and adaptations of famous stage musicals, such as *Guys and Dolls* (1955) or *Pal Joey* (1957). Rodgers and Hammerstein alone had six stage shows made into movies: *Oklahoma!* (1955), *Carousel* (1956), *The King and I* (1956), *South Pacific* (1958), *Flower Drum Song* (1961), and *The Sound of Music* (1965). *The Sound of Music* set new records for the highest gross income of a musical film and prompted moviemakers to waste fortunes trying to duplicate it. The people who understood film musicals and popular tastes were no longer in power in Hollywood. The Freed Unit was a thing of the past, and there was nothing to take its place. Success or failure, indeed entire careers, increasingly rode on the fate of a single film. To make their musicals greater attractions, producers frequently filled them with famous movie stars who could neither sing nor dance. Marlon Brando and Jean Simmons starred in *Guys and Dolls*, Deborah Kerr in *The King and I*, Richard Beymer and Natalie Wood in *West Side Story* (1961), Audrey Hepburn in *My Fair Lady* (1964), and Richard Harris and Vanessa Redgrave in *Camelot* (1967). Whether these adaptations were aesthetic and financial failures or successes, the real vitality in film musicals of the late-1950s and 1960s came from the stage, just as it had in the late-1920s when movie musicals were born.

But by the mid-1960s the stage was also declining as a source of musicals with mass appeal. Inflation dramatically increased the costs of productions and the prices of tickets, which forced reductions in cast size, production scale, and number of shows. Nor could Broadway match the opportunities or salaries that movies and television offered, so when talented young performers, such as Barbra Streisand, emerged, they tended to go into films or television, as had happened in the 1930s. Fewer and fewer good innovative musicals appeared, principally because reliance on affluent audiences and people on expense accounts did not encourage producers to take chances. Broadway musicals were also hurt by the indirect effect of rock music. For decades writers of musicals and popular music had worked in the same styles and traditions, cross-fertilizing each other. Broadway, Tin Pan Alley, Hollywood, and America sang the same songs. But that changed when rock and the youth market emerged. Traditional songwriters were no longer at the creative center of popular music, which had a stultifying effect on composers of stage musicals. As a result of these major changes, in the late 1960s and the 1970s, with some notable exceptions, Broadway tended to play it safe with revivals, shows derived from former hits, and all-black revues, revivals, and adaptations of classics. However successful they were, these shows lacked new musical concepts and new directions for the new age.

In 1968 a new show from Joseph Papp's People's Theatre workshop burst onto Broadway with the rebellious look and sound of the "hippies." Besides defying virtually every middle-class norm and moral belief, *Hair*, which included a controversial nude scene, also voiced strong protests against racial prejudice and the Vietnam War. With little structure or plot, the show's greatest strengths were its light rock score, which included "Good Morning Starshine" and "Aquarius," and its innovative staging, which had cast members walking through the audience on the arms of the seats, the band on the stage, and a concluding "love-in" in which the cast invited the audience members to throw off their inhibitions, go up on stage, and dance and sing about the coming of the age of Aquarius. Though it was no more realistic than *West Side Story*, *Hair* gave the overwhelmingly middle-class theatergoers of the late-1960s a chance to feel they understood and even briefly shared in the youth counter-culture, a chance to feel that flower children were just mildly rebellious, idealistic kids. Alive with intensity and energy, *Hair* ran for 1844 performances, and touring companies carried it throughout the country for years. But despite its great success, it did not usher in an age of Aquarius in stage musicals. The Broadway audiences generally preferred conventional musicals with traditional scores. By the late 1970s Broadway relied heavily on revivals.

The most important exception to the general decline of the musical in the 1960s and 1970s was the brilliant work of lyricist and composer Stephen Sondheim, who broke onto Broadway in a big way, writing the superb lyrics for *West Side Story* (1957) and for *Gypsy* (1959), two of the finest shows of the late 1950s. In 1962 his words and music enlivened the burlesque romp *A Funny Thing Happened on the Way to the Forum*. With shows such as *Do I Hear a Waltz?* (1965), *Company* (1970), and *Follies* (1971), Sondheim continued to develop his talents, growing artistically and musically more ambitious and innovative while audiences were growing more conservative and nostalgic. His *A Little Night Music* (1973), a waltz-filled score with sparkling lyrics, which included "Send in the Clowns," recalled the grand days of the integrated operettas of some half-century earlier and was a popular success. But his *Pacific Overtures* (1976), presenting the American intrusion into Japan from the Japanese point of view with an all-Asian cast, Oriental instruments, and poetic language, proved too demanding and difficult for audiences. It had a relatively short run. On the eve of the 1980s, his nearly operatic, musically serious *Sweeney Todd*, in which the songs carried the show's content, drew large audiences as well as enthusiastic reviews. But Sondheim's continual experimentation with the classic musical had relatively little influence on other Broadway composers or on producers, who had to face the realities of huge production costs, high ticket prices, and audiences looking for splashy, upbeat escapism.

In the mid-1970s, an innovative force found expression in film musicals, but it came from a new medium—records. It came not from the major labels that had capitalized on conventional stage and film musicals with best-selling original cast albums, but from the specialists in rock music. The independent record companies that catered to the affluent, free-spending youth market and had become experts in using radio to promote their recordings began to expand to other media. Instead of waiting for musicals with scores that might make successful albums, rock record companies produced coordinated albums and movies and used their promotion of the soundtrack albums and the films to reinforce each other. Robert Stigwood, who developed from a rock band manager into a power in the record business, led the move into film making. "We've given Hollywood a new way to go," observed Al Coury, president of the Robert Stigwood Organization (RSO), producer of the films *Jesus Christ Superstar* (1973), *Tommy* (1975), *Saturday Night Fever* (1977), *Sergeant Pepper's Lonely Hearts Club Band* (1978), and *Grease* (1978). "We have been able to utilize the marriage of music and film, and to use the music to sell the film in advance. With the right song, artist, and performance, and the mentioning of the film every time the music is played on the radio, it becomes a form of pre-selling."[24] The strategy involved issuing the album up to two months before the film and committing a large advertising budget to promote the record on radio stations that appealed primarily to the youth market. Single records from the album were released one at a time to maximize exposure. At one point, for instance, four of the five top singles on the pop chart were from the *Saturday Night Fever* cast album. Besides making money, the singles also promoted the album, which in turn built anticipation for the film and provided capital for promoting it when it was released, which then led to further sales of the album. As of June 1978 the film *Saturday Night Fever*, whose disco setting and dancing triggered a new fad, reportedly had grossed $90 million, and the soundtrack album had sold over twelve million copies. But no matter how profitable the rock film-albums were, they served a relatively narrow segment of the population—the youth market that had come to dominate both film and popular music by the 1970s.

On the eve of the 1980s the musical was a genre in trouble. The Broadway-Hollywood musical axis that had existed since sound pictures developed was broken because the two media no longer entertained the same audiences. Film musicals in the age of independently produced, big-budget movies again became major moneymakers. But the most popular film musicals had become cogs in the well-oiled, multi-media entertainment machines of the rock music entrepreneurs who mastered the high-powered promotional and marketing techniques that were the keys to the big spending youth market. At the same time, theaters around the country were filled every night with well-heeled audiences enjoying live musicals. But the shows were frequently twenty to fifty years old, and the stars were often of the same vintage. The stage was generating few notable new musicals. Rapidly escalating production costs meant high risks for investors and high ticket prices for patrons. As a result both producers and the public opted for the guaranteed appeal of famous stars and shows.

Ironically, the space-age technology of modern show business might offer the prospect for revitalizing the musical. Using satellites and cable systems combined with some revenue-collecting device, live performances could be broadcast directly into the homes of the nation's musical fans. This system might generate large enough revenues to allow producers to take risks, allow performers to work and develop on stage, perhaps in on-going companies, and provide Americans with an exciting range of new musicals. Perhaps because of modern technology a generation reared on entertainment machines might get a glimpse of what it has been missing and might seek out the unequaled, unforgettable experience of sitting in a dark theater with hundreds of strangers and being enthralled and entranced by a captivating live performance of a convincing musical fantasy.

Joe Smith and Charlie Dale relied heavily on verbal humor in their classic vaudeville routines, such as Dr. Kronkhite. Smith and Dale. *The Billy Rose Theatre Collection, New York Public Library at Lincoln Center.*

Gus and Max Rogers wore flamboyant costumes for their rollicking musical comedies. *The Rogers Brothers in Paris* (1904). *Harvard Theatre Collection.*

Rae Dooley and W. C. Fields used physical humor in a skit from *The Ziegfeld Follies of 1924. The Billy Rose Theatre Collection, New York Public Library at Lincoln Center.*

Gypsy Rose Lee and Bobby Clark gave sparkling vitality to a typical, sexy burlesque gag. *Star and Garter* (1942). *Harvard Theatre Collection.*

Silent movies excelled at action, including Mack Sennett's slapstick Keystone comedies. *Film Stills Archive, Museum of Modern Art.*

Harold Lloyd's thrill comedy depended on the realism of film for its tension. *Safety Last* (1923).

The intimacy of close camera work enhanced the emotionally engaging humor of Charlie Chaplin. Charlie Chaplin and Jackie Coogan in *The Kid* (1920). *Film Stills Archive, Museum of Modern Art.*

The visual puns of Buster Keaton exploited both the illusions of film and the fantasy of silent movies. *Our Hospitality* (1923).

The Marx Brothers—Groucho, Harpo, Zeppo, and Chico—brought their physical and verbal anarchism from the stage to early talkies. *Animal Crackers* (1930).

Mae West's sexy one-liners and suggestive innuendo spiced up pre-censorship sound movies. Cary Grant and Mae West in *She Done Him Wrong* (1933).

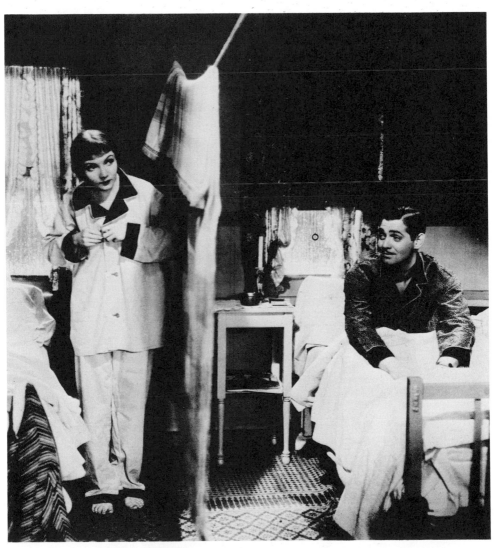

Frank Capra's *It Happened One Night* (1934), starring Claudette Colbert and Clark Gable, established the primacy in feature film comedy of directors, actresses, and actors who were not specialists in comedy.

The combination of Cary Grant, Katharine Hepburn, director Howard Hawks, and the pet leopard "Baby" created one of the best of the wacky, wholesome, romantic comedies that flourished in the tight censorship after 1934. *Bringing Up Baby* (1938).

The sexy comedy of Marilyn Monroe and Jack Lemmon in Billy Wilder's *Some Like It Hot* (1959) lured people to movie theaters in the age of television.

Combining qualities of the masters of silent film comedy with those of the standup, nightclub comedian, Woody Allen created a distinctive comic persona. Diane Keaton and Woody Allen in *Play It Again Sam* (1972). *Film Stills Archive, Museum of Modern Art.*

The records of Spike Jones, who used pistols, washboards, kazoos, cowbells, and other odd instruments in his musical parodies, had great appeal in the 1940s and 1950s when 78 rpm recordings were dominated by music. *The Billy Rose Theatre Collection, New York Public Library at Lincoln Center.*

Long-playing record albums, which held full comedy routines, enabled nightclub comedians such as Bob Newhart to become national stars and move into other media. *The Billy Rose Theatre Collection, New York Public Library at Lincoln Center.*

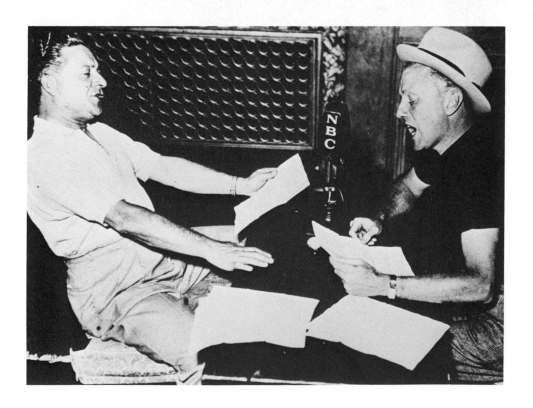

Despite playing to listeners who could not see him, stage veteran Ed Wynn used the funny hats and mugging of a theatrical comic in his early radio shows. *The Billy Rose Theatre Collection, New York Public Library at Lincoln Center.*

With their expressive voices Charles J. Correll (left) and Freeman Gosden created an entire cast of black characters on the *Amos 'n' Andy Show,* which began in 1928. *The Billy Rose Theatre Collection, New York Public Library at Lincoln Center.*

Jack Benny established a *radio* comedy style based on characterization and situation comedy. The Sportsmen and Jack Benny on *The Jack Benny Program. The Billy Rose Theatre Collection, New York Public Library* at *Lincoln Center.*

Milton Berle became Mr. Television in 1948 with his controversial, bigger-than-life antics, which were perfect for early, small-screen, black and white television sets. Milton Berle as Cleopatra on *Texaco Star Theater. National Broadcasting Company.*

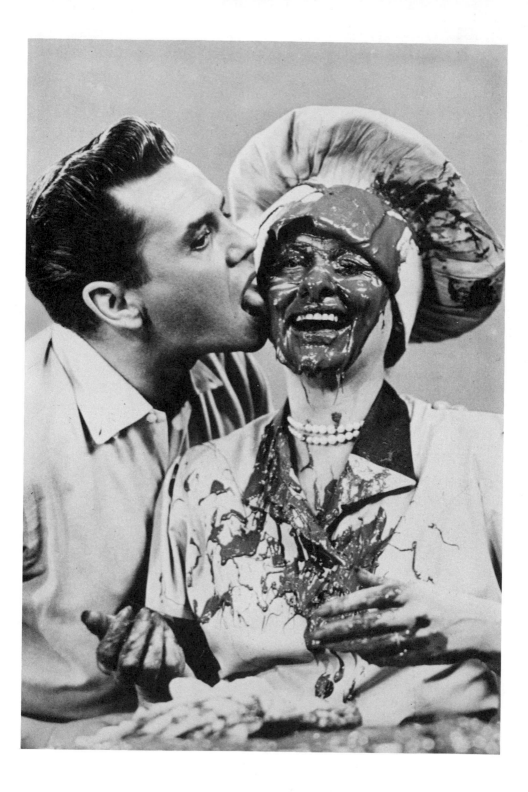

Rowan and Martin's Laugh-In used videotape technology to create a program with a faster pace than any previous comedy show. It also introduced such future stars as Ruth Buzzi (seated on piano) and Goldie Hawn (standing on piano). *National Broadcasting Company.*

Lucille Ball's great clowning made *I Love Lucy* one of television's most popular shows. Desi Arnaz and Lucille Ball in the 1952 "Candydipper" episode of *I Love Lucy. The Billy Rose Theatre Collection, New York Public Library at Lincoln Center.*

Jean Stapleton and Carroll O'Connor, playing Edith and Archie Bunker, used fine acting to make *All in the Family* a comedy that blended belly laughs with serious messages about distressing problems of modern life. *Columbia Broadcasting System.*

6

The Other Side:
Crime and the Media

Blazing gun battles, bruising fistfights, breathtaking chases, dramatic showdowns, and life-and-death struggles between good and evil have long been popular features of American show business. When set on the frontier, these stories of lawbreakers and law enforcers were called "westerns." Set in cities, the stories were called "crime." The crime genre generally drew its cast from three major character types: the criminal, often a member of an organized gang; the police officer, a member of society's organized law enforcement agency; and the private detective, either an amateur sleuth or a professional private investigator who was rarely a member of any organization. Besides being about law and order in general, the crime genre reflected American attitudes toward *urban* criminals, government officials, and private crime fighters, attitudes that varied with changes in social, political, and economic conditions and with changes in the entertainment media.

In the nineteenth century, stage shows rarely used cops, robbers, or detectives as central characters. Moralistic melodramas, of course, contained villainous crooks, but they were usually bankers, landlords, or other "white-collar" criminals who threatened foreclosure on mortgages and debts and were foiled by traditional, pure-at-heart heroes and heroines, not by policemen or detectives. Though stage producers ignored the dramatic potential of Edgar Allan Poe's pioneering detective stories, "The Purloined Letter" and "Murders in the Rue Morgue," some crime dramas proved popular by the 1890s, most notably Ameri-

157

can actor and playwright William Gillette's *Sherlock Holmes* (1898), a thriller loosely based on the A. Conan Doyle stories. Gillette played the role for decades, which was the normal pattern for stage hits when audience demand was large and the number of seats available for each performance was small. Even counting the many revivals of crime-detective hits like *Sherlock Holmes*, there were still few such shows in American theaters at the turn of the twentieth century. Crime had an urban focus, and nineteenth century popular plays, whether performed in cities, towns, or villages, tended to focus on rural heroes such as Davy Crockett and Buffalo Bill Cody.

But in the early twentieth century, the public eye began to turn to the city as reform-minded writers exposed corruption, inequities, and injustices in many areas of American life. As part of this muckraking, newspapers in 1912 used screaming headlines and shocking details to describe urban gang killings and vice scandals involving the police, which stimulated public interest in the exotic and alien urban underworld. Show business quickly cashed in on the curiosity that such exposés piqued. The popular stage began to feature what one contemporary journal called a "flood of melodrama featuring criminals hunted by detectives and police." These plays, whether George M. Cohan's *Seven Keys to Baldpate* (1913), with its suspenseful plot twists and surprises, or Elmer Rice's *On Trial* (1914), with its tense courtroom drama drawn from actual trial transcripts, were usually set indoors because the modern theater, despite its realistic special effects, could not compete with the outdoor action of films. In 1912 D. W. Griffith at the Biograph studio in New York made the silent film *The Musketeers of Pig Alley*, which the studio explained was "simply intended to show vividly the doings of the gangster type of people."[1] Shot on location in the dingy streets and alleys of New York's "other side" with genuine gangsters in the cast, the short movie packed in an armed robbery, an attempt to drug an innocent woman, a gangland shootout, and a police roundup of the hoodlums. The slum setting and the violent action demonstrated the advantages film had over the stage. But gangsters, cops, and detectives did not immediately become the subjects of many popular movies. The times were wrong for the crime genre.

The early twentieth century found its most popular action-adventure hero in the West, the frontier, and the cowboy, rather than the East, the city, and the cop. In fact, the most popular policemen of the era were Mack Sennett's bumbling Keystone Kops, who were more like slapstick circus clowns in blue uniforms than crime-fighting heroes. The spate of serious crime plays and movies after 1912, which ran counter to the general trend of the period, had been sparked by the eyecatching newspaper stories about urban corruption and largely passed from the nation's theaters when the popular press found its exciting stories in the European war that pitted vicious Huns against heroic Allies.

In the mid-1920s, lurid newspaper coverage again riveted public attention on criminals, this time colorful racketeers and bootleggers like Al Capone, who supplied America with liquor during Prohibition. In the upbeat, self-indulgent Jazz Age, gangsters fascinated the public with their sensational wealth, power, gambling, sexuality, and violence. Popular entertainment again followed the headlines, and gangsters became larger-than-life characters in both stage shows and films. The fad began to boom on stage with *Broadway* in 1926, and within the next few years, James Cagney, Joan Blondell, Edward G. Robinson, and Paul Muni became stage stars portraying gangland characters. But only movies could add the careening chases and exciting shootouts that were such a major part of the crime genre. In 1927 *Underworld*, an action-packed, romantic melodrama about a powerful gangster, was such a success that it thrust gangland pictures to the forefront of the silent movie business. "Here's to crime," a reviewer wrote in 1928. "Ever since *Underworld* came through with flying colors, most every producer including its particular sponsor, Paramount, had been trying to duplicate it."[2] The largest number of gangster movies released in any one year had been seven until 1928 when Hollywood produced twenty. And that was just the beginning.

The great outburst of cops and robbers movies produced in 1928 was not just the result of Hollywood imitating its big successes. It also reflected Hollywood's search for material and stars that showcased the new dimension sound added to movies. Musicals and verbal humor were the most obvious choices since they had been impossible to film effectively in the silent era. Less obviously, the crime genre also provided Hollywood with new sound attractions. The punchy slang of city streets, the screech of burning tires, and the chatter of tommy guns became part of crime movies only with the addition of sound. Hollywood producers turned to the stage not only for singers, dancers, and comics, but also for actors such as James Cagney and Edward G. Robinson, who already had developed the swagger and lingo of their cocky, tough-guy characters. At first, crime talkies looked like other static, early sound pictures adapted from stage plays, but by 1931 the combination of efficient sound technology, exciting cinematic action, explosive sound, and sharp dialogue produced gangster movies with powerful impact. The medium of sound motion pictures was perfect for the crime genre, which often relied as heavily on dialogue as on action—unlike the western, which was primarily visual and excelled in silent film. The crime genre was also perfect for the early 1930s.

In early 1931 a new picture opened with a somber night-time shot of a bleak gas station. A car pulls in, a figure darts into the office, shots ring out, the figure races out, and jumps into a waiting car, which squeals off into the dark night. The sight, sounds, and pace of a violent, small-time holdup introduce the story of Caesar Enrico Bandello, who rises from robbing a gas station to reigning as the *Little Caesar* of a Chicago mob. After the heist, Rico joins a gang and ruthlessly shoots his way to the top, killing the police commissioner, taking the gang away from the old boss, and living like a bandit king. Fearing that his old pal Joe, who had gone straight, will tell the police that Rico killed the commissioner, Rico and his number two man go to kill Joe. But Rico, the otherwise cold-blooded killer, cannot pull the trigger on his old friend. The police arrive, kill his sidekick, and drive Rico into hiding in miserable flophouses. When newspapers publish a policeman's charge that Rico is yellow, he phones the cop, who traces the call and finally guns down Little Caesar on a rainy streetcorner.

The bulk of *Little Caesar* was an American success story twisted and perverted by the despair and dismal conditions of the Depression, when survival, let alone success, seemed doubtful to a great many Americans. "I think the popularity of my role as Little Caesar can be attributed to the public preoccupation with the American dream of success," Edward G. Robinson reflected. "Rico was a guy who came from poverty and made it big. Remember, almost everyone was poor in those days. . . . Rico made it straight up the ladder and everyone could identify with his climb." In the traditional mold, Rico rose to the top of his trade through hard work and dedication. But his business was crime; his craft was murder; and his fall was never more than a gunshot away. But Robinson also felt that Rico's final words, "Mother of mercy, is this the end of Rico?" "probably expressed a feeling that millions of people had about their own lives" in the Great

Depression that destroyed careers and shattered dreams almost as quickly as the policeman's bullets riddled Rico's body.[3]

Little Caesar and the army of gangster films that followed in its wake burst with frenetic energy, ear-shattering gunfire, and the spicy slang of big city streets. Even no-nonsense hoods who could "take it" and "dish it out," who never "ratted" on their pals, and who had no trace of "yellow" might still get "taken for a ride" or "bumped off," just like the real-life mobsters in the news. As breathtaking as any other action-adventures and as up to date as the latest headlines, gangster movies were a great rage in the early 1930s. *Public Enemy, Scarface,* and scores of other hard-boiled films created major new movie stars. Many crime pictures of the early thirties, such as *The Mouthpiece, Lawyer Man, State's Attorney, Scandal for Sale, Scandal Sheet, Five Star Final,* and *The Dark Horse,* also portrayed corruption in such basic institutions as the police, courts, prisons, press, and city government.

In movie after movie in the despair of the early Depression, tough, gutsy men and women fought with whatever weapons they could muster to survive and get ahead in a crumbling, unjust society, and millions of average Americans paid their precious money to watch and root for them. The greatest attraction of the very popular *Public Enemy* (1931), the story of a poor Irish kid who rises from petty theft, through bootlegging and strong-arming bar-owners, to leading a gang, was the performance of James Cagney as the quick-tongued, fearless hero who exuded power, violence, confidence, and male supremacy. When a great many men who traditionally had been the breadwinners for their families felt frustrated, inept, and helpless because they could no longer be providers, Cagney and other tough guys gave them an emotional outlet. The gangsters directed their take-no-guff aggression not only at men but also at women, who were kept in their places as either doting mothers or sexy window dressing. Though Cagney, like Robinson, was physically short, he seemed ten feet tall when he looked trouble in the eye, sneered at it, and whipped it, or when he got mad at Mae Clarke at the breakfast table, picked up a half grapefruit, and squished it into her face. In 1932 a movie fan from Arkansas wrote to *Movie Classic* magazine that "what we need now is a well-placed sock from the one and only Cagney to lift us out of this mental depression and replace the old smile and cheerio on the face of millions." Cagney, too, worried about the debilitating effects of the Depression on the American people. "The thing I'm most afraid of is the *slave complex,*" he observed. "There is such a thing. I've watched it growing. Fellows who once had salt in their blood and steel in their nerves, who were four square on their feet and as independent as all hell, have gone cringy and fearful. Fearful of losing their jobs. Cringy to their bosses and to those in power."[4] Gangsters like those played by Cagney never cringed. They stood up to anyone who got in the way—hoodlums, businessmen, policemen, or politicians—as they lashed out at society in an outburst of violent rage.

In the early 1930s state censors attempted to limit the glorification of gangsters and the contempt for law enforcement in a campaign that included New York censors requiring Howard Hughes to add the subtitle "The Shame of the Nation" to his especially violent film *Scarface* (1932). Studios made concessions like having the gangsters killed in the end or urging movie theater managers not to make the gangsters seem like heroes in advertising campaigns. But without powerful national censors, movie studios followed the dictates of the box office, and Hollywood continued to turn out movies centered on lawbreakers. The crime pictures of the early thirties were only part of movies' general assault on traditional American values, an assault that extended from musicals like *Gold Diggers of 1933*, through the anarchistic comedy of the Marx Brothers, to the mocking sexuality of Mae West. In response, groups of citizens led by the powerful Legion of Decency of the Catholic Church, which urged Catholics to boycott movies it judged indecent, demanded strict censorship of pictures when the movie business was slumping badly between 1930 and 1933. Whatever the role of the censorship campaign in this Depression decline, moviemakers had to listen to any large, vocal group threatening to boycott films. As a result, the movie industry in 1934 gave the Production Code Administration the power to censor films by making it commercially impossible for unapproved movies to be shown. For producers of crime pictures this meant giving sympathetic treatment to law enforcement and the courts, rather than portraying them as inept or corrupt and making heroes of criminals. While Hollywood was putting teeth in the censorship code, President Franklin Delano Roosevelt was beginning to restore hope that America could get back up on its feet—with a big helping hand from the government. The national mood was changing, and so were the movies.

"Public Enemy Becomes Soldier of the Law," ballyhooed Warner

Brothers about its 1935 feature, *G-Men* starring James Cagney. "Holly-wood's Most Famous Bad Man Joins the G-Men and Halts the March of Crime." Instead of just assuming that Cagney was playing a govern-ment agent, the movie acknowledged the gangster tradition by show-ing how a kid from the slums could make something of himself and end up on the side of the law. Yet, it was a gangster who got Cagney out of the slum and into law school. Determined not to be a shyster mouthpiece for the mob and initially unwilling to join the F.B.I., Cagney struggled to survive as an honest lawyer until gangsters mur-dered his unarmed friend, and Cagney decided to get revenge by fight-ing for the new forces of law. "Arm your agents," a Justice Department spokesman told a Congressional committee in *G-Men*, "and not just with revolvers. If these gangsters want to use machine guns then give your special agents machine guns, shotguns, tear gas—everything else. This is war!"[5] War it was. In *G-Men* and the many movies about fed-eral agents that followed it, Hollywood sustained, perhaps even in-creased, the level of violence that had proved so popular in the gang-ster movies of the early 1930s while also developing heroes who did not have to be killed in the end, as gangsters did, and who could fall in love and marry, which added the appeal of happy endings to the urban shoot-em-ups.

The new hero was not just a policeman, he was a *federal* agent. Gangsters might outsmart, outshoot, or bribe local cops or judges, but they could not stand up to the G-men who made a federal case of it. As *Special Agents* (1935) simply put it, "Uncle Sam won't stand for it." This movie message, that the agents of the national government were the answer to the society's problems, was no accident when Roosevelt's federal New Deal was attempting to get the country going. A Missouri theater owner told *Time* magazine about *G-Men* that "we honestly believe every theater should play this for the reason that it leaves a lot of people thinking our government is okay." In 1936, as if to under-score the change in crime heroes, Edward G. Robinson, who triggered the rage for gangsters with his portrayal of *Little Caesar*, followed James Cagney in switching sides. In *Bullets or Ballots*, Robinson played an undercover agent, who as a disgraced cop joins and takes over a gang. When he finally learns the identity of the "Big Boys," the crooked bankers who control crime in New York, Robinson is mortally wounded but gets the names to a special crime investigator before he dies. "What makes it a good film," *Time's* critic observed, "is that it brings Edward G. Robinson . . . back into the crime fold, this time on the side of the law."[6]

In the late-1920s early crime movies had also made heroes of crime fighters, but instead of being tough cops who fought gangsters they were refined, private detectives who lived and worked in a world far removed from the slum world of the mob. The first movie detectives came from the literary tradition of upper-class, genteel amateurs who dabbled in solving crimes as a hobby. As early as 1903, Biograph made a short Sherlock Holmes film. Many other detective pictures followed in the silent movie era, though they tended to be action, not sleuth, movies because stories that relied heavily on interrogations of suspects, on verbal reasoning, and on explanations of how the crimes were solved were not well suited to the medium of silent film. "A detective story depends on dialogue," director Howard Hawks observed from first-hand experience. "It is essential to it. When I was given *Trent's Last Case,* we actually had a scenario for a talkie, but Fox couldn't get rights to make it as a talking picture. I had to shoot it as a silent. It was quite a challenge to tell a story that depended on dialogue while keeping dialogue at a minimum."[7] Besides the technological limitations of the medium, another major reason for the detective story's relatively slow development in silent pictures was that many of the most popular fictional detectives—Philo Vance, Hercule Poirot, Sam Spade, Nero Wolfe, and Nick and Nora Charles—had not yet been created. The golden age of detective fiction began in the mid-1920s. So when sound movies became popular, so did detectives.

Totally unlike gangster movies, detective pictures of the late twenties and early thirties virtually ignored the Depression. Instead, they offered moviegoers an escape into the leisured world of wealth and privilege, the world of penthouses not flophouses. The polished, articulate gentleman became the detective hero, as if Fred Astaire were taking time out from dancing with Ginger Rogers to solve a few crimes. In 1929 dapper Ronald Colman portrayed Bulldog Drummond, and suave William Powell used his well-modulated voice, polished diction, and genteel bearing to play Philo Vance, a debonair bon vivant who, as a hobby, used his intuition and instinct to solve forgeries, murders, stock manipulations, blackmail, and other crimes that intruded into his upper-class world. Vance did not battle thugs; he outsmarted criminals. The only way he would ever see a tommy gun was in a gentleman's gun collection.

In 1934 William Powell left Warner Brothers, with its stable of tough guys, and moved to MGM, the studio that specialized in films of grace, beauty, and fantasy. His first MGM picture, *Manhattan Melodrama*, teamed him with Myrna Loy, a film husband and wife team that lasted fourteen years and created a new image for the screen detective. In 1934 Loy and Powell played Nora and Nick Charles in *The Thin Man,* which became so popular that MGM made six sequels in the next 14 years. Powell played a retired detective who managed the affairs of Loy, his spunky heiress wife. As if screwball comedy characters had joined the fight for law and order, the attractive sophisticated couple engaged in a running battle of playful insults and quips that underscored their love for each other as they solved crimes. By flirting and teasing as movie lovers often did *before* they were married, Nick and Nora Charles showed that couples could remain lovers and continue to have fun together after they were married, which was a most unusual image for movies. The original *The Thin Man* appeared the same year as *It Happened One Night* and bore a closer resemblance to that romantic comedy than it did to contemporary crime movies. Over the course of *The Thin Man* series the comic tone was maintained, and a family focus was added when Nick, Jr., was born at about the same time that MGM's Andy Hardy series was enjoying great success with its wholesome, all-American family saga. By the 1940s family and comedy dominated the most famous genteel, upperclass detective movies.

In the 1930s crime generally had been portrayed as either a life and death war between armies of policemen and criminals for control of the society or as an intriguing, if rather bothersome, intrusion into the otherwise carefree upper-class enclaves. But in the 1940s, movie portrayals of crime and crime fighters changed markedly. The broad battle between gangsters and G-men gave way to crimes against individuals, and the victims increasingly turned for help to professional private investigators, often called private eyes, who solved crimes for a living. Unlike England and Europe, where the vast majority of crime fighters came from either the government or the upper classes, America developed its own democratic crime fighter, the working-class private eye whose popularity reflected not only America's traditional distaste for aristocrats but also its distrust of government power, especially police forces which could be corrupt and oppressive.

The private eye, a tough, individualistic working stiff, who was his own man with his own code, struggled to survive in a shady area between the mobster and the family man. Unlike the uppercrust amateur sleuth, the private eye usually worked in sleazy surroundings, often a grimy little room with filthy walls, a beatup desk, and an old metal file cabinet that held little more than a half-empty whisky bottle. Operating on the borderline of the law and using the criminal's violence, knowledge of the streets, and understanding of the sordid side of human nature, the hard-boiled private eye was the urban counterpart of the western gunfighter, who would violate the law but not his own sense of right and wrong. Often an ex-cop who had left the force because of the restrictions imposed on him, the private eye was a loner, an outsider, the farthest thing from an organization man. Except for his own code, his only allegiance was to the client who hired him as a one-man private police force to fight a single battle against an individual crime or criminal. The cynical private eye who had seen it all knew better than to try to fight the hopeless war to eradicate injustice.

Though the development of the private eye was part of a gradual Americanization of the dilettante detective, his emergence as a popular character in movies dates from 1941 when Humphrey Bogart starred as Sam Spade in *The Maltese Falcon,* the third movie to be made of Dashiell Hammett's 1930 novel. Warner Brothers' 1931 version was lost in the rattling tommy guns and screeching tires of the action-packed gangster movies of the early thirties. Its 1936 remake, a comedic version with Bette Davis, was also unsuccessful. So, when the studio planned to reshoot the twice-worked vehicle with novice director John Huston, George Raft, then a star, turned down the apparently unpromising part of Sam Spade. Bogart, who had shot into the movie limelight playing gangster Duke Mantee in *Petrified Forest* (1936) but had become type-cast as a ruthless, cold-blooded killer in pictures like *Dead End* (1937) and *The Roaring Twenties* (1939), was chosen for the part of the cynical private eye who is tricked into joining the search for the Maltese Falcon, a legendary statuette rumored to be of incredible value. Taken off guard by the sob story and vulnerable look of beautiful Brigid O'Shaughnessy (Mary Astor), Spade takes her case. When his partner, Miles, is killed, Spade is sucked into the cutthroat competition for the Falcon among: Astor's O'Shaughnessy, who will

lie, make love, cry, or kill to further her own interests; Sydney Greenstreet's Kasper Gutman, a refined fat man with a taste for the finer
things, a rich voice, and a total absence of scruples; and Peter Lorre's
Joel Cairo, a small, soft-voiced man who seems about to explode in
psychotic violence at any moment. Thrust into this ruthless triangle
with no knowledge of what is happening or how much is at stake,
Spade survives by keeping his tough façade, following his own code,
and learning to distrust even his own client, though he is falling in love
with her. At the end of the picture, after the Falcon is found but
proves worthless, Astor offers herself to Bogart if he will help her escape. Despite his love for her, his code prevails, and he turns her over
to the police. "I don't care who loves who, I won't play the sap for
you," he explains to her with deadpan voice and face. "You killed
Miles and you're going over for it."[8] The well-cast, well-directed picture's greatest strength was Bogart's portrayal of Sam Spade, which
revealed the very human man behind the tough, cynical shell, the man
whose hand shook after he bluffed his way out of a tight spot with
Greenstreet's thugs, the man who fell for Astor even though he knew
she was an opportunist who would do anything and use anyone to get
the Falcon.

During World War II when America was united in its war against
fascism, Bogart expanded his portrayal of the cynical tough guy with
a heart in *Casablanca* (1942) and *To Have and To Have Not* (1943),
wartime movies in which the hard-nosed loner who claims to be out
only for himself cannot help joining the great cause. In 1946, with the
war won, Bogart played Raymond Chandler's detective Philip Marlowe in *The Big Sleep*. Bogart's Marlowe is thrust into a world where
little makes sense and where few things or people are what they seem.
Hired by a dying millionaire to stop the blackmailing of his daughter,
Bogart quickly finds himself caught up in murders, seemingly unex-
plained violence and brutality, and frequent double-crosses. With a
plot so difficult to follow that even director Howard Hawks claimed he
did not understand all of it, the story portrayed a horrifying world
gone mad, a world in which people acted with no apparent motiva-
tion, a world in which sinister forces might arbitrarily plague even the
most innocent.

After World War II a number of pictures with this world-view, often
called *film noir*, became popular. Rather than the victorious war for
freedom and the Western way of life ushering in a new golden age,

America was hit hard by a series of crippling strikes, disillusioning political scandals, menacing Communist takeovers of Eastern Europe and China, and divisive searches for American Communists from Washington, D.C. to Hollywood. It was as if the evil that had once been contained in gangsters, criminals, and fascists had broken loose and infected the whole world. The movies of the late 1940s, especially crime movies, reflected this sense of discord, chaos, and peril. In *Kiss of Death* (1947), for example, an ex-con (Victor Mature) lives out a nightmare, trying unsuccessfully to go straight, having to return to crime to support his kids, getting caught again, informing on a gang that beats the rap, and being stalked by a maniacal killer (Richard Widmark) who sadistically shoves a crippled old woman down a flight of stairs before Mature finally kills him. In *White Heat* (1949), a ruthless psychotic gangster (James Cagney) with an Oedipal complex ends his ranting, raving, murdering life by fleeing from the police to the top of a huge gasoline storage tank, being critically wounded, screaming "Top of the world, Ma!," and firing into the tank, providing the picture and his life with a fiery climax. In movies, as in the real world, unseen and uncontrollable forces seemed to be leading to senseless destruction. But in the early 1950s, with Dwight Eisenhower as President, westerns, with their heroic models of rugged American individualists blazing the way for civilization and progress, replaced tough private eyes and G-men as the screen's most popular action stars. But by that time America had crime fighters in its homes as well as in its theaters.

In the early years of the Great Depression when sponsored, professional radio programming became a major force in American popular entertainment, crime became the major action genre on the new entertainment machine in the home. Crime stories relied heavily on dialogue, exposition, and sound effects, which were radio's great strengths. Generally, radio crime shows reflected the same broad patterns as crime movies, which is no surprise since they both tried to reach the broadest possible audiences and had to appeal to the same changes in public moods and tastes. But even in the early Depression when movies glamorized gangsters, radio did not. The primary reason for this different approach lay in the fundamental difference between the two media. The people who paid for movies, the studios, only had to worry about making pictures that would draw large audiences of ticket buyers. The people who paid for radio, the sponsors, had to worry not only about finding shows that would draw large audiences but also about finding shows that would make listeners feel good enough about the entertainment to buy the products advertised. Sponsors could not afford to offend potential customers, and since radio programs were broadcast into people's homes, they had to be family entertainment. When crime shows came to radio, their heroes were crime fighters, not gangsters.

Though some crime fighting shows and characters, such as Ellery Queen, were hits in both movies and radio, by the mid-1930s radio had developed its own crime shows that capitalized fully on the medium and were in many cases not successful in movies, just as many popular movie characters did not succeed on radio. Philo Vance, for instance, was very popular in films in the 1930s but not on radio, while *The Shadow* was a long-running radio hit but was featured in only one serial in movies. Radio and movies generally gave the public similar types of crime stories, but they did it in ways that reflected the differences between the entertainment machine in the theater and the entertainment machine in the home. Radio lacked visual effects and famous action stars, but it had regular listeners, an intimate relationship between shows and audiences, time slots that varied from fifteen minutes to an hour, and the need for a great many programs. The best and most distinctive radio shows made all these qualities into assets.

In 1935 original radio crime fighters joined movie G-men in the violent war on criminal mobs. Opening with sounds that triggered the listener's imagination with visions of explosive action—shattering glass, clanging burglar alarms, screaming sirens, chattering machine-guns, and the shuffling feet of convicts marching into their cells—*Gangbusters* used a realistic, documentary tone for its weekly re-creation of local police stories, which reassured listeners that their community police were as vigilant, relentless, and effective as G-men. From the commission of the violent crimes, through the spine-tingling chases and the ear-popping shootouts, to the climactic capture or killing of the criminals, the show used the full power of radio sound effects. And since each story ran only half an hour, minus time for commercials, the episodes could maintain a high level of action without the pacing needed in full-length movies. At the end of each story, *Gangbusters* described a real criminal who was wanted by the police. "If you have seen this man," the announcer pleaded, "notify the F.B.I., your local law enforcement agency, or *Gangbusters* at once!"[9] In its first three years, the show claimed to have helped capture 110 criminals. This documentary approach to crime programs was to work repeatedly on entertainment machines in the home, which had the credibility of a medium that brought people news and the advantage of short time slots that did not have to make a spare, factual style interesting for an hour and a half as movies did.

Among its great many crime fighters, radio developed distinctive heroes who capitalized on the medium's lack of visuals. "Who knows what evil lurks in the hearts of men?" asked the deep and mysterious voice. "The Shadow knows!," it answered with a laugh. The Shadow, an elusive figure devoted to "righting wrongs, protecting the innocent, and punishing the guilty," was the secret second identity of Lamont Cranston, a wealthy young man about town who, while traveling in the Orient, learned "the hypnotic power to cloud men's minds so they could not see him."[10] Using the dual identities of a prominent social figure and an ephemeral character who was at home in the darkest alley of the bleakest slum allowed the creators of *The Shadow* to combine the appeal of Philo Vance's penthouse with that of Sam Spade's underworld. Radio freed writers from the need to create scenes that could be translated into concrete reality, as they had to do for stage or film. On radio The Shadow could throw his voice for miles, receive telepathic messages from ancient spirits, control other people's minds with his will power, and make himself invisible without stretching listeners' credulity. Aided by the expressive voice of Orson Welles, who played the part from 1937 to 1939, the audience seemed to have no trouble believing that the invisible Shadow could terrorize and destroy hardened criminals, twisted scientists, or corrupt politicians with nothing more than his taunting, mocking voice and laughter. But a 1937 motion picture serial of *The Shadow* did not catch on with movie fans, perhaps because much of the magic and mystery were lost when the imaginative impressions created in people's minds by radio had to be played out on screen. The Shadow, never successfully adapted to film or television, was the epitome of a *radio* hero.

Many of radio's greatest crime fighters had hidden identities and dual personalities. But that was only the beginning of radio's potential for developing fantastic heroes. With no need to worry about realistic, visual special effects, radio was free to stimulate listeners' fantasies, free to develop a hero who was "faster than a speeding bullet, more powerful than a locomotive," and "able to leap tall buildings at a single bound"—a hero who could fly. "Look! Up in the sky! It's a bird! It's a plane! It's Superman!"[11] *The Adventures of Superman* began as a syndicated radio show in 1938, when the character was merely a feature in *Action Comics*. Unlike The Shadow or The Green Hornet, who were ordinary people using disguises to hide their identities, Superman was an alien from outer space masquerading as an ordinary human being. Having arrived from his native planet Krypton with X-ray vision, the strength to bend steel, and the ability to fly, Superman committed himself to fighting evil and injustice. Normally disguised as timid, mild-mannered newspaperman Clark Kent, whenever trouble occurred he stripped to his red and blue cape and tights, lowered his voice, and became Superman. Except that his X-ray vision could not pierce through lead and that Kryptonite could neutralize his power, Superman was invincible. To make him seem more human and to make the shows more suspenseful, his friends Lois Lane and Jimmy Olsen were frequently captured and tormented, which meant that the flying man of steel had to proceed carefully with his cases to protect his friends, instead of just flying in and effortlessly crushing the criminals.

Radio created a whole range of dazzling crime fighters. They were thin, fat, tall, and short; American, Oriental, English, and French; private eyes, lawyers, playboys, policemen, district attorneys, and fantasy figures with extraordinary powers and secret identities. During World War II radio's crimefighters joined the war against fascists at home and abroad. After the war they returned to conventional crimes and retained their great popularity. In 1945 radio stations were broadcasting an estimated 90 minutes of crime shows every day, with each show drawing over five million listeners. But before long, radio crime fighters faced a new adversary they could not defeat—television. Many radio crime fighters moved successfully to the new medium, as television initially drew much of its programming from radio, which by the mid-1950s was dominated by recorded music rather than the action, comedy, mystery, and musical variety shows that it had brought into America's parlors and bedrooms for twenty-five years.

The radio crime show with the greatest initial impact on television, *Dragnet*, premiered on radio in 1949 and differed greatly from most other radio programs. Jack Webb, creator and star of *Dragnet*, built his show on a deliberately low-keyed documentary style which, unlike *Gangbusters*' action-packed approach, traced the methodical work of two ordinary policemen solving crimes. The believable program demonstrated that a popular police show need not be all action, shooting, and bizarre criminals. *Dragnet* opened with a crisp, punchy announcement beginning with, "Ladies and gentlemen, the story you are about to hear is true. Only the names have been changed to protect the innocent," and ending with Webb saying simply, "My name's Friday. I'm a cop." The announcer explained that, in cooperation with the Los Angeles Police Department, "you will travel step by step on the side of the law, through an actual case, transcribed from official police cases. From beginning to end, from crime to punishment, *Dragnet* is the story of your police force in action."[12] With routine leg work, thorough checking and re-checking of clues, evidence, and leads, and short, to-the-point questions calculated to get "just the facts," Sergeant Joe Friday and his partner systematically pursued and caught a criminal in each episode. Despite its understated, matter-of-fact approach and its use of flat, often weary, voices, the show was far from dull, in part because it ran only half an hour, but principally because it took audiences behind the scenes to see how real policemen worked. It also actively involved audiences in solving the cases by revealing facts only as Friday and his partner learned them. The show was a great success on radio and on television, where it ran from 1953 to 1959. The transfer to television, obviously, meant creating realistic visuals, which Webb did by filming the show. But the basic program remained the same—the story of two good cops routinely doing their jobs. Its focus on people rather than action also beautifully suited the television medium. *Dragnet*'s business-like, documentary style of crime solving provided the model for a number of successful television police programs, from *The Lineup* (1954-59) to *Adam 12* (1968-75), from *Highway Patrol* (1955-59) to *The F.B.I.* (1965-74).

Like radio, television did not glamorize or make heroes of gangsters or law-breakers. But it did produce a number of programs that questioned the efficiency and justice of law enforcement. On *Perry Mason*, from 1957 through 1966 in prime time and ever since in reruns, lawyer Perry Mason defended people who had been unjustly accused of crimes. Created originally in novels by Erle Stanley Gardner, Perry Mason appeared on movie screens before he came into American homes. But the movie Mason differed sharply from the radio and television Masons. In 1930s' films, lawyers were often portrayed as crooked shysters, but Mason was played as a refined upper-class lawyer who spent little time in courtrooms and operated a large, well-oiled legal firm out of plush quarters. In 1943 Perry Mason appeared on radio as a "defender of human rights, champion of all those who seek justice."[13] The fifteen-minute show ran five days a week as a continuing story in the afternoon when soap operas dominated radio. The complex "who-dun-it" plots with surprising twists and revelations remained common to Mason in all three media, as did his conflicts with the police and district attorney. But in movies he was a slick, cultured businessman and in radio a somewhat flighty soap opera character. Neither characterization fully developed the human appeal, intriguing puzzle-solving, or powerful courtroom drama that television did.

In 1957 Perry Mason came to television, played masterfully by Raymond Burr, in a one-hour, prime-time format that allowed time to develop the complexity of the plot and still drive to the electrifying courtroom showdowns. Television's Mason was primarily a courtroom lawyer who was brilliant at thinking on his feet, at deduction, at interrogating witnesses, and at forcing the guilty to break down in court, admit their guilt, and prove that Mason's clients were innocent. The concentration on tense courtroom drama was also perfect for television. Each episode captured viewers' interest from the start. Even before the titles run, the audience hears a heated conflict that ends with a death. Then, someone begs Mason to defend the person the police are seeking or have arrested. Once Mason accepts the case, the viewers know that the suspect is innocent, no matter how damning the motive and evidence appear to be. But they do not know who has committed the crime. While Mason and his private investigator, Paul Drake, gather evidence and witnesses, the police and district attorney complacently await the trial, which is the focus of the show. As the district attorney confidently lays out the government indictment, Mason fights a legal holding action, and Drake searches for new leads. Finally, Mason figures out the case, recalls key witnesses, and exposes the killer. Week after week, year after year, just getting the facts led police Lt. Tragg to arrest the wrong suspect and district attorney Hamilton Burger to prosecute innocent people. Only because of Mason's private sleuthing and his devastating courtroom questioning were the guilty caught and the innocent freed. The show's implicit message was that the government's legal forces could be ineffective and even menacing to good, honest citizens whose only recourse was to hire a private crime fighter.

In 1959 when crime shows began to challenge westerns as television's most popular action genre, leading the charge were private detectives, ranging from the swingers of *77 Sunset Strip* and *Hawaiian Eye* to the hard-hitting *Peter Gun* and the analytical investigators of *Checkmate*. With major movie studios filming series for television, crime on the entertainment machine in the home for the first time could offer some of the visual excitement of the entertainment machine in the theater. The longest running of these private eye shows, *77 Sunset Strip* (1958-64), the first effort by Warner Brothers to extend its television production from westerns to crime shows, featured handsome detectives, played by Efrem Zimbalist, Jr., and Roger Smith, who operated out of a Hollywood nightclub. The show, which brought sexy glamor and a light-hearted tone to television crime shows, ushered in a number of handsome, young private eyes who chased pretty women as well as crooks. The programs were part of ABC's first major success in the television ratings race, which reportedly prompted CBS executive Jim Aubrey to order: "Put a sexy dame in each picture and make a *77 Sunset Strip* if that is what is necessary, but give me sex and action."[14]

But probably the most influential crime show of the late 1950s, *The Untouchables,* featured tough cops and explosive violence. Returning to the blazing style of James Cagney in *G-Men, The Untouchables* starred Robert Stack as Eliot Ness, the leader of tommy-gun-toting, untouchable federal agents who had a free hand to hunt and eliminate members of rum-running mobs. Set in the Prohibition era of the 1920s, the show used a documentary approach to justify the new level of bloodshed it brought to television. By the end of its first year *The Untouchables* was nearing the top of the ratings. The key to its success was clearly its violence, or as television executives called it, its "action." ABC, which had run a distant third until it emphasized violent action series, assigned a script supervisor to ensure that each episode was packed with violence. He praised one early script for opening with "a lot of action—a running gunfight between two cars of mobsters who crash, then continue to fight in the streets. Three killed. Six injured. Three killed are innocent bystanders." The story built from there with scenes of a mail-truck holdup in which the driver is killed and a hoodlum is beaten unconscious and thrown into a river. The episode climaxes at a small air strip where the mobsters are waiting for one of their planes. Instead The Untouchables fly in, catch the hoods off-guard, and shoot the gang boss as he tries to flee. When the action in the series lagged, network officials urged executive producer Quinn

Martin "to give careful attention to maintain this action and suspense in future episodes. As you know, there had been a softening in the ratings, which may or may not be the result of this talkiness, but certainly we should watch it carefully."[15] Writers found enough ways to mix shooting with talking to keep the show running until 1963 when it was killed off by protests against its use of Italian names for its gangsters and against its excessive violence, which seemed even worse in the wake of the assassination of President John F. Kennedy that year.

In the mid-1960s, the era of the Vietnam War and the heating up of the Cold War, spy and war shows tended to replace crime as television's top action programs. But in the late-1960s when American fought American at home over the Vietnam War, racism, and radicalism, tough police shows returned to prominence, offering the public at least symbolic reassurance that the forces of law and order could control the new level of violence that seemed to be tearing the country apart. Efrem Zimbalist, Jr., who had played one of the free-spirited private eyes of *77 Sunset Strip*, symbolized the new tone of television crime shows in 1965 by becoming the leader of the somber organization men of *The F.B.I.*, a show that had the personal endorsement of J. Edgar Hoover. Every week for nine years bright, efficient F.B.I. agents caught criminals and crushed conspiracies. In 1967 Jack Webb, using his low-keyed documentary style, re-created *Dragnet*, which had been off the air since 1959. In the late 1960s, television was filled with police programs set in places as far apart as New York and Honolulu.

Perhaps most significantly of all, Raymond Burr, whose Perry Mason series had carried the message that inept policemen and district attorneys tried to put innocent people in jail, changed sides and messages by starring in a new show, *Ironside*, in which he played an ex-chief of detectives on the San Francisco police department who, despite being paralyzed from the waist down by a would-be assassin's bullet, carried on his fight against crime as the head of a small, special investigative unit in the police department. With a young white policeman and policewoman and a young black assistant whose job was to drive his van and carry him when necessary, Ironside took on crime. He also took on the serious, new problems of the age—getting along with a new generation of young people, dealing with militant blacks, and responding to charges of racism. As a gruff, demanding, but concerned father figure, Ironside not only built his inexperienced young officers into an effective team but also created emotional bonds between them as they worked closely together on tough cases. The key to his success was that in a time when many adults questioned their own beliefs and looked to young people for answers, Ironside never doubted his own traditional values and never accepted anything less from his young staff than complete dedication to his rules. He was a tough man of honor and commitment who judged people by their performance, not their age, sex, or race. Even Mark, Ironside's angry, racially sensitive, black assistant, who at first suspected that he was hired as a token, was won over by Ironside's insistence that Mark do his job and that he had no one but himself to blame if he did not make something of himself. During the series Mark completed school, became a lawyer and a police officer, and joined Ironside's team and family as an equal. In this popular show, which ran from 1967 to 1974, fighting crime was more than an end in itself; it was also a way to bridge the gaps between generations and races, a way to build a loving family from totally different people who committed themselves to preserving traditional American values, a pattern that was adapted by other police shows such as *The Mod Squad* (1968-73) and *The Rookies* (1972-76). In a real, if unconscious, way *Ironside* was television's answer to the youth rebellion and racial violence of the era.

In the early 1970s, American society seemed to be crumbling. Crime and violence mounted; the police and the courts seemed ineffective; an American Vice President and a President resigned in disgrace; and public confidence in many basic American institutions and in the nation's future was shaken. It was in this context that television developed a wide range of crime fighters who used every weapon and tactic they could find to fight an all-out war for order and control that paralleled the war fought against gangsters and disorder in the 1930s. Traditional tough cops made a strong comeback in such popular and long running new shows, as: *Streets of San Francisco* (1972-77), which teamed young Michael Douglas and veteran actor Karl Malden in an action show devoted to catching criminals, not to solving social problems; *Kojak* (1973-78), with Telly Savalas as a tough, stylishly dressed cop with a shaved head, a Tootsie pop in his mouth, a defiant sneer on his face, and a contemptuous "Who loves ya, baby?" on his lips as he caught the worst thugs in New York; *Hawaii Five-O* (1968-79), which starred Jack Lord as the relentless, hard-hitting head of the Hawaiian state police; and *Police Story* (1973-77), an anthology format with different stars each week portraying police officers as human beings who paid great prices in their personal lives for their dedication to fighting crime.

When the forces of disorder seemed to be succeeding in their assault on American society, television also created a new breed of police officers who looked, lived, and fought like the street criminals they battled, much as inept societies in movie westerns hired unscrupulous professional killers to fight other professional killers. But television's street cops had a commitment to society and justice that was lacking in the movie western's hired guns of the period. Beginning in 1975, *Baretta*, an unconventional, streetwise, plain-clothes cop used the unorthodox tactics of the street-fighter to bring order and justice to his down and out neighborhood. Also in 1975, *Starsky & Hutch*, featuring two young, plain-clothes cops with a hopped-up car and quick trigger fingers, opened fire on violent lawbreakers. Lacking the social concerns of *Baretta, Starsky & Hutch* was a straightforward, violent action show in the mold of *The Untouchables*, giving audiences heavy doses of auto chases, fist fights, and shootouts while reassuring viewers that this violence was being used on the side of law enforcement. By the late-1970s, organized protests against the high level of violence on television doomed programs like *Starsky & Hutch* because networks and sponsors were reluctant to offend viewers and consumers.

But movies in this same period had no need to curb their violence, since a great many tickets were being sold to pictures that made *Starsky & Hutch* look like child's play. In 1971 Clint Eastwood, who had become a movie star playing cold-blooded western killers, brought a similar approach to crime pictures, playing *Dirty Harry* Callahan, a fearless policeman who becomes a virtual vigilante because of his frustration with the restrictions placed on the police in their fight against crime. While tracking Scorpio, a vicious madman who kills innocent people, including children, Dirty Harry demonstrates his bravado and his contempt for criminals. After breaking up a bank robbery, Harry calmly levels his possibly empty gun at a burglar who has to decide whether to call Harry's bluff and draw his own gun or to surrender. "Tell you the truth," Harry observes, "I lost count myself. Now, what you got to do, considering this is a 44 Magnum, the most powerful hand gun in the world and will blow your head off if it's loaded. What you've got to do is ask yourself, 'Are you feeling lucky, punk?'"[16] The burglar wilts, surrenders, and then asks if the gun is empty. Harry smiles stoically, levels his gun at the crook, pulls the trigger, and the

hammer clicks on the empty chamber. Then Harry returns to his
search for the maniac who is terrorizing the public. After Scorpio kills
a young girl, Harry breaks into Scorpio's room, catches him, tortures
him into telling where the girl's body is, and arrests him. But because
his rights have been violated, Scorpio is released, and Harry is ordered
off the case. Finally, Harry takes matters into his own hands, rescues a
busload of children Scorpio has kidnapped, shoots and kills Scorpio,
and throws his badge away as the picture ends. In many ways, Harry
represented the traditional western hero who rode into a corrupt frontier town and cleaned it up so a civilized society could develop. The
major difference was that Callahan *began* as a member of the legal
establishment in a supposedly civilized society, took the law into his
own hands as a result of social and legal decay, and ended by turning
his back on the basic legal institutions of his society. The picture, with
its virile, vigilante hero fighting the senseless violence that plagued
helpless people, was a great hit.

In 1973 Eastwood starred in *Magnum Force,* a sequel with even
more menacing implications than *Dirty Harry.* Before the movie begins, Eastwood repeats his lines about the 44 Magnum being powerful
enough to blow your head off, asks whether you feel lucky, points the
gun at the camera, and fires. In the first action of the picture, a motorcycle policeman wearing a helmet uses a Magnum to murder a racke-
teering labor leader who has been unjustly acquitted of killing a rival
and his family. As the picture unfolds, policemen, hamstrung by legal
restrictions, murder crook after crook. Eventually, Dirty Harry, who
viewers assume is the murderer in uniform, realizes that young police
officers are the vigilantes—as if television's *Rookies* had gone from social do-gooders to avenging assassins. Harry, who remains committed
to the system even though he continually fights against the way it is
implemented, sets out to stop them. After a bomb kills his partner and
nearly kills him, Harry takes the information about the young cops to
his superior, who turns out to be their leader. Though the assassins
turn on Harry, a chase and shootout end with the three young cops
and their leader dead. The nightmare of lawless policemen is ended,
and the integrity of a basic institution is preserved. Dirty Harry might
quit the police department in disgust, but he also fought to keep it
from being used to corrupt the very traditions of law and justice that
it was charged with defending.

Eastwood's highly successful crime pictures expressed the fear that many people felt in the 1970s—that criminals and corruption were virtually immune from the law and the courts. Even vicious murderers and rapists seemed to be set free by the courts or prison authorities at alarming rates. *Dirty Harry* offered a specific, personal solution to one miscarriage of justice. But when *Magnum Force* offered the broad, general solution of organized vigilantes in uniform, even Dirty Harry Callahan rejected it. But he had no other solution. Nor did many other people in the 1970s, when strong, outraged citizens took the law into their own hands and dished out their own versions of retribution, revenge, and justice in movies such as *Walking Tall* (1974), *Death Wish* (1974), and *Taxi Driver* (1976).

Ironically, in the early 1970s, one of the most talented of American film-makers, Francis Ford Coppola, found a symbol of honor, justice, and family values in a violent crime boss who built an empire of vice, corruption, and murder. Based on the best-selling novel by Mario Puzo, *The Godfather* (1972) became one of the most popular pictures of all time and raised the gangster to the level of the mythic hero seen at his benevolent, fatherly best. The film provided an image of what the Public Enemy or Little Caesar might have become if they had survived, built large institutions, and become administrators. The world of *The Godfather* is a hierarchical world of organization men, a world of patriarchy and inherited position, far different from the world of independent, self-made men who catapulted from the slum to the mansion in the gangster movies of the thirties. That period of upward mobility, which had also thrust Vito Corleone from being a poor immigrant to being an autocratic ruler of an empire, had passed long before the picture began. Instead, the film told the story of an old man who wanted respectability for his family, but was the captive of his own success. He and his family could not escape from his violent business and from the corruption of modern America.

Though Don Vito Corleone, the Godfather, played beautifully by Marlon Brando, ran his crime syndicate with an iron hand, using murder as one of his weapons, especially for revenging unjust offenses against his family, Coppola portrayed him as an honorable man who believes in traditional values and refuses to enter the lucrative drug traffic because it is immoral, which leads rivals to try to assassinate him. Corleone's youngest son Michael (Al Pacino), who was supposed to become "a senator or something" respectable and have nothing to do with the mob, foils the second assassination attempt, kills the rival in revenge, and flees to Sicily to hide. When his wife is killed by a bomb, he returns to New York to revenge her murder and to head the family business. Coppola's sequel, *The Godfather, Part II* (1974), flashed back to the young Vito being orphaned in Sicily, emigrating to America, and becoming a tough, young man (Robert DeNiro) who begins his brutal rise to power in order to build a good life for his poor family. The picture also follows the career of Michael, who expands the empire, uses a corrupt Senator to avoid being indicted by a Senate investigating committee, and ruthlessly murders anyone who stands in his way—rivals, friends, or family. As a result, Michael rules unchallenged, but alone. At the peak of his power, he is a failure, having lost the family, traditions, and moral values that his father had stood for. *The Godfather* saga reflected the widespread longing in the 1970s for old-fashioned family values. It also reflected the pessimistic belief that Old World morality inevitably disintegrated in the face of New World realities and that there was nothing anybody could do about it.

In the early 1980s movie theaters were filled with nightmarish blends of crime and horror movies in which psychopathic killers, human and inhuman, slaughtered and dismembered victim after victim, often attractive young women, in graphically portrayed bloodbaths. In October 1980 *The Variety Market Guide* listed about forty such movies in circulation or about to be released. In 1981 one of these pictures, *Friday the 13th Part II*, a sequel to a horrifying hit, opened with a woman being decapitated with an axe and moved on to a woman stabbed in the temple with an icepick, a policeman beaten to death with a hammer, a man in a wheelchair split open with a hatchet, and a couple impaled on a spear while making love. Though such movies did not fit in any classic crime category, they did reflect the broad sense of powerlessness felt by a great many people in an era of runaway inflation, growing unemployment, oil and gasoline shortages, international terrorism, and violent street crime. Television, with its broad audience and strict censorship, did not directly reflect this vicious, gory trend in its regular programming, though some movies made for television used a similar tone, if not similar detail. Generally, television ducked the crime problem by concentrating on sexy shows and comedies, which were occasionally blended with some action in popular shows such as *CHiPS*, about handsome young California highway patrol officers who devoted as much energy to being playboys as to solving major crimes.

Based on the history of the genre, it seems likely that show business crime fighters will reassert the rule of law and order. When and how that might happen is unpredictable, but it is likely to coincide with the return of hope and the feeling that people can take control of their lives. It probably will come from movies, which have a free hand to use all the violence necessary to create a hero as tough as the times. Television, with its restrictions on violence, has its hands tied behind its back. Even if network television cannot provide America with a new breed of crime fighting heroes, the ever more varied technology of modern show business in the home enables the American people to get almost any type of entertainment almost anytime they want it. No doubt crime shows in some form will remain a fixture of show business as long as crime remains a fixture of modern life. Public moods and tastes, hopes and fears, will decide whether the focus of crime shows will be cops, private eyes, or criminals, and whether the tone will be reassuring or threatening.

7

Goodness Had Little To Do with It: Sexuality and the Media

Sexy men and women have always been features of popular entertainment. Each period in the history of American show business has had certain stars who especially captured the sexual tastes, ideals, and fantasies of the times. The qualities of these sex symbols have changed over the course of the twentieth century as public attitudes, mores, and moods changed and as new entertainment media developed.

Though sexy entertainers had been luring Americans to performances for decades, many of these shows were widely considered to be indecent and disreputable. But in the 1890s, Florenz Ziegfeld began to create sexy shows and stars with a glamor and style that made them respectable as well as enticing. As part of his approach, Ziegfeld began to perfect many of the promotional techniques that producers would use throughout the twentieth century. Focusing his publicity on the *personal* charms of little known entertainers, Ziegfeld used well-planned public relations campaigns to create stars whose principal appeals were their sex appeal, personality, and fame—rather than their talent, character, or performances—sex symbols whose personal and performing images were identical. In the public's eye these entertainers often seemed to be uninhibited people who acted out their private impulses in public rather than skilled performers. But this only added to their appeal as long as they did not go too far beyond the bounds of respectability. Ziegfeld's first promotional triumph came in 1893 when he transformed a fairly ordinary entertainer into an exotic sex symbol by using backstage gossip and revealing photos of the scantily-clad performer. Ironically, the first creation of the man who became famous for "glorifying the American girl" was Eugene Sandow, a strong man, not a glamor girl. But Ziegfeld quickly moved from "beefcake" to "cheesecake."

In 1896 Ziegfeld signed Anna Held, a pretty, young European with an hour-glass figure, an exotic French accent, and a saucy sexuality. After making her arrival in New York a glamorous event, Ziegfeld out-fitted a hotel suite to look like Marie Antoinette's boudoir, filled it with a feast and champagne, dressed Held in a seductive negligee, gave her provocative answers to obvious questions, and invited in the press. Be-cause of such promotions and Ziegfeld's stories about her milk baths, kissing contests, auto-racing, and expensive wardrobe, newspapers and magazines made Held a famous celebrity and a great attraction before she ever set foot on an American stage. This pattern would be followed time after time by twentieth-century promoters. "She would not be a 'sensation' at all," complained the *New York Times* reviewer of her American debut, "if the idea had not been ingeniously forced upon the public mind that she is . . . naughty."[1] Held lived up to the publicity with her French accent and her suggestive renditions of songs like "Come and Play with Me" and "I Can't Make My Eyes Behave." She also inspired Ziegfeld to produce *The Follies of 1907*, an Americanized version of a racy Parisian revue, a fast-paced blend of comedy, produc-tion numbers, and pretty women, from a Salome dancer to bathing beauties singing "Come and Float Me, Freddie, Dear." Over the years, the *Ziegfeld Follies,* which grew more lavish, more star-studded, and more daring, became the very epitome of glamorous, exciting big-time show business.

In the early twentieth century, live show business grew increasingly risqué exploiting female sex appeal. No one was a better example of that than Eva Tanguay. In the era of the refined Gibson Girl, when young women were expected to strap themselves into corsets and to blush at the mere mention of courtship, Tanguay exploded on stage with wild, uninhibited renditions of double-entendre songs like "I Want Some One To Go Wild with Me" and "It's All Been Done Before But Not the Way I Do It." "She is a tornado, a whirlwind, a bouncing bundle of perpetual motion," one reviewer observed of her vaudeville act. "She screams, she shouts, she twists and turns, she is a mad woman, a whirling dervish of grotesquerie. She is unlike any other woman on the stage."[2] Tanguay was also keenly aware of the importance of publicity and made certain that she got her share. When Salome's Dance of the Seven Veils swept show business, Tanguay called a press conference to unveil her new costume. Then, she walked in fully clothed, smiled, looked down at her clenched fist, slowly opened her hand, and asked the reporters how they liked the costume. With her eyecatching publicity stunts and her stunning performances, Tanguay projected an image of untamed, liberated female sexuality that made her one of the most popular and most highly paid vaudeville stars. In the early twentieth century, when traditional sex roles were being challenged on stage and off, Tanguay may have been "unlike any other woman on stage," but it was not for a lack of competition.

In 1896 when Ziegfeld began to promote Anna Held and motion pictures were still novelties, the Edison Company released a very short movie of middle-aged stage stars John C. Rice and May Irwin re-enacting an incident from their hit play *The Widow Jones*. The brief interlude created a great sensation because it was a closeup of the lovers kissing. "Magnified to gargantuan proportions," fumed Chicago critic Herbert Stone of *The Kiss*, "it is absolutely disgusting. . . . Such things call for police intervention."[3] Stone's strong reaction to an innocent romantic encounter was an early demonstration of the great emotional power of the movie industry to excite audiences with its portrayals of romance and sexuality. But even though early movies did offer audiences what were then considered to be revealing glimpses of women's legs in pictures like *A Girl Climbing an Apple Tree* or *The Flatiron Building on a Windy Day*, in the nickelodeon era, when the movie business was struggling to establish itself as an independent entertainment form with its own theaters and was facing licensing and censorship problems, few films were as sexually daring as stage shows.

The first movie stars were young adolescent women with lithe bodies, blonde curls, and pretty faces—actresses such as Mary Pickford and Lillian Gish. Under the direction of D. W. Griffith, they portrayed Victorian girl-women who were, as Gish described them, "the essence of virginity—purity and goodness, with nobility of mind, heart, soul, and body."[4] Pickford, with her ringlets, winsome sweetness, vivacious youth, and wide-eyed innocence, became America's Sweetheart by appealing to Victorian images of the "good girl." Before 1917 Pickford regularly played girls who blossomed into adolescent maidens or young women. When movies got sexier after World War I, audiences rejected her portrayals of women, forcing her to preserve her youthful innocence by playing only children, even boys, throughout her movie career. Through Pickford, audiences held on to their fantasy images of an earlier, more innocent age.

The films of D. W. Griffith, especially those starring Lillian Gish, who played a much wider range of roles than Pickford, offer a clear insight into the sexual values of the period. Like many early-twentieth-century men, Griffith retained the conflicting sexual values and double standards of the Victorian age. Consciously, as a proper moralist, he was shocked that Marguerite Clark would take her stockings off before the camera. Yet, unconsciously, as a man and as a producer of popular pictures, he filmed Blanche Sweet, another of his pretty, blonde teenagers, wearing what Gish described as "a crepe shift and a tiny pair of panties, which proved no protection during one scene in which she had to ride a horse sidesaddle."[5] Griffith generally avoided open eroticism in favor of teasing audiences by placing a pretty, virginal, young blonde into a sexually charged, menacing situation often with an older, darker man, as he did when he made delicately beautiful Lillian Gish the object of sexual assaults in two of his and her finest films, *Birth of a Nation* (1914) and *Broken Blossoms* (1919). Griffith's unconscious manipulation of the sexual symbols and fantasies his generation inherited were tremendously popular when movies and the American public were moving from the nineteenth into the twentieth century.

Griffith's innocent, girlish, movie heroines also had their naïve, boyish counterparts. "Nobody ever did it like Fairbanks," recalled John Wayne of his boyhood hero. "And he always had this beautiful grin on his face as he was doin' these impossible tricks. God, how I wanted to be like him. I dreamed of being like him."[6] Boys and men all over America and the world wanted to be like Douglas Fairbanks in the years around World War I when he ruled screen adventure. And women around the nation and the world wanted to find men like Fairbanks, who brought to the screen a romantic figure combining the athletic grace of a gymnast, the dashing figure and winking eye of a lover, and the youthful naïveté and enthusiasm of a boy, which made him a movie star rivaling Chaplin and Pickford in popularity.

Though he was already a stage star when he entered pictures in 1914, film offered Fairbanks almost unlimited potential for exciting action and intimate closeups. By 1916 the *Motion Picture World*'s reviewer applauded Fairbanks for being "in a class all by himself, at once an athlete of resource and daring and a subtle interpreter of the amusing side of human nature."[7] The public loved his joyous frolicking, and by 1917 no other movie star received more publicity. In the many interviews he gave, Fairbanks projected himself as a regular guy having a wonderful time. In 1917, he did his first historical adventure, wearing a period costume, fighting enemies with dazzling sword play, and racing over rooftops. In the 1920s, these colorful, exciting elements, with the addition of spectacular stunts and courtly romance, gave pictures such as *The Mark of Zorro* (1920), *The Three Musketeers* (1921), *Robin Hood* (1922), and *The Thief of Baghdad* (1923) the look of fairy tales.

While he reigned on screen as the dashing, swashbuckler king of adventure, off screen Fairbanks lived out an even more fantastic fairy tale when in 1920 America's boyfriend married Mary Pickford, America's sweetheart—a dream wedding possible only in Hollywood. The storybook couple—the boy next door and the girl next door—held court at their palatial Pickfair estate like American royalty, receiving almost every notable visitor to Southern California. Yet, they never lost their image as fun-loving, real folks who had struck it rich but who had not lost the common touch. Fairbanks, for instance, lived out the fantasies of men and boys all over America in the sports-crazy 1920s when he sparred with Jack Dempsey, served a tennis ball to Bill Tilden, and pitched to Babe Ruth. Magazines and newspapers filled their pages with stories about Pickford and Fairbanks. Their fashions, cars, and pets, her cosmetics and hairstyles, his suntan and athleticism, all influenced an American public that relished every tidbit of information it could get about the stars known simply as "Doug and Mary." But though Pickford and Fairbanks continued to pack movie theaters by portraying idealized, innocent images of an earlier time, those images began to be challenged in 1916 when the first blatant sex symbol squirmed onto the nation's screens.

Today, the word "vampire" evokes a sinister masculine image, principally because of the performance of Bela Lugosi in the 1930 film of Bram Stoker's classic horror novel, *Dracula*. Before that, though, Hollywood's image of a vampire was a mysterious, man-killing woman, an image created by Theda Bara in the 1916 film *A Fool There Was*. The picture told the story of a woman who seduces and corrupts a young married diplomat, steals him from his family, and then leaves him to

a life of alcohol and drugs. To intrigue the public the Fox studio transformed Theodosia Goodman from Cincinnati into Theda Bara, who
supposedly had been born in the shadow of the Sphinx. Bara and the
vamp became one in a torrent of publicity featuring sensational stories
about her as a superstitious, crystal-ball gazing, amulet-wearing mar-
riage-wrecker and sexy photos of her barely covered by exotic clothing
and surrounded by snakes, skeletons, cobwebs, and skulls—like an ancient, erotic goddess sprung back to life. Claiming that some women
had "a strange, witch-like power over men," Bara boasted that "the
vampire that I play is the vengeance of my sex upon its exploiters. You
see," she concluded, "I have the face of a vampire, perhaps, but the
heart of a feministe."[8] In contrast to Griffith's male fantasy of the helpless, sweet girl-woman, Bara's vamp evoked male nightmares of powerful female avengers who would reverse traditional sexual roles, se-
duce men, exploit them, and then cast them aside.

Bara stunned audiences and critics in the age of movie innocence.
Reviewers found her sensuous, "purely animal" appeal revolting, but
fascinating, and the public lined up to see her pictures. By the end of
1916 an estimated 400,000 people saw a Bara movie every *day*. In three
years she made an incredible forty movies, including the vamp roles
of Carmen, Salome, and Cleopatra, but she also insisted on playing
non-vamps, pictures that drew good reviews, but few patrons. People
did not want to see Bara, the woman they loved to hate, the woman
who embodied the darker, demonic side of human nature, playing
angelic roles like Pickford's. But in 1919, Bara insisted that she "would
not slink and writhe and wriggle day in and day out." She demanded
"to bob my curls, and climb trees, and love for love's own sake."[9] Fox
refused to renew her contract, and she returned to the stage.

Bara's attempt to change media was no more successful than her attempt to change screen images. "The picture talked,' the *New York
World* reviewer sniped at her 1919 stage performance, "and we laughed.
The picture took into her live arms several men and squeezed them
into kisses, and we tittered. Her vampire speeches were uttered with
matter-of-fact and colorless rigidity."[10] Bara apparently did not realize
that silent film was fundamentally different from the live stage. Sound
was the most obvious difference. With an emotionally charged image
like Bara's, silent movie fans imagined how she sounded. In filming
silent pictures she could simply use her own voice because audiences
did not hear it, but when she spoke on stage, her mid-American "school

girl" dialect, as several critics labeled it, made her performance laughable when almost any foreign-sounding accent could have been convincing enough. But there was probably much more to her stage failure than that. Silent film, with its absence of sound, was a medium with fantasy at its heart, a medium that could successfully portray emotional intensity that would have seemed overdone in a more realistic medium. Bara's hypersexual vamp, like Chaplin's sentimentalized tramp, was a product of the silent screen, whose fans customarily took one-dimensional fantasy figures seriously. But on the realistic stage, Bara's exaggerated vamp looked like a parody, and audiences laughed. Despite a brief, unsuccessful movie comeback in 1925-26, Bara's career was effectively over on the eve of the 1920s when movie portrayals of sexuality were changing profoundly.

Beginning in 1918 Cecil B. De Mille created a series of pictures about women who were both sensual and respectable. In *Why Change Your Wife?* (1920), for instance, after Gloria Swanson's nagging drives her husband to another woman, she seduces him back. In *Don't Change Your Husband* (1919), a bored Swanson runs off with a young man, but returns to her husband when he promises to work at romance, not just at making money. In this series of racy movies combining infidelity, sexuality, and beautiful people in the very latest clothing and settings, De Mille implicitly preached that modern women should protect their marriages by adopting the vamp's erotic weapons and that men should realize that their wives needed affection and sex as well as food and shelter. De Mille also used flashbacks to scenes of ancient, hedonistic eroticism in Babylon, imperial Rome, or biblical times to add historical accuracy to his moralistic rationalization for portraying sex. "I am sometimes accused of gingering up the Bible with large and lavish infusions of sex and violence," he observed in his autobiography. "I can only wonder if my accusers have ever read certain parts of the Bible."[11] Whether or not critics and others read the Bible, many people bought tickets to see sexy movies like De Mille's.

The 1920s was a decade of jarring contrasts. It was the age of flappers, Dixieland jazz, bathtub gin, the Sultan of Swat, and the Charleston. But it was also the age of a Constitutional amendment outlawing alcoholic beverages, of the anti-evolution Scopes trial, and of the white-sheeted Ku Klux Klan burning crosses across the nation to protest against immorality, as well as against minorities. It was the age of licentiousness and the age of censorship, the age of experimentation and the age of repression. Show business was a major force for change and a major source of controversy because it brought the changes to the eyes of Americans as never before. Though stage shows were more openly erotic and provocative than movies, they also had much more restricted audiences. If the *Ziegfeld Follies* and Eva Tanguay did not appear in Butte, Montana, or Biloxi, Mississippi, Gloria Swanson and Rudolph Valentino movies did. Mass-produced films brought the sights of the latest Hollywood fads, fashions, and follies to the smallest, most conservative American towns. For the first time, almost everyone in the country could see what the most daring people in the country were doing.

Stage shows also grew racier. Glamorous revues, including the *Ziegfeld Follies,* which was the classiest of a growing lot, even spotlighted nude women. But, ironically, the woman who most typified the daring sex appeal of live show business in the twenties never took her clothes off on stage. Mae West entered vaudeville in the early twentieth century, when double-entendre songs, lusty women like Eva Tanguay, and alluring female impersonators like Julian Eltinge were the rage. Drawing on all three, West used her curvaceous figure and sexy voice to create a striking stage image. By 1912 when a New Haven, Connecticut, newspaper denounced her "enchanting, seductive, sin-promising wriggle," West's audiences and salary were growing rapidly. Wearing gowns like a rhinestone dress that fit "like a second skin" and was slit to the thigh and accentuating the lyrics to suggestive songs with "little private gestures," West became a top vaudeville star. Delivery was the key to her appeal. "It isn't what you do," she often explained. "It's how you do it." And she certainly knew how to do it. In 1926 West's first full-length show, *Sex,* got her arrested and convicted in New York for "lewd, profane, lascivious, or obscene" behavior. "Miss West's personality, looks, walk, mannerisms and gestures," she quoted the prosecutor as arguing, "made the lines and situations suggestive."[12] The publicity was invaluable. By 1927 Mae West had become the queen of innuendo.

West found the right type of material for her style when she played an 1890s Bowery tavern owner, Diamond Lil, "one of the finest women that ever walked the streets." Unlike Bara's joyless vamps who never fell in love, West, with her waved blonde hair, huge false eyelashes, and figure-hugging gowns, fell in love time after time after time, and she loved sex. "Never have I seen an actress pawed from hip to buttock as Miss West's avid leading man pawed her in that bedroom set with the golden swan bed," critic Ashton Stevens observed. Despite all her visual and sexual appeal, West needed the realism of the stage and later of sound motion pictures to give her blatantly hedonistic caricatures general appeal. With her lusty voice, suggestive one-liners, and superb comic timing, she balanced her brassy, aggressive sexuality with mocking, tongue-in-cheek humor, leaving no doubt that it was all in fun. "Haven't you ever met a man who can make you happy?" she was asked. "Sure I have," she fired back, "lots of times." Or, she provocatively asked a man, "Is that a gun you got in your pocket, or are you just glad to see me?"[13] Stage audiences laughed *at* Bara; they laughed *with* West, which allowed her and them to strip away normal hypocrisy and to enjoy sexy stage antics.

Until 1920 American leading men had been fair-skinned, wholesome, All-American boys, personified by Douglas Fairbanks and Wallace Reid. But in 1921, dark, sultry Rudolph Valentino burst into the movie world with an explosive performance in *The Four Horsemen of the Apocalypse* as a young, sexy Argentine dilettante. Valentino first appears ten minutes into the picture wearing a gaucho outfit, clenching a cigar in his teeth, and striding into a cantina and up to a dancing couple. He taps the man on the shoulder, looks the woman in the eyes, beats the man to the floor with his whip, and sweeps the woman into his arms for a slow, sensuous tango that climaxes with a passionate kiss. In a normal movie of the time a Fairbanks or a Reid would have bounced out of the crowd, thrashed the masher, and whisked the woman away. But Valentino was the hero, not the villain, and the picture made him a rising star.

His next movie almost made him a god. As *The Sheik,* a dashing Arab warrior, he meets an Englishwoman traveling in the desert alone, pulls her off her horse onto his, and commands, "lie still, you little fool" as he takes her back to his opulent tent. "Why have you brought me here?" she asks. "Are you not woman enough to know?" he replies. If she did not know, everyone else did, at least once the studio publicity department finished with the ads, which featured a large photo of him sweeping her from her horse to his and the warning: "Shriek for the Sheik Will Seek You Too!" Lest there be any doubt, the ads explained that "he wanted only one thing and she knew what it was, and it would be only a matter of time before he got it."[14] In one sense, it was a scene right out of Griffith—a dark, powerful man sexually threatening an innocent blonde woman. But in this case, instead of killing herself rather than submit, as Mae Marsh had done in *The Birth of a Nation,* the woman falls in love, and they marry.

Though called a "he-vamp," Valentino actually had a much more complex appeal than Bara. He did dominate women, but in pictures like *Blood and Sand* (1922) he also fell victim to vamps, a weakness which only made him more attractive to women who could fantasize about being forcefully subjected to his every whim, but also about subduing or even mothering him. This vulnerability, which Bara's vamps totally lacked, humanized his roles. But Valentino's displays of softness caused a number of men to question his masculinity, as the *Chicago Tribune* did when it condemned him in an editorial as a "pink powder puff."[15] After Valentino, who died at age thirty-one in 1926, American action heroes tended to be either hard-shelled, tough guys showing no weakness and taking no lip from women, or adventurers, almost totally absorbed in the male world of combat and awkwardly shy around women. Romantic heroes tended to be played by comic actors, not action stars.

The major symbol of female sexuality in the silent movies of the 1920s sprang from American college campuses. In 1923 movie actress Colleen Moore, who had been wearing long curls to play Pickford roles, was startled to meet college coeds with short, bobbed hair and "an air of independence about them." Realizing that she "shared their restlessness, understood their determination to free themselves of the Victorian shackles of the pre-World War I era and find out for themselves what life was all about," Moore became a star by portraying these qualities in *Flaming Youth* (1923). The picture which included suggestive scenes of men and women undressing around a swimming pool, focused on Moore as a saucy flapper who teased, flirted, drank, and danced wildly, though she remained a "good girl" to the end. In the 1920s flappers of all sorts appeared in movies. Moore portrayed the "glamorous dream of youth and gaiety and swift tapping feet," as writer Margaret Reid described the types in 1927. Constance Talmadge represented "the deft princess of lingerie—and love—plus humor; and Joan Crawford was "gowned to the apex of sophistication." But more than anyone else, Clara Bow, in 1927, epitomized the flapper, "pretty, impudent, superbly assured, as worldly wise, briefly clad, and 'hardboiled' as possible."[16]

After getting into movies by winning a fan magazine contest, Bow played small parts in over two dozen movies between 1923 and 1925, including *Enemies of Women,* in which she danced on a table top, reportedly without wearing panties, which prompted star Lionel Barrymore to quip, "you can see all the way up to the Virgin Islands!"[17] She also posed for pinup photos that left no doubt she was nude under a sheet. In 1926 she became a star with her performances in *Mantrap,* *Whoopee,* and especially *Dancing Mothers,* in which she flirted, teased, stayed out drinking and dancing all night long, and tried to steal her mother's boyfriend. In 1927 she played the *It* girl, a role she lived up to off the screen with her well-publicized, uninhibited escapades. On screen Bow had a believable, thoroughly American sex appeal—direct, honest, and vulnerable. Not so beautiful that female fans could not identify with her, she regularly played ordinary working women—manicurists, dancers, and store clerks—women who freshened up their makeup when they saw a man, flirted with him, and followed him into the glamorous, uppercrust world, but always put the brakes on when things were about to go too far—until the wealthy man married her. In movie after movie Clara Bow played out what must have been many young working-women's fantasies of updated, sensual versions of the Horatio Alger myth in an era when many people believed everyone could get rich.

But by the early 1930s, show business and its sexual images were changing radically. Faced with the huge costs of converting to sound motion pictures, with the economic despair of the Great Depression, and with competition from free radio shows, Hollywood had to make movies that would entice people to part with their precious money. Musicals, verbal humor, and crime pulled people in. So did sex. "In a state of panic and chaos," Cecil B. De Mille complained in 1931, movie producers "rush for the bedspring and the lingerie the moment the phantom of empty seats rises to clutch them." The complaint might seem strange coming from De Mille, the master of racy romances and sexy biblical epics, but he was right. As MGM director Hunt Stromberg had explained in 1928 to young David O. Selznick, "tits and sand sell tickets."[18]

Jean Harlow proved that Stromberg was at least half right. The way she bounced along without a bra got her the female part in *Hell's Angels* (1930) and made her a star. Harlow changed the nature of female sex symbols in movies. Unlike flappers, who focused the audience's attention on their legs, Harlow raised audience sights—to the breast. Her bra-less look created a sensation, as did her blonde hair. Until then, blonde hair in movies had signified the "good girl." Pickford was a blonde, Bara a brunette, and Bow a redhead. Harlow reversed this long standing light-dark, good-evil dichotomy. But her looks were only part of her quick rise to stardom. Following the familiar pattern, the studio cranked out sexy photos, stories about her love life, and provocative one-liners for her to deliver to the press. Asked how she liked to wake up in the morning, she smiled and said, "I like to wake up feeling a new man." Though critics panned her acting and voice, moviegoers loved her tough, sexy, wisecracking performances. She played so many floozies that once when her agent called her about a movie role, she reportedly asked, "What kind of whore am I now?"[19]

In *Red-Headed Woman* (1932), a typical Harlow picture, after using her body to catch a wealthy man and then trying to blackmail and sleep her way to acceptance by his peers, she is caught in an affair with the chauffeur. When reconciliation with her husband fails, she shoots him, avoids a murder charge, and begins life anew with a titled lover, a race horse, and the same chauffeur. The film's humor gave the movie a light tone, and Harlow won praise for "out-Bowing the famed Bow as an exponent of elemental lure and crude man-baiting technique." Harlow may have been sexier than Bow, but she also played a different role. In her movies, Bow had settled for marrying the boss. Harlow *started* with the boss and then was driven to seek more lovers and more riches, just as the heroes of the gangster movies of the period were continually driven to expand their empires. To succeed at this gold-digging, Harlow had to be sexy, but she also had a traditionally feminine side that added to her appeal. "Jean Harlow," observed director George Cukor, "was very soft about her toughness."[20] Harlow, who died at the height of her popularity in 1937 at age twenty-six, had a bold, brassy sexiness that captured the mood of the early 1930s when the public wanted to watch and hear "little people" make something of themselves.

In the early years of the Depression when movies featured lusty, conniving female sex symbols, male images on screen hardened and toughened. The popular, trigger-happy gangsters had little time for women in their action movies, but by the end of 1931 Clark Gable was becoming a new romantic star and being hailed as "Valentino in Jack Dempsey's Body," a he-man who fought with his fists, took no guff, and loved women on his own terms. Gable generally played a lower-class guy who met a rich woman, turned her into a passionate lover, and refused to let her dominate him because of her class. Adding a seductive sense of humor to this image, Gable won an Academy Award for best actor and became a top movie star with his sparkling performance in the hit comedy *It Happened One Night* (1934). His cocky, all-man working stiffs, combining elements of the gangster hero with elements of the romantic lover, had great appeal. "He was boyish, mannish, a brute—all kinds of goodies," Hollywood actress Joan Blondell remembered. "When he grinned you'd have to melt. If you didn't want him as a lover, you'd want to give him a bear hug. He affected all females, unless they were dead." Film was an excellent medium for Gable because the closeups brought viewers face to face with what one writer in 1932 described as "a bull with little boy's eyes."[21]

Gable played many variations on his basic character. "He's tough, uneducated, got a hell of a temper, can fight his weight in wildcats— you know, Frances," script writer Frances Marion was told by the studio, "typical Gable stuff, with sex that drives the women crazy." In *Broadway Melody of 1938*, teenage Judy Garland expressed the sentiment of girls and women all over the country when she gazed moon-eyed at a photo of Gable and sang "You Made Me Love You." But Gable's basic image appealed to men as well as to women. In 1938 when he stepped out of character to play a martyred Irish patriot in *Parnell*, his fans deluged MGM with protests. "Let others portray historical figures," one incensed fan wrote. "Gable is cut out for roles where he gets tough with women. That's what he's good at, and that's what I'll pay to see."[22] Ironically, the following year Gable found his greatest, most popular role in an historical drama in which he was unusually tender.

As soon as the public learned that Margaret Mitchell's *Gone with the Wind*, a best-selling novel about the South in the era of the Civil War, was to be filmed, it clamored for Gable to play Rhett Butler, the cynical outsider who laughs at idealistic southern gentlemen for thinking they could win a war with "cotton, slaves and arrogance." Butler's only adversary is strong-willed, independently minded southern belle, Scarlett O'Hara, who originally rejects him as a crass outsider, but is finally won over by his manhood and wealth and marries him. Gable and the role were perfect for each other. In one famous scene, when Scarlett locks him out of her bedroom, he accepts it, but makes sure she knows that "if I wanted to come in, no lock could keep me out."[23] The role also gave him a new tenderness. When Scarlett has a miscarriage, tears stream down Butler's face in one of the rare instances of an American male character crying with no loss of manhood.

Gable's acting career in a real sense peaked in the role of Rhett Butler, but his popularity seemed unlimited. He numbered among the top ten box-office attractions every year between 1932 and 1949, except when he served in the armed forces. Until his death in 1960, he remained a major romantic star, having courted leading women from Jean Harlow to Marilyn Monroe. "What Gable had in a measure that no other star quite matched—or projected as ferociously as he did—was a true masculine personality," observed the *New York Times* in its obituary of him. "He was consistently and stubbornly all Man."[24] Sound movies beautifully projected these qualities. Besides seeing closeups of his ruggedly handsome face with his twinkling eyes and smirking grin, audiences could also hear his sexy voice and his unique delivery of lines, like "Frankly, my dear, I don't give a damn." In the fullest sense, Gable epitomized the rugged, sound motion picture hero —the tough guy as lover.

In the early 1930s, with exciting new stars like Harlow and Gable drawing masses of people to movies and with free radio shows entertaining even more people at home, stage shows lost their mass audience and never regained it. The only live entertainment form that prospered in the 1930s was burlesque, which drew large audiences all over the nation with fine performers like Gypsy Rose Lee and Ann Corio doing tantalizing, seductive, striptease dances that made men forget their problems. With the dire plight of "legit" shows, burlesque expanded into Broadway and other respectable theater districts, which provoked mounting censorship activity from church and civic groups. In 1937 New York City closed all its burlesque houses and issued new licenses only to theaters that had dropped the name burlesque and the striptease. Despite funny responses like Ann Corio appearing on stage in a black evening gown with a padlock on the zipper and singing "I Would If I Could, But I Can't," burlesque was nearly eliminated from the mainstream of American show business. With the suppression of burlesque, the crippling of vaudeville, the decline of revues, and the shift of musicals to upperclass audiences, the live stage ceased to be a major purveyor of popular images of sexuality in show business.

The other major change in entertainment media in the 1930s, the maturation of radio, had relatively little influence on popular portrayals of sexuality. With its ability to use sound effects, music, and voices to stimulate listeners' imaginations, radio may have had the potential to be the most erotic of all entertainment media, since it allowed listeners to project their own private fantasies and feelings as they visualized scenes. But while radio as an entertainment form was very well suited to performing sexual material, the medium's financial, legal, and institutional structures required that radio be very restrained in its treatment of sexual subjects. Broadcast over the publically owned air waves by government licensed stations, received in people's homes, and paid for by sponsors who wanted to sell their products to listeners, radio programming emphasized family fare and was designed to offend as few people as possible.

The sexiest shows on radio were the daytime domestic serials created for women who worked at home. Called "soap operas" because companies like Procter & Gamble sponsored many of them, they differed from other serials with continuing stories because they focused on women as major characters, on the home as the major setting, and on personal, often marital, problems as the major themes. The typical heroine in shows like *When a Girl Marries, John's Other Wife, Young Widder Brown,* and *Our Gal Sunday* had to face an incredible array of problems, from blindness to kidnapping, from amnesia to suicide. But perhaps most prominent was her problem with men. In soap operas married women continually had to fret about their husbands, who were generally weak and might at any time give in to the temptresses who seemed to be everywhere. "To hold a man's love, what should a young wife be?" asked the introduction to a hit soap opera. "Business partner? Dancing companion? Playmate? Should she place her home and her children above all else? How can she make her life secure from her rivals? These are some of the questions the modern woman faces . . . some of the questions that must be answered . . . when a girl marries."[25] Many of the problems grew out of huge social gaps between the major characters. Our Gal Sunday moved from a little mining town in the West to seek happiness with a wealthy, titled Englishman; Backstage Wife had been a simple, Iowa secretary before marrying a sophisticated Broadway star; and John's Other Wife worried about keeping up with her business tycoon husband. Unlike the eternally faithful, eternally worried wives, single women in the soaps could have careers, as did Helen Trent, who designed dresses, Young Widder Brown, who ran a tearoom, and Portia, who practiced law in *Portia Faces Life*. Single women were also free to become involved in complicated, perplexing, and exciting romances and dilemmas. Passionate love affairs, menacing abductions, and sinful infidelities regularly spiced up the stories, tormented the heroines, and titillated the listeners. Though the language and descriptions were restrained, soap operas provided their huge audiences, estimated at over half of American housewives, the stuff of which domestic, romantic, and sexual fantasies were made.

But radio programming in general included little sexual material because sponsors and network officials reviewed scripts and rehearsals in advance, made changes to avoid anything potentially embarrassing, and fired any performer who repeatedly used offensive material. Problems occurred most often in variety and anthology formats that used different performers for each show. An Adam and Eve skit on *The Chase and Sanborn Hour* in 1937 included suggestive lines like: "Would you, honey, like to try this apple sometime?" and "If trouble means something that makes your blood race through your veins like seltzer—Mmm, Adam, my man, give me trouble!"[26] If Eve did not get the trouble she wanted from Adam, the network got plenty of trouble it did not want from the Federal Communications Commission, which warned the network that its stations would not be relicensed if it aired such material again. NBC not only banned Mae West, who had played Eve, from appearing on the network, but also ordered that her name not even be mentioned. Radio wanted nothing to do with anything that threatened its station licenses and its livelihood.

Without government licenses or sponsors to worry about, movie studios were theoretically free to make any pictures the public would pay to see. The public clearly would pay to see suggestive movies that ranged from Harlow's tough sexpots and Marlene Dietrich's aggressive seductresses to the sophisticated sensuality of director Ernst Lubitsch's comedies, *Love Me Tonight* (1929) with Jeanette MacDonald and Maurice Chevalier, *Trouble in Paradise* (1932), and *Design for Living* (1933), the design being for Miriam Hopkins to love two men at the same time in a ménage à trois. But the film industry was not free from censorship pressure. The sexy movies of the early 1930s brought to a head long-smoldering demands for censorship that dated back to 1896 and reaction to *The Kiss*. Censoring stage shows had always been a sporadic local process because each performance of each production in each theater could be different. Live show business was inherently decentralized. So was the early movie business. But by the 1920s films could be censored effectively because they were fixed, manufactured goods and because control of their production, distribution, and exhibition had been centralized in a handful of huge studios. In 1922 as movies got much racier, the motion picture industry, faced with possible legal censorship in thirty-six states, had acted to police itself. It hired Will H. Hays, Postmaster General of the United States, a man with political contacts and skills, to head an office charged with establishing and maintaining moral standards for the industry. The Hays Office eliminated efforts at legal censorship and issued movie guidelines, but it had no power to enforce them.

In 1930 a new, stricter code was drafted, but the censors still lacked enforcement power, so movie studios, to lure Depression audiences away from free radio shows, ignored censors and made sexier pictures. No one forced the issue of censorship more than Mae West who brought her lusty innuendo to movies in 1932. In *Night after Night,* when a hatcheck girl says to West, "Goodness, what beautiful diamonds," West pauses, suggestively shoots back, "Goodness had nothing to do with it, dearie," and then slowly sashays up a staircase with her swaying rear end to the camera. In *She Done Him Wrong* (1933), *I'm No Angel* (1934), and *Belle of the Nineties* (1934), she continued to belt out her steamy one-liners. "Mae couldn't sing a lullaby without making it sexy," *Variety* observed in 1933. Martin Quigley, one of the authors of the 1930 code, singled out West's *I'm No Angel* as "a vehicle for a notorious characterization of a scarlet woman whose amatory instincts are confined exclusively to the physical. There is no more pretense here of romance than on a stud farm."[27] Hollywood could not ignore such protests once they became well organized. In 1934 a committee of Catholic bishops formed the Legion of Decency to tell Catholics which movies to boycott, and the Federal Council of Churches warned Hollywood that it would seek federal censorship unless the industry enforced its 1930 code. Between 1930 and 1933 movie attendance dropped 25 percent; ticket prices were cut by a third; nearly one out of every three movie theaters closed; and Paramount, RKO, Universal, and Fox all faced financial disaster. In this crisis the industry gave Joseph I. Breen the power to withhold a seal of approval from any picture that violated the code, and the studios pledged not to distribute or show films that lacked a seal, which would have meant disaster for any movie in the days of studio theater chains and block bookings.

The Motion Picture Production Code became a reality in Hollywood in 1934. Guaranteeing never to "lower the moral standards" of viewers or to make them sympathize with "the side of crime, wrongdoing, evil, or sin," the Code devoted seven of its twelve sections in whole or part to sexuality. Though censors could not take the twinkle out of Maurice Chevalier's eyes, the smirking smile off Gable's face, or the provocative look away from Harlow, they could and did force moviemakers to be much more circumspect and restrained. Despite some specific restrictions, such as a ban on nudity and a provision that adultery and illicit sex never seem justified, most of the Code was more in the nature of general principles, such as the requirement that bedroom scenes be treated with "discretion," "restraint," and "good taste." The Code's subjectivity and flexibility allowed it to change a little with the times, as movies became the major medium bringing sex appeal to the mass market after 1934.[28]

The major movie stars who emerged in the late 1930s represented subdued sexuality and a greater emphasis on romance, as called for in the early years of the new censorship. With a lighter, gentler image than Gable's, Cary Grant became one of America's most beloved, most enduring screen lovers—the epitome of the urbane, romantic leading man. Grant got his first movie contract in 1931 at age twenty-eight. But he did not become a big star until the late-1930s when his refined bearing, boyish good looks, and not-too-stuffy British accent made him an excellent foil for fast-talking, wisecracking, strong-willed heroines played by Constance Bennett, Irene Dunne, Katharine Hepburn, and Rosalind Russell, with whom he co-starred in daffy screwball comedies such as *Topper* (1937), *The Awful Truth* (1937), *Bringing Up Baby* (1938), and *His Girl Friday* (1940). With such roles Grant became a well-established star playing the jaunty lover with a sense of humor, a debonair manner, and an emotional vulnerability. For over thirty years, in films ranging from frothy romances to spellbinding mysteries, Grant charmed movie audiences. In 1959, over a quarter of a century after he had broken into motion pictures, Pauline Kael, in a review of *North by Northwest*, observed that Grant "seems to have gotten younger and better-looking, yet he's probably older than Jessie Royce Landis, who plays his mother."[29] Actually they were both fifty-five.

By the late 1930s, in the golden age of movies, major movie stars portrayed a wide range of sexy women and men. Tall, broad-shouldered, Swedish-born Greta Garbo, who became an American star in the silent era playing the strong, sensual femme fatale, became an even bigger star in the 1930s when she used her husky voice and enigmatic face to portray exotic, mysterious women who were aggressively independent, sometimes anti-male, until they fell in love, lost their aloof power, and suffered tragically. German-born Marlene Dietrich vamped men and enchanted audiences with her hard-boiled roles. But most female stars were home-grown, including Carole Lombard and Katharine Hepburn, who played witty, young women with minds of their own; Joan Crawford, who went from 1920s' flappers to wealthy play-girls; and Bette Davis, who rose to fame with beautifully etched portraits of evil vengeful women who destroyed men. In the 1930s, the males who were seen as sex symbols in movies were as diverse as the female sex symbols.

The 1940s were a different story. America went to war in 1941, and war meant men leaving for battle and women serving at home in a wider range of jobs than ever before, changes the movies reflected. War action pictures were highly popular, providing vehicles for stars like John Wayne, John Garfield, and Robert Mitchum to fight hero-ically against fascism. While presenting idealized images of men as heroic warriors battling for liberty, war movies generally devoted little attention to sex and romance. But in *Casablanca* (1943) the war produced one of the most enduring screen romances. Humphrey Bogart, playing a tough yet tender cynic who operates a nightclub in Casablanca and is determined to think only of himself, finds himself embroiled in the anti-Nazi cause of Underground leader Paul Henreid and in a rekindled romance with Ingrid Bergman, who is torn between her duty to her husband and her love for Bogart. Finally, Bogart, sacrifices his own happiness with Bergman, who would have stayed with him, to get Henreid and Bergman to freedom where they can continue the war effort.

With many men away at war, Hollywood in the early 1940s, more than at any other time, concentrated on women's lives and problems because the audiences were heavily female. In movies women were defense workers, nurses, WAVES, WACS, teachers, novelists, editors, business executives, and Congresswomen. But even Hollywood's strong, independent woman, who rose to the top of her profession, still found full satisfaction only in traditional romance and marriage. Perhaps the clearest example of the treatment of strong women in the 1940s came in the series of pictures Katharine Hepburn made with Spencer Tracy, pictures which represented the romantic battle of the sexes at its American best.

After successfully playing heiresses in *Bringing Up Baby* (1938) and *Philadelphia Story* (1940), Hepburn portrayed a political activist and newspaper columnist in *Woman of the Year* (1942), a change of roles that symbolized the wartime shift from flighty screwballs to serious working women. Though Tracy is a low-brow sportswriter uninterested in politics and Hepburn is intensely political but uninterested in sports, they develop a squabbling, sparring romance leading to a conflict-ridden marriage that begins on their wedding night with her sheltering a defecting European scientist and his compatriots, while he hosts his rowdy, drinking pals. Much later, when she wins the "Woman of the Year" award, he refuses to attend the banquet because she "isn't a woman at all." After a long running battle of digs and quips, *she* gives in and attempts to master the traditionally feminine domestic duties of the kitchen and home. "We were perfect representations of the American male and female," Hepburn observed. "The woman is always pretty sharp, and she's needling the man . . . and then he slowly puts out his big paw and slaps his lady down, and that's attractive to the American public. He's the ultimate boss of the situation, and he's very challenged by her. It isn't an easy kingdom for him to maintain. That—in simple terms—is what we did."[30] They did it nine times. No screen couple ever did it better.

In the early 1940s, while working women toiled in tailored clothes, a new generation of glamor girls put on tight sweaters, shortened their skirts, and lifted men's spirits. Lana Turner stretched sweaters and men's imaginations as a buxom, blonde beauty who had graduated from an Andy Hardy movie to co-starring with Clark Gable as the screen's "hottest new team" in *Honky Tonk* (1941). In 1943 Betty Grable was the number one box office attraction with her "million dollar legs" and the war's most popular pinup photo, a shot of her in a tight bathing suit, her shapely rear end to the camera and an enticing smile on her face as she looked over her shoulder—an alluring vision of the pink, soft, cuddly all-American girl with a come-hither look. Adding spicy variety, voluptuous Rita Hayworth, with her flaming red hair, long legs, and wild abandon exuded raw, sultry sex appeal in pinups and in movies. Women of all kinds filled the screen in the early 1940s.

By the early 1950s the movie industry faced a crisis as crucial as the Great Depression. The studio system disintegrated at the same time that film-makers faced stiff competition from television, which brought the sights and sounds of entertaining family amusement into the home. But television, which inherited radio's inhibitions and censorship along with its formats, shows, and stars, broadcast little that could in any way be considered sexy. Many of the women who starred in early television series, for instance, were comics not noted for their sex appeal, stars like Gertrude Berg, Imogene Coca, Gracie Allen, Joan Davis, Eve Arden, and Lucille Ball. In fact the boldest, brassiest female character in early television was Milton Berle in drag. Until the late-1950s, when movie studios brought dashing, action heroes to television, men in television were not much sexier than women. There were certainly appealing men and women who were goodlooking, but the action was very tame. When Elvis Presley appeared on the *Ed Sullivan Show*, for instance, the camera filmed the swivel-hipped singer only from the waist up. But if early television was sexually bland, it was enjoyable free entertainment, loaded with the music and comedy America loved. As television spread, movie attendance fell.

Hollywood responded to television's family shows by experimenting with new attractions that the small-screened entertainment medium could not match—three-dimensional pictures, wide screens, high fidelity sound, and monumental epics. But movies found their greatest anti-television weapon in an old attraction—sex, especially new sex symbols who could entice people into theaters. Busty blondes with submissive, girlish personalities became very popular in the postwar era that saw women put back in their traditional places, as dutiful, nurturing wives and subservient, sexy playmates. Marilyn Monroe perfected the new image after playing a number of small movie parts in the late 1940s and early 1950s. Besides her full, ripe figure, breathless, little girl voice, blonde hair, puckered red lips, half-closed, doe-like eyes, and erotic movements, Monroe also projected an innocence and vulnerability that appealed to both women and men. Unlike the brash, assertive Jean Harlow, Monroe seemed sweet, tender, and unthreatening, almost a naïve little girl living in a woman's body. Though her movie roles—usually dumb blondes with warm hearts—were less important than the image she conveyed, she had a nice, light comedy style that sparkled in pictures such as *Seven Year Itch* (1955) and *Some Like It Hot* (1959). Above all, people *liked* her. In a 1962 poll, not one person questioned considered her immoral or distasteful; women *and* men saw a quality of innocence in her, which suggests why she was so much more successful than blatant, heavy-handed competitors like Jayne Mansfield, who virtually based her career on the impossibility of keeping her forty-inch bust in bras, dresses, or swimsuits.

In the early 1950s while established actors such as Clark Gable, Gary Cooper, Cary Grant, Humphrey Bogart, and John Wayne continued to play their usual roles, new male stars emerged who combined raw sexuality, rebelliousness, and emotional vulnerability. In 1951 Marlon Brando burst into movies with a new power and energy in *Streetcar Named Desire* playing Stanley Kowalski, a violent, passionate working man who sexually controls women, but who is also an immature, psychologically weak strongman. Brando continued this image in *The Wild One* (1953) as the leader of a motorcycle gang, a tough guy who wears long sideburns, a cap with a visor, and a black leather jacket with a skull and crossbones on the back. With a chip on his shoulder, a sneer on his face, and mumbling incoherent speech, he and his gang take over a little town. But he also reveals a soft side, when he falls in love with a "good girl" he rescues from a rival gang and treats gently. Finally, not knowing how to express himself, he leaves her his trophy, smiles, and rides off on his motorcycle. This performance became the prototype for other rebellious, young characters who were tough, inarticulate, but tender beneath their hard shells, an image indelibly stamped on moviegoers' consciousness in 1955 by James Dean in *Rebel Without a Cause*. In 1956 the youth culture found its greatest sex symbol in the rebellious eroticism of rock 'n' roll singer Elvis Presley, who excited his young radio, record, television, and movie fans with his gyrating pelvis, rich, sensual voice, and thumping rhythms.

Of the many young actors who began in the Brando style in the 1950s, Paul Newman proved to have the broadest and most enduring popularity. Between 1950 and 1975 only John Wayne made the list of top ten box office attractions more often than Newman, who first reached the list in 1963 and remained there until 1976. Newman's career revealed the changing roles of men in the post-World War II era. After a Brando-like performance in 1956 playing Rocky Graziano, a tough street kid who rose in the world on the strength of his fists, the blue-eyed, handsome Newman, played sexy, young roles in *The Long Hot Summer* and *Cat on a Hot Tin Roof* and became a major star. In the 1960s, he grew even more popular with portrayals of tough loners with their own values and a sensitive side that had to be suppressed in the conflict-ridden world. In 1967 when America was wracked with violent dissent and discord about race relations and the Vietnam War, Newman starred in *Cool Hand Luke* as a defiant, alienated prisoner on a chain gang who escapes over and over again until he is killed. When he escapes for the last time, he goes into a church and talks to God. "It's beginning to look like you got things fixed so I cain't never win out. Besides, I'm tired of all them rules and regulations and bosses, You made me like I am. The thing is—where am I supposed to fit in . . . I guess I gotta find my own way." When a great many people, especially the young people who were coming to dominate movie audiences, were trying to find their own ways with protests and the youth counterculture, the picture and Newman had great appeal. In 1969 Newman and Robert Redford, who himself became a top star in the late 1960s, co-starred in *Butch Cassidy and the Sundance Kid*, a light-hearted, tongue-in-cheek story of two western bank robbers who engage in a running verbal duel that sparkles with the wit and one-upmanship of the male-female sparring of screwball comedy or the masculine teasing of Bob Hope and Bing Crosby in their Road pictures. As far as sexuality was concerned, the most important point about the highly popular picture was that it was about an affectionate relationship between two men. "You know," Newman observed, "I don't think people realize what that picture was all about. It's a love affair between two men. The girl is incidental."[31]

Male stars dominated the screen in the late 1960s and early 1970s to the virtual exclusion of women from major parts. In such very popular, very different buddy pictures as *The Odd Couple* (1968), *Midnight Cowboy* (1968), *Easy Rider* (1969), *M*A*S*H* (1970), *Deliverance* (1973), *Papillon* (1973), *The Sting* (1973), and *The Longest Yard* (1974), women were absent or unimportant. Some of the films were explicitly homosexual, some implicitly, and some neither. But all were men's movies. Between 1967 and 1976 there was never a single year in which more than two women were among the top ten box-office attractions, and in six of the ten years there was only one woman. Only singer and actress Barbra Streisand, with six appearances on the list, proved to be a consistent female drawing card. In contrast, between 1957 and 1966 three or more women had made the list in eight out of the ten years. The overwhelming dominance of men, which began in the mid-1960s, probably resulted in large part from the emphasis on violent action pictures in which women were often relegated to roles as pretty window dressing. Also, the number of movie comedies and musicals, which had been major vehicles for women, declined sharply because of competition from television. And ironically, as movies became more explicitly sexual, female stars became *less* important, as if the only thing that mattered about women were their bodies.

By the mid-1960s the treatment of sexuality in movies was changing markedly. The old Code and its enforcement began to disintegrate in 1953 when Otto Preminger successfully released *The Moon Is Blue* without a seal of approval because he refused to delete the word "virgin." The American movie industry was caught between the appeal of increasingly risqué European films—with stars ranging from lithe, sex kitten Brigitte Bardot to busty, hot-tempered Gina Lollabrigida—and the appeal of wholesome, free entertainment on television. It had to become more permissive. By 1955 the Legion of Decency reportedly found over a third of movies objectionable, though in 1960 nudity was still virtually nonexistent in pictures shown in America. But it was just a matter of time until that barrier fell. The Code was virtually unenforceable in the modern movie industry, where a small number of studios no longer controlled everything from production to exhibition. In the era of independent producers, independent distributors, and independent theater-owners, the movie business was decentralized and uncontrollable. The change in the audience was also a major factor in the change in film-makers' attitude toward sexuality. The family audience that in the past had threatened boycotts now generally stayed home to watch television. Moviegoers were younger and younger. For many of them, condemnation of a picture by the Legion of Decency or by the Code Office probably offered an added enticement. The pressure continued to mount on the thirty-year-old censorship structure, until it finally collapsed.

In 1965 a motion picture with a frontal shot of a woman's bare breasts won Code approval for the first time. Though *The Pawnbroker* was a serious film in which the partial nudity was artistically essential, the implications of the decision were obvious. In 1966 the Production Code was revised. The new opening sentence stated that it was "designed to keep in close harmony with the mores, the culture, the moral sense and the expectation of our society."[32] The Code, in short, was to become *relative,* not absolute, reflecting current values not fixed morality. Under the new system pictures with nudity or highly suggestive content would have to carry the warning "Suggested for Mature Audiences" in their ads. By 1968 when over half the movies passed by the censors carried this warning, the system was changed again. No longer would there be censorship or approved pictures. Instead, movies would be labeled: "G" for general audiences; "PG" parental guidance suggested; "R" restricted for people under seventeen unless accompanied by parent or guardian; and "X" no one under seventeen admitted. With no taboos except what the marketplace would bear, movies got sexier in subject matter, language, and exposure. Even the long-standing line between acceptable sensuality and unacceptable pornography became blurred. In 1972 *Deep Throat,* a movie with clinical closeups of all sorts of sex acts and the premise that the female star's clitoris was located in her throat, became a popular fad, and reportedly earned over $3 million on its $25,000 investment. Though not nearly as graphic or as focused on sex acts as *Deep Throat, Last Tango in Paris* created great controversy in 1972 with its nudity, loveless sex, totally submissive young heroine, and foul-mouthed, domineering, older hero—played by Marlon Brando. Though few major films fit into the pornographic category, movies in the 1970s exploited sexuality with an abandon never seen before.

In the mid- and late-1970s there was also a rebirth of serious pictures starring actresses in strong roles that reflected women's points of view and problems. The changing career of Jane Fonda in many ways represented the changing screen images of women. The daughter of famous star Henry Fonda, Jane broke into movies in 1960 as a cheerleader, winning praise for a "smile like her father's and legs like a chorus girl." In the early sixties, she seemed headed for a career as a sex star, playing light, frothy comedies in America while at the same time in France her husband, Roger Vadim, was grooming her as his new Brigitte Bardot. These performances prompted critic Judith Crist to crown Fonda "Miss Screen Nude of '67."[33] But Fonda's career took a different turn in 1969 with her sensitive portrayal of a Depression marathon dancer in *They Shoot Horses Don't They,* which she followed in 1971 with a sexy, but serious, Academy Award-winning performance as a prostitute in search of her own identity in *Klute.* In the late 1970s, Fonda played several strong, interesting women including: Lillian Hellman in *Julia* (1978), the story of Hellman's development as a writer and of her close relationship with her longtime friend, Julia; and an astute reporter investigating the threat of a nuclear power plant disaster in *China Syndrome* (1980).

When the motion picture business discovered how many people would pay to see serious films starring actresses, it began to turn out "women's pictures" on subjects ranging from career professionals, through broken marriages and quests for personal independence, to union organizing, pictures such as *The Turning Point* (1977), *An Unmarried Woman* (1978), *Kramer vs. Kramer* (1979), and *Norma Rae* (1980). But at the same time, women and sexuality were also being portrayed in ways that reached a new low in major feature films. In the late 1970s, girls such as Jodie Foster and Brooke Shield, who were closer to ten than to fifteen years old, were playing sexy movie roles including prostitutes in *Taxi Driver* (1976) and *Pretty Baby* (1978). There was also a rash of highly popular, vicious horror movies in which psychopathetic men tormented, victimized, assaulted, and brutally murdered women. It was as if some male moviemakers and moviegoers, threatened by women's liberation and by mature, assertive females, were retaliating by focusing their lust on inexperienced, undemanding girl-women and their anger on helpless female victims.

While sexuality in movies was changing radically after the mid-1950s, sexuality on television was changing gradually but dramatically. Television's first major sex symbols were the new male stars who emerged from the action-adventure shows filmed by movie studios beginning with the wide range of western heroes who became so popular in the late-1950s. Some, such as Clint Eastwood (*Rawhide,* 1958-66) and Steve McQueen (*Wanted Dead or Alive,* 1958-60), who had relatively inexpressive faces and used few words but projected powerful, action images, found their greatest success on large movie screens. Many others became essentially *television* stars, who used the same manner, style, and characterization in a wide range of roles. Gene Barry, for instance, gained fame as stylishly dressed, debonair Bat Masterson, a role he played from 1957 to 1961. He carried that style with him as a millionaire police chief in *Burke's Law* (1963-65), as

Amos Burke, Secret Agent (1965), and as a newspaper publisher in *The Name of the Game* (1968-72). Similarly, James Garner took his tongue-in-cheek, roguish, cowardly character from the western gambler he played on *Maverick* (1957-62) to a gun-fearing, sheriff-conman in *Nichols* (1971-72) and private investigator Jim Rockford on *The Rockford File* (1974-80). Barry and Garner typified television stars. They had the right style for the medium. Television's small screen and frequent closeups require understated, subtle actors with mastery of a great many refined facial gestures and vocal intonations. Performers with enduring television appeal, including sex appeal, have had relatively low-keyed, personal images.

Television was much slower to develop major female sex symbols even though women were among its first and greatest stars. In general although many women on television were attractive, few female stars dressed, moved, or performed in essentially sexy ways until the 1970s, the major exception being on the soap operas which carried on radio's tradition of racy daytime programming and made it even spicier. The one area in which television's evening portrayals of women even approached the veiled eroticism of 1940s' movies was advertising, which was, after all, the reason that free television existed. "The director explained that actual singing was of little import," actress Susan Barrister recalled of her audition for an automobile commercial. "It was the sensuality, the passion with which I related to the car standing before me now, that was important."[34] In such ads, the sex appeal did not have to have anything directly to do with the product as long as it held the male viewer's interest and suggested that the product somehow carried sex appeal with it. But except for some suggestive commercials, television remained very tightly censored. In 1952 Lucille Ball could not even use the word "pregnant" to tell Desi Arnaz that she was going to have a baby, and in 1960 when Jack Parr used the phrase "water closet," a European term for a toilet, the network censors deleted it from the broadcast. In the late 1960s, this extremely restrictive censorship began to be relaxed, pushed by the popular double-entendre jokes and bikini-clad dancers of *Rowan and Martin's Laugh-In* and the biting, topical satire of *The Smothers Brothers Comedy Hour.*

It was in the mid-1970s, after movies had dropped even the semblance of censorship, that the entertainment machine in the home began to feature erotic women in action shows, perhaps because

organized protests had diminished the amount of crowd-pleasing violence on television. Women had been in action shows since the early
days of television on programs like *The Roy Rogers Show* (1951-57)
and *Annie Oakley* (1953-58). But in 1974 when shapely Angie Dickinson began starring in *The Police Woman* (1974-78), there was an eye-
catching difference. Dickinson often did undercover vice work, which
meant she wore revealing outfits and had to take them off after work.
"My producers do have me taking a lot of baths and showers," Dickinson observed. In 1976, *Charlie's Angels,* the story of three nubile
young women working as private investigators, made its debut and
quickly moved toward the top of the ratings. The reasons were neither
the action nor the plots. "When the show was No. 3, I figured it was
our acting," observed one of the Angels, Farrah Fawcett-Majors. "When
we got to be No. 1, I decided it could only be because none of us
wears a bra." The stories seemed chosen primarily to keep the bra-
less Angels running, jumping, dancing, swimming, and otherwise showing off their attractive bodies. "We love to splash them with water,"
the show's producer admitted. "It makes them look so sexy."[35] Farrah
Fawcett-Majors became the nation's newest sex symbol and one of its
most famous. A pinup poster of her in a tight, thin bathing suit sold in
the millions, and closeups of her with her long, fluffed up hair and her
toothy grin smiled out at America from magazine racks all over the
country.

Charlie's Angels pioneered what came to be called "jiggly" programming, which along with youth-oriented comedies and action shows
made ABC the top rated network for the first time. Premiering in 1977
ABC's *Three's Company,* the story of three young and attractive room-
mates—two women and a man—combined youth comedy and jiggles,
most of the jiggles provided by blonde Susanne Somers, who frequently wore towels and nighties around the apartment. Paul Klein,
NBC program chief at the time, doubted that *Three's Company* would
have succeeded three years earlier because "the girls wore brassieres
then." By the late 1970s there were virtually no subjects that were taboo
on television, including nymphomania, teenage sex, lesbianism, adultery, rape, homosexuality, group sex, male and female prostitution,
and incest. Though there was plenty of spicy talk about risqué subjects, the sexual action on television was verbal, not visual. "It's junior
high school sex," observed NBC's head of programming in 1978 of
Three's Company in particular and of the genre in general. "They talk

a lot about sex, but don't do anything about it. The boys smile a lot and the girls jump up and down."[36] Despite all the jiggling and the titillating talk approved by them, network censors could still be surprisingly prudish. In 1978 NBC censors cut out an open mouthed kiss with tongues showing, and CBS deleted a brief shot of nude female backs—*above* the waists!

Television sexuality remained far tamer than that of the movies. "The sexual breakthrough in TV," observed Frank Price the president of Universal Television in 1978, "has probably taken us to where the movies were in 1935." But it was far racier than ever before, and organized protests against television's sexual excesses mounted. Complaints to the FCC about obscenity, indecency, and profanity jumped in one year from about 6000 to over 20,000. There were also increasing threats to boycott the products of firms that sponsored the objectionable shows. But at the same time, the ratings for these shows were often so high that sponsors could ignore the relatively few, highly vocal critics to reach the great masses of invisible fans. "The viewers speak with forked tongue," claimed A. R. Van Cantfort, an official of an NBC station in Atlanta. "They say, 'Gosh, there's too much flesh shown on *Charlie's Angels*.' Then they go home, kick off their shoes, turn on the set and ogle those three broads on what is probably the poorest-written show on television."[37] In 1981 *Charlie's Angels*, after numerous cast changes and a five-year run, was cancelled, but only because of falling ratings.

In the 1980s the biggest influence on the portrayals of sexuality in popular entertainment is likely to come from changes in entertainment technology in the home, specifically from cable systems and satellites that carry specialized channels to interested individuals all over the country and from video recording systems that allow people not only to record broadcasts for subsequent re-viewing but also to buy or rent recordings of sound motion pictures, to show in their homes when they wanted. "X" rated films and pornography proved initially to be very popular. The trend is clearly toward individuals' ability to enjoy exactly the entertainment they want. People will certainly choose a wide variety of entertainment including erotic shows, as the gap between theatrical and home entertainment narrows.

8

Leave 'Em Laughin':
Comedy and the Media

Americans love to laugh. They always have. While American show business was still in its formative stage in the 1840s, comedians became some of its most popular stars, especially in minstrel shows and circuses, which popularized a wide range of enduring comedy styles. Using distorted black dialects, raucous blackfaced minstrel comics traded puns, one-liners, and riddles and fought running verbal battles with the formally dressed, grammatically precise master of ceremonies, the interlocutor. Minstrel comedians also blustered through overblown, malaprop-laden monologues that ridiculed the pompous and poked fun at everything from education to women's rights. The shows concluded with farces that blended music, production numbers, and slapstick in parodies of hit shows, current events, and popular fads. In the circuses of the 1830s and 1840s, which were small one-ring shows with only one act performing at a time, the clown became America's first standup comedian, cracking snappy jokes, singing comic songs, and interrupting and insulting the high falutin' ringmaster. All these elements—wordplay, verbal dueling, monologues, burlesques, slapstick, musical parodies, and common people mocking the uppercrust—became permanent parts of American entertainment as it evolved and matured.

By the end of the nineteenth century when live show business was in its heyday and many popular entertainment forms had developed and taken to the road, the American people had more opportunities to

211

laugh than ever before. Comedy was just about everywhere there
were shows, and there were shows just about everywhere. Though
many popular plays, like *Uncle Tom's Cabin,* and many book musicals, like *Evangeline,* made heavy use of humor, these forms were not
primarily comedic. Neither was the circus, but it did develop a distinctive comedy style. When circuses expanded into three-ring extravaganzas with more going on at once than any one person could concentrate on, the clown changed from a solo, verbal comedian to one
of a group of basically pantomime comics staging sight gags heavy
with eyecatching, slapstick stunts and frantic chases. While the minstrel show continued with the varied, blackface comedy that audiences loved, it faced stiff comedy competition. The American burlesque
show began to emerge as a distinctive entertainment form in the late
1860s after the great success of Lydia Thompson and the British
blondes, who showed off their hips and legs by wearing men's trousers
while portraying male roles in plays and parodies. Sex appeal and comedy became the hallmarks of the American burlesque show, which grew
racier over the years. To keep getting laughs from audiences primarily
interested in looking at pretty women, burlesque comedians had to ex-
cel at their craft. But because the burlesque show was America's most
overtly erotic entertainment form, it had relatively low status, and it
narrowly restricted the range of its comedians' repertoires. So, many of
the great comics who started in burlesque, Fanny Brice, Bert Lahr, and
Bud Abbott and Lou Costello among them, moved to other entertainment forms where they could get broader recognition and could develop their talents more fully.

If comedians and fans had been asked in the early twentieth century which live entertainment form was best for comedy, a great many
of them would have answered "vaudeville." Since it presented scenes
from hit shows and lavish production numbers as well as single acts,
vaudeville could almost be considered a compendium of show business's
greatest hits. But whatever else was on a typical, varied, nine-act bill,
the show was usually half-comedy. In the early twentieth century, the
many levels of vaudeville theaters and circuits scattered around the
country gave young comedians plenty of time and plenty of chances to
get on-the-job training where they could make mistakes and work out
their own styles without ruining their careers. Out of that experience
came many of America's most popular comics. "I didn't know it, but I
was learning even as I bombed," Milton Berle recalled of his difficult

days in vaudeville as a young comic of sixteen or seventeen. "The timing was tightening up, and I was learning about material, why a joke worked one time and not another, why some jokes I used that were not as good as others in my act got a bigger laugh. It was because they went with the personality that was beginning to go across the footlights."[1]

Almost all great comedians who emerged from the live stage tried out several acts, images, and names before finding the approach that best utilized their talents. For over ten years before he became a star, George Burns was a singer, rollerskater, dancer, and comic, who worked with groups, men, women, dogs, and seals, even taking second billing to a seal as "Flipper and Friend." When he first teamed with Gracie Allen, she did the straight lines while he, dressed in a flashy comic's costume, delivered the punchlines. But when the audience laughed at her instead of at him, Burns changed the act, giving Allen the punchlines and focusing on her "illogical logic." As soon as Burns learned that while he understood the comedy, she knew how to deliver it, Burns and Allen were headed for stardom with the distinctive image, funny material, well-rehearsed routines, and perfect timing that spelled success.

Live show business, especially vaudeville, was a superb medium for comedy of all sorts, whether it was Red Skelton's pantomime clowning or Will Rogers's folksy monologues, Fred Allen's dry quips or the Marx Brothers' physical and verbal fireworks. But the stage did have limitations as a comedy medium. In vaudeville, comedians usually had to work with very limited space, props, and sets, often in front of a drop curtain, because many of the other acts on the bill were production numbers that had to be set up while the comics were on. As a result, vaudeville comedians tended to concentrate on wordplay rather than on action and to perform as solo acts or "two-acts," such as Smith and Dale or Gallagher and Shean. The comedy also had to be clear and strong enough to project to the last row of huge theaters. But the top comedians produced by vaudeville and burlesque learned lessons that kept them in the spotlight throughout much of the twentieth century, despite radical changes in show business. As new entertainment media developed, each medium found a way to make America laugh. Since it was one genre featured in every phase of modern show business, comedy provides the clearest evidence of the diversity and complexity that resulted from the application of modern technology to popular entertainment.

The audiences who patronized vaudeville and burlesque also flocked into nickelodeons. Many short early movie comedies were little more than indoor stage scenes made with few of the motion picture's unique camera or editing techniques. So, when an early director applied only part of D. W. Griffith's type of film artistry to comedy, he was immediately crowned the King of Comedy, even though his films were generally unimaginative. But Mack Sennett took the first few steps toward what soon became the fine art of silent movie comedy.

Mack Sennett, born in 1880, broke into show business in 1899 playing the rear end of a horse in a burlesque show in New York's Bowery Theatre. After touring in burlesque and learning that the public liked slapstick and pretty women, Sennett went to work as a bit actor for Biograph in 1908. He studied Griffith's camera and editing techniques and in 1911 began to make his own comedy shorts, drawing material from burlesque slapstick and circus clowning. But Biograph officials, who had earlier complained about Griffith's innovative film work, objected to Sennett's violent comedy. "Too many people fall downstairs or out of windows, or get shot or run over," Biograph complained to Sennett. "Can't you be funny without being so rough?"[2] Sennett's rough and tumble comedies drew big crowds, and in 1912 he left Biograph to join the new Keystone Movie Company as a partner with full control over his pictures. Like many other early directors, Sennett put the familiar, visual comedy of the stage into his pictures.

What made Mack Sennett's comedy shorts stand out from most others of his time was the way he used the special qualities of film. His greatest trademark was the apparently chaotic, free-for-all chase, which often began with two characters and spread and spread until the whole world seemed caught up in Sennett's crazy antics—flying pies, head-on collisions, trolleys running down pedestrians, and cars crashing through buildings or side-swiping trains. But the chases were actually carefully structured, filmed, and edited to create the impression of breakneck, daredevil action. Besides taking his cameras into the streets for the authentic look of real cars, people, explosions, and collisions, Sennett used a far greater variety of camera angles than did his contemporaries; he cut scenes to half their normal length; and he sped up the action by having the cameramen crank their cameras at about half the normal pace and by taking out every third or fourth frame of the film, which also created the jerky look often associated with silent comedies. Sennett also used the camera for special effects.

To show trains or trolleys roaring down the tracks and screeching to a halt inches away from a hero or heroine, or speeding cars racing toward a head-on collision, Sennett started the vehicles at the end of the scene and had them race at full speed in reverse while the cameraman wound the camera backwards. When the film was run forward, the exciting effects were produced. Giving a new twist to the old circus gag in which a whole group of clowns pile out of a tiny car, one by one, Sennett made scores and scores of Keystone Kops seem to tumble out of one patrol wagon by filming a group of men falling out of the wagon, stopping the camera while they got back in again, and repeating the process until he had all the footage he wanted. Sennett then edited his film to a rapid-fire pace that cut between shots with lightning speed, producing a feeling of wild, uninhibited frenzy.

Sennett's pictures established one of the fundamental qualities of silent comedies—a quality of fantasy that stage shows lacked, as critic-historian Walter Kerr has brilliantly argued. Live shows—the stage, the sets, and the props—were totally artificial, but during a performance, audiences could accept the consistent illusion as reality. In silent pictures the realism of film footage of actual people, places, and events was continually contrasted to the artificiality of the absence of sound. Speeding trains did not roar; detonated bombs did not explode; closing doors did not slam; moving lips did not speak. This artificiality gave silent films a dimension of make-believe and fantasy that allowed audiences to suspend their normal credulity, meaning that comedians could ignore the laws of cause and effect when they wanted to. They could fall off high buildings, be run over by cars, be shot in the seat of the pants, or hit over the head, and walk away unhurt. In this atmosphere Sennett could carry his slapstick to violent extremes and never offend or shock audiences, who knew the realistic-looking brutality was harmless play. But audiences also learned that in certain cases cause and effect *always* applied. As soon as they saw a comedian near an open manhole, a hot stove, or a snarling bulldog, they started to laugh knowing there was absolutely no way he could escape his funny, painless fate.[3]

Mack Sennett demonstrated the great popular appeal of silent movie comedy, but it was Charlie Chaplin who made silent film comedy a respected, popular art form. Chaplin came to motion pictures from the stage, where he performed with Fred Karmo's English Pantomime Troupe from 1906 to 1913 and learned to entertain audiences in Europe and America without speaking. After seeing him perform only once, Sennett had Keystone hire him, an offer of triple his salary convincing the young man to overlook the contempt he felt for early movies. With his background in pantomime, Chaplin stepped easily into silent films. Working at the incredible pace of early moviemakers, he appeared in some 35 short Keystone comedies in 1914-15. By the end of his first year in film, the *New York Herald* declared that "the Chaplin craze seems to have supplanted the Pickford craze."[4]

Chaplin left Keystone in 1915 for Essanay to direct and star in fourteen short comedies. Essanay allowed Chaplin weeks instead of Keystone's usual few days to make each film and to develop his style. By 1917 he had made over two dozen films of his own (fourteen for Essanay and twelve for Mutual) and had fully developed his unforgettable style. Basically, Chaplin thought in terms of *character* not caricature, in terms of the individual not the group. He slowed down the pace, moved the camera in, and actively involved the audience in the fate of his character, who frequently turned from the action, looked straight at the viewers, and communicated his feelings and reactions directly to them. Chaplin created a character with human depth and complexity. "You know this fellow is many-sided," he recalled telling Sennett of his evolving screen character, "a tramp, a gentleman, a poet, a dreamer, a lonely fellow, always hopeful of romance and adventure. He would have you believe he is a scientist, a musician, a duke, a polo player."[5] Chaplin also used pathos and poignancy to add emotional depth to his characters.

What Chaplin brought to silent comedy was *acting,* rather than clowning. He was a masterful pantomimist. With his expressive face and a body that he controlled with the grace and fluidity of a ballet dancer, Chaplin could say more without words than most people could with them. Though the silent screen had real problems expressing the serious messages of traditional drama without dialogue, Chaplin explored the most basic and most moving human emotions. His intense, highly evocative acting style was beautifully suited to silent films because it spoke strongly enough for both sound and sight. Though he played many roles in his films, his masterpiece was the Little Tramp, the lonely, poverty-stricken outsider with the funny little moustache, cane, baggy pants, tight formal coat, bowler hat, and oversized shoes. The Little Tramp, who wanted desperately to be accepted and loved, appealed to people of all ages, sexes, races, and nationalities.

Using his character acting, Chaplin pulled people's heartstrings and tickled their funny bones at the same time with the plight, antics, and resourcefulness of poor outsiders struggling for survival and love in a cruel, inhumane world. In *The Tramp* (1915), for instance, he saves a pretty, young woman from thieves, but while protecting her home from another attack he is shot by her father. She nurses the Tramp back to health, which he mistakes for love, and when she leaves him for another man he dejectedly limps off down a dirt road. But, then, he pulls himself together, twirls his cane, perks up, and bounces jauntily off into the distance as the scene fades out. In *The Kid* (1920), one of Chaplin's finest films, the Little Tramp finds a baby in a garbage-filled slum alley and raises him as his son. Five years later they have their own business. Young Jackie Coogan breaks windows, and the Tramp repairs them. Throughout the picture Chaplin blended comedy and tender emotion as the bonds between the man and the boy grow stronger as they fight to stay together. Early in the film when the child tries to kiss the Tramp, he avoids the commitment that could make him emotionally vulnerable by ducking and giving the boy a little kick. But much later, after an orphanage truck has carried off the kid, who cries and begs to be rescued, after the Tramp races over rooftops in pursuit, and after they finally are reunited, the Tramp hugs the boy tightly and kisses him again and again on the lips, a rare moment of uninhibited and unequivocal love in Chaplin's films.

Chaplin took his film-making very seriously. As his popularity and his control over his films increased, his output decreased: from twelve films in 1916-17 to eight between 1918 and 1922 and down to only two between 1923 and 1930. The two, however, were *The Gold Rush* (1924) and *The Circus* (1928), which won him Academy Award nominations as best actor and best director. Chaplin became a determined perfectionist. For his twenty-six-minute movie *The Immigrant* (1917), he shot as much footage as D. W. Griffith had for his two-and-a-half-hour epic *The Birth of a Nation* (1915). For *The Kid*, Chaplin reportedly shot 50,000 feet for a scene of the Kid making pancakes while the Tramp gets out of bed and makes his blanket into a lounging robe. The scene in the film ran 75 feet. Because of such perfectionism, Chaplin starred in only four pictures in the 1920s. Because of his artistry and the universality of his emotional humor, he never lost his popularity with his massive audiences, but his central image—the poverty-stricken Little Tramp facing a brutal, class-conscious world where people were either very rich or very poor and where a poor person's greatest hope was survival—was at odds with the upbeat climate of the 1920s.

This optimistic period called for a new comic vision. Harold Lloyd supplied it with films that outgrossed Chaplin's and Keaton's in the 1920s. It took Lloyd, a craftsman not a natural genius like Chaplin, about a hundred films to develop his own distinctive image and style. In 1917, after seventy pictures, Lloyd donned horn-rimmed glasses to play an awkward, ambitious, inept young man described by Lloyd as "no different from anybody else. But he did the things that other people would like to have done."[6] As the cowardly title character of *Grandma's Boy* (1922), he finally gained confidence, caught a murderer, beat up a bully, and won the girl. In *The Freshman* (1925), he thought he was a real keen guy but was actually a campus laughing-stock until he went from waterboy to football hero. Over and over, Harold, as Lloyd's character was called, survived humiliation and embarrassment to make something of himself by the end of the picture, which captured the 1920s' belief that anyone with determination could succeed.

Through Lloyd's Harold many people's dreams came true, but Lloyd did not produce the deep emotional impact that Chaplin achieved with superb acting. Realizing this, Lloyd intensified his audience's involvement with his character by combining the dangerous thrills of a Mack Sennett chase with Harold's quest to be important. Chaplin grabbed his audience by bringing tears to their eyes; Lloyd grabbed them by bringing gasps to their lips. Lloyd thrust awkward, clumsy, bumbling Harold into situations that forced him to attempt death-defying stunts. In *Safety Last* (1923), his most famous thrill comedy, Harold is a department store clerk who turns human fly to scale the outside of the tall store building as a publicity stunt. With his fingernails scratching handholds in the stone, Harold precariously climbs the building to a height of twelve or thirteen stories despite new hazards at every floor. When a vicious dog chases him out onto a flagpole, it breaks, leaving Harold clutching desperately to the minute hand of the building's clock. As thrill builds on thrill and laugh builds on laugh, the clock hand slips from eleven down to six. And then, the entire clockface begins to pull loose from the building with Harold hanging by its springs. He gets back to the building, keeps climbing, and is nearly to the top when a swinging, four-armed wind gauge, which the audience sees but Harold does not, punches him off the top of the building and leaves him dangling upside down with his foot caught in a rope. At last, he makes it to the top and falls into the arms of his adoring sweetheart.

For such thrill comedies, Lloyd made full use of film, but he did not rely on camera trickery. He shot *Safety Last* on location, made the climb, and apparently did the stunts himself. Using four cameras, he made sure that nearly every shot, even closeups, was filmed from above with streets full of people, cars, and trolleys far below, reinforcing the authenticity of the shots and intensifying the feelings of tension and danger. The basic concept of *Safety Last* was a *film* concept. It could not have succeeded in the theater.

Though never as popular as Chaplin or Lloyd, Buster Keaton, the unsmiling stoic who rarely even moved his lips, made the fullest use of the unique comic potential of silent film. As Walter Kerr observed, Keaton regularly reminded audiences that film was an illusion. He put his fingers over a lens to cover up a woman in a bathtub; he tilted the camera so a boat sailing upstream seemed to be going uphill; and while paddling a canoe in a river, he jarred viewers by suddenly standing up, lifting the canoe out of water with his legs sticking out of the bottom, and walking to the river bank. In *Sherlock, Jr.* (1924) he focused on the relationship between viewers and the film illusion. After Keaton, playing a movie projectionist, falls asleep in the booth, a ghostly double leaves his body, walks into the theater, and leaps into the picture to save the heroine, only to have the villain throw him off the screen and into the audience. When Keaton gets back into the movie, the picture repeatedly cuts to new settings before he can rescue the woman. Like moviegoers, no matter how involved he gets in the picture, Keaton's character has no control over the action because he believes in the reality of the fantasy.

The silent movie era produced many top comedians, some of whom such as Stan Laurel and Oliver Hardy successfully moved into the sound era. But the masters of silent comedy—Chaplin, Lloyd, and Keaton—were all bound to their era, though for different reasons. Chaplin needed the *silence* so he could pull out all emotional stops in his visual portrayal of the deepest human feelings. Adding dialogue might have destroyed the delicate balance between tender emotions and hearty laughs and pushed him over the dividing line between sentiment and sentimentality. Even after all other major American film-makers had converted to sound dialogue, Chaplin continued to work in pantomime. In contrast, Lloyd needed *film* and the 1920s, but not really the silence. His eager-beaver, persevering all-American boy who made something of himself by stumbling through dangerous stunts might have been just as effective if there had been sound motion pictures in the 1920s, but he was not well suited to the Great Depression of the 1930s. Keaton, who worked in movies almost until his death in 1966, was most effective when the silence allowed him to focus on the *film illusions* he turned into masterful visual puns.

When the times and the medium changed abruptly in the late 1920s, so did comedy. The transition from silent to sound motion pictures had a greater impact on comedy than on any other genre, except musicals. First of all, silent comedy's special dimension of fantasy was lost when sound was added to film. So, initially, was much of the freewheeling, fluid movement of silent comedy. Crude, early sound equipment virtually imprisoned film-makers in small sound studios and shackled performers to stationary microphones. Editing, too, was at first very difficult because sound and picture were recorded together. As a result early sound comedies lacked Sennett's complex chases, Chaplin's ballet-like moves, Lloyd's gymnastic thrills, and Keaton's clever film pranks.

The first person to take full advantage of the new sound technology for comedy was graphic artist Walt Disney, who began working on animated cartoons in the 1920s. Animation, the technique of photographing a series of drawings each showing a slight change in position of the images so that the pictures appear to move when shown in rapid succession, had been part of show business since early in the century but had been considered little more than film curiosities. Except that the major characters were animals who dressed and acted like people, cartoons had basically the same qualities as most silent movie comedies, in which the laws of gravity and cause and effect need not apply. But early cartoons lacked the unique appeals of the silent comedy masters. Only after talkies removed the fundamental dimension of fantasy from most film comedy did the animated cartoon come into its own—with Walt Disney leading the way.

In 1927 Disney created a new character—"a romping, rollicking little mouse."[7] What set Mickey Mouse off from all other animated cartoon characters and from most film comedians was that his career and sound were born together. By the time sound became the rage in early 1928, the Disney brothers, Walt and Roy, had two silent Mickey Mouse cartoons ready to release but held them back and plunged into creating sound cartoons. Unlike the early sound moviemakers working with actors, the only limitations cartoonists faced were the limitations of their imaginations and their drawing abilities. Their only technological problem was coordinating sight and sound, which they solved by creating the movement in the cartoon to the rhythm of a metronome and marking the beat on a working print. Then Disney and his staff watched the film and created a score using tin pans, whistles, cowbells, and washboards as well as conventional musical instruments. By having the conductor take his beat from the marks on the film, the score was perfectly coordinated with the action. Drawing cartoons to a musical beat had the added advantage of giving the animated cartoons a smooth, rhythmic movement that made them a pleasure to watch. Many early sound comedies were not.

"Steamboat Willie," the first Mickey Mouse cartoon released, included a scene of pure fantasy right out of the best of silent comedy, and it was a big hit. After Mickey saves his girl friend Minnie from his evil boss, Pegleg Pete, who chases the couple down into the hold of the ship, the story stops, and the musical fantasy begins. When a goat eats Minnie's sheet music and she cranks its tail, the notes of "Turkey in the Straw" come out of its mouth and out of the theater speakers. Minnie and Mickey, then use other animals as musical instruments, a cow's teeth serving as a xylophone and a sow's teats as a bagpipe. The normal soundtrack added a dimension of reality to the fantasy of moving drawings of animals who acted like people, which allowed audiences to care about the characters and still accept the unrealistic qualities that made the characters such a delight. By 1929 the Disneys had released four sound Mickey Mouse cartoons which so beautifully exploited the new entertainment medium and were so popular that they received top billing on theater marquees, a rare honor for shorts.

By 1929 Hollywood was learning to make appealing conventional sound comedies. Film director Ernst Lubitsch, who had brought European sophistication and sensual urbanity to American silent films with polished comedies about upper-class life, such as *Forbidden Paradise* (1924), demonstrated that talkies could be both cinematically artistic and wickedly amusing with films such as *The Love Parade* (1929),

One Hour with You (1932), and *Merry Widow* (1934). But in the transition to sound, Hollywood generally turned to the stage, especially to veterans of vaudeville and musicals such as the Marx Brothers, Mae West, and W. C. Fields, comedians who combined visual and verbal appeal.

Like many other early talkies, the first two Marx Brothers pictures, *The Coconuts* (1929) and *Animal Crackers* (1930), were just films of their stage shows. Both pictures had sound problems that at times made the fast dialogue and the fast moving brothers difficult to understand, but both were great financial successes. *The Coconuts* netted Paramount close to $2 million in the year of the stock market crash and the onset of the Great Depression, while *Animal Crackers* was the studio's top money-maker in 1930. The Marx Brothers brought to the screen what amounted to a sampler of existing comedy styles. Groucho played an outrageous, wisecracking, sharp-tongued anarchist; Zeppo was a young and handsome straight man; Chico carried on the tradition of crude Italian dialect humor, blended with a scheming hustler's eye for an angle; Harpo played a mute, horn-tooting, harp-playing, sticky-fingered romantic. As a foil they often used matronly Margaret Dumont who played a huffy dowager trying to keep her composure and sanity while the brothers demolished the world around her.

In the early Depression when America's basic institutions seemed to be disintegrating, the Marx Brothers ridiculed institution after institution and group after group. With their verbal anarchism, they made everything into a laughing matter. In *The Coconuts* (1929) they lampooned real-estate swindlers, con men, and the get-rich-quick mentality of the 1920s. In *Animal Crackers* (1930) they turned on high society. In *Monkey Business* (1931), at the height of rum-running, they mocked bootleggers and mobsters. In *Horse Feathers* (1932) they took aim at higher education. In *Duck Soup* (1933) they lambasted government, patriotism, and political leadership. Groucho played the ruler of Freedonia, a tiny nation he plunges into war over an imagined personal insult. "While you're out there risking life and limb," he cynically tells Harpo as he goes off to fight, "we'll be in here thinking what a sucker you are."[8] In these films, everyone was either a self-centered scheming phony or a silly naïve fool. Disorder, misunderstanding, and confusion were the rule. The normal courtesies, values, and assumptions did not apply. Just as silent movie comedians had suspended natural laws to portray people in control of the world, the Marx Brothers suspended social and political laws to show the world in control of people.

America, movies, and comedy were changing radically in 1934. Franklin Delano Roosevelt and his New Deal were beginning to restore hope by convincing the public that all it had to fear was fear itself and that with the government's help America could put itself on its feet again. At the same time, the film industry, facing boycotts and growing protests because of the immorality of its pictures, established powerful censors to control the content of movies. Films like Mae West's lost much of their spice and vinegar after 1934, and the Marx Brothers turned their sights to non-controversial targets like opera, horse racing, and play production. But the new code did not stop W. C. Fields, with his bulbous nose, ruddy face, darting eyes, and distinctive voice, from playing characters with a taste for booze, a distaste for animals and children, and a wacky irreverence. His bitter cynicism was summed up in the title of one of his movies, *Never Give a Sucker an Even Break* (1941).

In 1934 a different sort of film comedy swept the nation, a comedy of reconciliation and hope that had a lasting effect on movie comedy. *It Happened One Night* won the 1934 Academy Awards for best picture, director, writer, actor, and actress. But neither of the award-winning stars who delighted audiences and critics with their comedy was a comedian. Clark Gable was a versatile young actor on the way up, and Claudette Colbert was an experienced movie actress who had played many roles, including a silent movie version of Cleopatra. Gable and Colbert demonstrated that it was not necessary to be experienced stage comedians to succeed in film comedy. The picture's director, Frank Capra, who had grown up in the silent movie business, had directed a wide range of films, not just comedies.

It Happened One Night began with a class-conscious battle of the sexes between a headstrong heiress, played by Colbert, and a cocky, streetwise newspaperman, played by Gable. Thrown together on a bus because she is fleeing her possessive father and he is out of work and in search of a story, the two are drawn together by her need for his survival skills and his need for a scoop about the "spoiled rich kid." Despite the great differences in their backgrounds and their frequent fiery spats, the two strong-willed, proudly independent people fall in love and marry after she has left a playboy at the altar to run off to Gable. Throughout most of the film, Capra used simple camerawork.

To focus on the sparkling dialogue and the sharp personality conflict, for instance, he shot the couple from one camera angle, beginning with a long shot and unobtrusively moving the camera slowly in for close-ups as the viewer became more and more involved in the scene. One of the funniest scenes in the film clearly revealed Capra's experience with silent movie comedy. When Gable and Colbert are stranded on a country road, he, as the man of the world, confidently lectures her on the fine art of thumbing a ride and then demonstrates his technique. When car after car passes him, she calmly steps out to the road and hikes up her skirt. The first passing car screeches to a stop as she quips, "the limb is mightier than the thumb." Capra filmed the pantomime scene simply, without moving his camera, but then used masterful editing to build the timing and pacing to a funny climax. Such under-stated but tremendously effective film technique brought out the best in the dialogue, performers, and story.

The frequently imitated film was a fantasy, a wish fulfillment that said class, upbringing, and wealth did not matter, that love conquered all, that all conflicts were merely misunderstandings, and that there were no irreconcilable differences. It was the perfect fantasy for the era of the Great Depression when the public desperately wanted to believe that the American national family could be reunited if people would just be people and forget preconceived ideas and prejudices. After the anarchistic outbursts of the early Depression—whether the machine-gun-toting Jimmy Cagney, the morality-flaunting Mae West, or the nihilistic Marx Brothers, the American public in the mid-1930s turned to entertainment featuring warm, reassuring images of recon-ciliation, entertainment expressing traditional values of the world as it should be.

The many romantic comedies that filled the screen in the late thirties, like many of the film musicals, crime stories, and radio comedies of the same period, focused on the themes of unity and cohesion in the face of discord and conflict. Even the upper classes, frequently the butt of American humor, were part of this spirit of healing through laughter. In the "screwball comedies" of the period, such as *My Man Godfrey* (1937) or *Joy of Living* (1938), which featured headstrong, wealthy eccentrics, the rich could be pompous stuffed-shirts and stuck-up snobs. But they could also be strong, down-to-earth individualists ridiculing pretensions and providing attractive evidence that the upper classes, played with bright sophistication and playful charm by stars such as

Carole Lombard, Fred MacMurray, Katharine Hepburn, Cary Grant, Irene Dunne, Jean Arthur, and James Stewart, could be "real folks" just like anybody else. Well, maybe not *exactly* like anybody else, but at least fun-loving people who just happened to be wealthier and crazier than most folks.

In *Bringing Up Baby* (1938), one of the funniest screwball comedies of the period, Katharine Hepburn played a witty, wacky heiress with a pet leopard and a crush on serious anthropologist Cary Grant, who is devoted to completing a dinosaur skeleton—until her dog steals the last bone. The zany antics that follow include Grant singing "I Can't Give You Anything But Love" to the leopard to calm it down, taking his clothes off and putting on Hepburn's fluffy robe, only to be confronted by her puzzled aunt, and Hepburn getting them out of jail by posing as a gun moll. Finally, he gets the last dinosaur bone; she gets him; but the dinosaur skeleton is demolished when they knock it over as they embrace. Despite all their idiosyncrasies, rebelliousness, and independence, even the most eccentric of the comedy screwballs realized in the end that love and marriage were the roads to happiness and fulfillment. The wackiness and craziness of the early Depression were not gone from the screen, but they had been redirected from attacks on traditional values and institutions to affirmations of them.

By the early 1930s, when Hollywood had completed its transition from filming stage shows to making sound films, distinctive movie comedy had emerged. In feature-length comedies, versatile film directors like Frank Capra, Howard Hawks, and George Cukor took the place of comedy specialists just as versatile actors and actresses replaced comedians. Before World War I Charlie Chaplin had realized that the most effective film comedy came from *acting*. No matter how ridiculous an incident or situation might look to viewers, Chaplin's characters took them seriously. They did not act like comedians telling jokes, but like people facing reality that others laughed at. "If what you're doing is funny," he explained simply, "you don't have to be funny doing it."[9] In the late 1930s, when Howard Hawks was trying to explain the key to successful screen comedy to Katharine Hepburn, he pointed not to the stage, but to the masters of the silent screen—to Charlie Chaplin, Harold Lloyd, and Buster Keaton, who "weren't out there making funny faces. They were serious, sad, solemn, and the humor sprang from what happened to them. They'd do funny things in a completely quiet, somber, deadpan way."[10] What Hollywood discovered was that the feature-length film as a medium needed stories and story-tellers more than gags and gagsters. With some notable exceptions, feature film comedy after the mid-1930s became the domain of actors, actresses, and directors who were specialists in *film*, not necessarily in comedy.

As competition between media intensified and each began to specialize in what it did best, comedy became less central to the appeal of movies than it did to the appeal of radio and, later, television. One major reason was that the motion picture was essentially a narrative medium requiring character development, unfolding plots, and well-paced laughs, which was not the best showcase for the talents of pure comedians whose stock in trade was piling laugh upon laugh in ten- to twenty-minute non-stop bursts. Full-length movie comedy tended to use humor as only one of the several components in a picture, whereas radio developed shorter shows that tended to be dominated by humor. Another major reason that movies relied less heavily on comedy than radio did was that film also excelled at musicals, westerns, and sexuality. Radio had more need to specialize, and it proved to be an excellent medium for stage comedians who did verbal comedy.

For comedians who learned their trade on the live stage, radio required major adjustments. On stage, comics could clown and use visual humor ranging from slapstick to subtle gestures. Traveling constantly and playing to new audiences every night, they could refine one piece of material and use it over and over for years and years. They could also adapt their basic routines to local audiences, inserting special material or dropping references people might not like. All that changed with radio. The listening audience could not see the performers, who had to create all their effects with their voices and with sound effects. The radio audience was also fundamentally different from theater audiences because it was a *national* audience. No longer could comedians localize jokes or make entire careers of a routine or two, regardless of how good they were. Once radio comedians told a joke, they had to assume that everyone had heard it, which meant they continually needed new material. Since the broadcasts went into people's homes, the comedy also had to avoid anything offensive.

Comedy had played a relatively small part in early, pre-network, pre-sponsor radio, which was dominated by music. Then, Charles J. Correll and Freeman F. Gosden created an absolute sensation with *Amos 'n' Andy*, which tied people all over the country to their radios at 7:00 p.m. every week night after it became an NBC network show in the summer of 1929. This situation comedy, with its emphasis on creating believable characters and putting them in funny predicaments that unraveled slowly episode after episode, set many enduring patterns for radio shows. Correll and Gosden, who had little stage experience before creating their distinctively *radio* comedy, capitalized on the lack of visuals by using only their two voices to create an entire neighborhood of black characters who had their roots in stereotyped minstrel comedy but the pair were also likeable people who ingeniously struggled to make ends meet during the Depression with their "Fresh Air Taxi Company of America, Incorporated," which consisted of one rundown, old car that cost $25.00. Hard-working Amos kept the cab running and drove it while lazy Andy was "workin' the books," "restin' his brain," or looking for a way to make a quick buck, which kept them in debt week after week. But they never lost their optimistic belief that "times like dese does a lot o' good 'cause when dis is over . . . people's like us dat is livin' today is goin' learn a lesson."[11] They kept up America's hopes by conveying their social sermons with laughter. But, despite *Amos 'n' Andy's* pioneering radio style, format, and popularity, radio initially turned for most of its humor to the live stage, which had been crippled by the double whammy of the Great Depression and the new entertainment media. Many stage singers, dancers, actors, and actresses went into movies; many vaudeville comics went into radio.

Drawing on vaudeville did not, however, mean drawing on a single type of humor or on the type that was best suited to radio. As he had done on stage for years with his soft Oklahoma drawl, rich metaphorical language, and common-sense approach, Will Rogers used his monologues to satirize American institutions, fads, and follies. But there was only one Will Rogers, so his verbal style did not set a general radio trend. In the early 1930s, highly visual clowns, such as Eddie Cantor and Ed Wynn, did have a broad impact. But regardless of style, the first major adjustment all stage comedians faced in radio was the empty studio. All their performing lives they had learned to play to a live audience, responding to laughs, adjusting their timing and material, and catching the audience up in the infectious quality of laughter. So, in early radio, comedians demanded live studio audiences, which allowed comics like Wynn and Cantor to retain their physical humor and to assume that if they made the studio audience laugh they would also make the folks at home laugh, even though they could not see what was happening. Beginning in 1932, Ed Wynn starred in Texaco's *The Fire Chief*, using the stage props, crazy costumes, oversized shoes, tortoise-shell glasses, and funny hats that had become his trademarks. With his silly outfits, mugging grins, and bobbing eyebrows, Wynn clowned his way through a steady stream of jokes, gags, and two-man patter designed to produce a laugh every twenty seconds. Eddie Cantor, whose *Chase and Sanborn Hour* topped the ratings in 1933 and 1934, wore outlandish costumes, broke eggs over the heads of cast members, hit and kicked his announcer and guest stars, made funny faces, and did anything else he could think of to make the studio audience laugh.

Such visual comedy worked well on radio at first because listeners were predisposed to laugh at famous stars, because the studio audience's laughter was contagious (it later became the basis for using recorded, "canned" laughter), and because announcers described the action. One Hallowe'en, Cantor's announcer described Eddie "wearing one golf shoe and one lady's slipper, one silk stocking, and one plaid golf sock, tweed knickers and a tutu, a woman's blouse with a man's vest over it, a necktie, a blond curly wig and a Sherlock Holmes fore-and-aft cap."[12] *That* was funny whether you could see it or not. But it was not *radio* comedy. It was stage comedy described over radio. Transferring material from one major medium to another without substantial adaptations worked only until comedians developed material that took full advantage of the special qualities of radio. Wynn's rating began to fade in 1934, and in 1935 Texaco cancelled his show. He returned to radio, but never regained his popularity there, though he later excelled on early television with its visual dimension. Cantor blended sentimentality, patriotism, and family values with his humor and maintained his position. But radio comedy in the late 1930s belonged to a new comedy style.

The new *radio* humor, though continuing to use conventional stage humor, utilized *Amos 'n' Andy*'s format: creating strong, likeable comic characters and putting them in situations that would produce laughs. Using continuing characters capitalized on radio's intimacy by allowing regular listeners to get to know the characters and to anticipate their reactions. This format also greatly diminished the problem of creating enough material for a new show every week because writers could use running gags that grew out of the characters' personalities.

Radio comedy, in short, was a comedy about people—warm, intimate, and human as well as funny.

Jack Benny led the way for vaudevillians who adapted their styles to the qualities of radio. By the late 1920s, Benny had developed a distinctive stage image, dressing debonairly, affecting a sophisticated personality, and glibly telling stories about newspaper headlines, current events, and troubles with his girl friends, which seemed to be things that actually happened to him instead of jokes. By 1928 after nine years as a single, he was well established in vaudeville with a national reputation as a comic master of ceremonies, but he was not a top star. In 1929-30 he played small roles in two movies and toured with a racy revue, but had still not found the right medium. Having seen his friends George Burns and Gracie Allen get their own radio show in 1932, he jumped at the chance to appear on Ed Sullivan's radio variety show, where he was so successful that he was offered his own program. The first problem that he, like other stage comedians, faced was doing an entirely new show every week. "There I was, a man who would book three days in Scranton to break in one new joke before I'd try it in the big-city theaters, and now I would have to break in new jokes every single week to the whole country without any tryout at all!"[13] At first, Benny continued with the act he had developed for the stage. Relying on conventional comedy writers, he wisecracked his way through show after show. Interspersing monologues, dialogue with the band leader, and a wide range of music, he was bringing vaudeville to radio. But realizing that that would not work in the long run, he began to develop a distinctive character that was especially well-suited to radio.

After two years on the radio, Benny became a pretentious braggart boasting that he was the "Beau Brummel" or the "Clark Gable of the Air." The central comic thrust of the show became the continuing cast's deflation of the star's overblown ego. On one show, he was delighted to hear that Mary Livingston thought he would make a great movie star, another Boris Karloff. "But I'm not a Karloff, Mary," he protested. "No," she shot back, "but you certainly bore us."[14] In the following years Benny fleshed out a character who vainly worried about his balding head and his toupee, refused to admit that he was over thirty-nine, even though he collected an old-age pension, and was so cheap that he drove an ancient Maxwell car, paid his cast piddling salaries, and hoarded his money in a vault buried deep within the earth and guarded by a man who had been there so long he did not know who had won the Civil War. "Audiences howled at Jack, the self-confident man who made a fool of himself," recalled his wife Mary. "Audiences laughed *at* him, but also *sympathized* with him because, invariably, his best-laid plans blew up in his face. Jack was Everyman: the pleasant guy striding down the sidewalk supremely confident he was making a tremendous impression until he stepped into that rain-slick puddle and fell on his ass."[15] As early as 1934 a nation-wide poll named Jack Benny the most popular radio comedian. In the summer of 1936 his then thoroughly developed show first topped the ratings. It remained in the top five for ten years.

Characterization and intimacy were the keys to Benny's enduring success with situation comedy. Using the premise that the broadcast was a radio rehearsal held in Benny's home, he made the program an informal affair that seemed to take listeners behind the scenes and to show real people at work and play. As early as 1934 he understood that "the use of situations involves comic characters which grow in value as they become more and more familiar to the audience."[16] Each cast member became a character as clear-cut as Benny's egotistical cheapskate. His wife played Mary Livingston, Jack's wise-cracking, ego-deflating girl friend; announcer Don Wilson, a bulky ex-football star, teased Benny about his stinginess, took a ribbing about his girth, and kept trying to sneak in extra plugs for the sponsor; bandleader Phil Harris played a wild-living, hard-drinking hipster who called Benny "Jackson"; boyish tenors Frank Parker, then Kenny Baker, and finally Dennis Day, added the innocence and naïveté of youth to the extended family of the cast, and Eddie Anderson, the first black regular on radio, played Rochester, Benny's spunky butler who had a taste for nightlife and gave as much guff as he took from the "boss." Besides the major characters, actors such as Sheldon Leonard, Frank Nelson, Artie Auerbach, and Mel Blanc created a wide range of continuing characters and sound effects, which added a rich store of recurring comedy bits to Benny's repertoire, including the vault, the sputtering, coughing Maxwell, the racetrack tipster with his: "Psst! Hey, Bud . . . c'mere!", the department store floorwalker with his unctuous "Yeeees?", Polly the parrot with its wisecracks, and the railroad clerk who announced the train for "Anaheim, Azusa, and Cuc . . . amonga." Once listeners pictured Benny and the familiar cast members in a situation, they could already anticipate the conflicts and running gags to come and might begin laughing before they heard anything else.

The other keys to Benny's success were his perfectionism and his sense of timing and pacing. Benny carefully crafted every element in the show, sometimes spending an entire hour to perfect a single line. "Every laugh was carefully constructed," Mary Benny explained, "built up gradually, so when it finally came, the audience was ready to respond."[17] He and his cast also made masterful and dramatic use of pauses, which had especially great impact on radio, a medium usually continually filled with sound. The audience's anticipation of what his character would do and say combined with the added expectation created by pauses could be devastatingly funny. Reportedly one of the longest laughs ever obtained from a studio audience came when a robber stopped Benny and ordered: "Your money or your life!" As the audience began to titter at the mere mention of money to the skinflint, Benny paused, and paused, and paused, until the astounded and frustrated bandit screamed: "Quit stalling! I said your money or your life." Finally, Benny spoke: "I'm thinking it over."[18]

Jack Benny could entertain America's radio listeners for over twenty years with essentially the same characters and situations because he thoroughly understood the medium and created a funny, diversified *program* rather than a personal vehicle. "Practically, all comedy shows owe their structure to Benny's conceptions," observed Fred Allen, one of the giants of radio comedy. "He was the first to realize that the listener is not in a theater with a thousand other people, but is in a small circle at home. The Benny show is like a *One Man's Family* in slapstick. When they tune in to Benny, it's like tuning in to somebody else's house. Benny was also the first comedian to realize that you could get big laughs by ridiculing yourself instead of your stooges. Jack became the fall guy for everybody else on his show."[19] With all cast members delivering laugh lines, audiences never knew where the next quip was coming from, which in effect created a studio full of comic characters the audience knew, liked, and laughed at.

By the late 1930s, largely because of Benny's astounding success, situation comedy dominated radio humor, though variety shows remained very popular, as did Fred Allen's *Town Hall Tonight,* one of radio's wittiest programs. It combined Allen's caustic, satirical commentary on current events with comedy skits, people with unusual jobs, and dialogues with guest stars and with his wife Portland Hoffa who played a wacky scatterbrain. A great many of the popular situation comedies were in one way or another family shows. Besides Benny's gang having many qualities of an extended family and the show being set in his home, Goodman and Jane Ace played an urbane, married couple in *Easy Aces; The Goldbergs* was a portrayal of a Jewish immigrant family; and *Vic and Sade* and *Fibber McGee and Molly* added small-town families to the dialful of family-oriented situation comedies in the 1930s and 1940s. Radio, as a medium, called for situation comedies, but it was the public mood that decided that they would have a *family* focus. During the discord of the Great Depression and the Second World War, radio fans loved comedies centered on strong families and tight-knit groups that quarrelled but ultimately pulled together to overcome their problems, just as movie audiences poured in to see screwball comedies of reconciliation.

The major radio and film comedy styles that evolved in the mid-1930s continued through the 1940s with some notable variations and changes, especially the emergence of Bob Hope as a major comedy star. Hope had been broadcasting since 1932 and realized that to reach the top he needed "something different and ear-catching," which he found in a return to snappy, topical monologues and Ed Wynn's goal of three laughs a minute. For Hope's own show, which premiered in 1938, he hired a large staff of writers to arm him with enough ammunition to fire at the audience with the staccato pace of a human machine gun. For each show Hope had two different groups of writers each prepare an entire script on the same theme. Then he combined the best of each into one ninety-minute script, which he and the cast performed to a live audience, whose response determined what went into the weekly, thirty-minute show.

Though Hope had a diversified variety format, it was his monologue that distinguished his shows. While other programs opened with music or a commercial, he began with a greeting, a mention of where he was, a plug, and a joke, all in one sentence. "How do you do, ladies and gentlemen," he might start off, "this is Bob 'deep in the heart of Texas' Hope telling you Texans to use Pepsodent and your mouth won't be a scandal."[20] Then he cut loose with a flurry of one-liners and short jokes, using over twenty in seven minutes, sometimes up to six or seven a minute. "My idea was to do it as fast as I could and still have the listeners at home get it and let the live audience in the studio laugh too," Hope explained. He wanted to grab the audience immediately and not let it go, to challenge it to listen carefully and be "with it" enough to get all the jokes. "You have to get over to the audience that there's a game of wits going on and that if they don't stay awake, they'll miss something."[21] Unlike Benny's, Hope's jokes were topical and political, as Will Rogers's had been, but unlike Rogers, Hope was not piercing or biting. Hope's humor slid quickly and smoothly over the surface of contemporary personalities and events, tickling the funnybone rather than stimulating the mind. From the very beginning of World War II Hope solidified his popularity with the public by entertaining servicemen at bases and hospitals at home and abroad. Broadcasts of these shows made people at home feel close to the boys at the front and grateful to Hope. By January 1943 he had the top-rated show on radio, a position he maintained through the war.

Hope also assumed some of Jack Benny's comic boasting about his courage, good looks, and lovemaking and the ego-deflating humor that went with it, which allowed audiences to identify with him as well as to laugh at his jokes. This brash, insecure characterization worked well on radio, but was most effective in films when teamed with Bing Crosby's understated, relaxed, self-confidence. Beginning with the *Road to Singapore* (1940), Hope and Crosby, like two brothers, playfully quibbled, wisecracked, and teased their ways through a series of adventures on the road to exotic places like Zanzibar, Morocco, and Utopia while fighting for the affections of sultry Dorothy Lamour. Mixing light-hearted comedy with toe-tapping tunes, colorful locations, and pretty women, the Road pictures proved that an unconventional family that fought affectionately but pulled together in the pinch would work, not just in American homes but also in far-away places with strange sounding names.

There were, of course, many other important comedy stars, pictures, and shows in the 1940s, but fundamental changes in comedy awaited the development of the last major entertainment machine to develop in the first half of the twentieth century. Television spread slowly following World War II because there were relatively few stations, sets were expensive, and the shows were little more than local productions. But that began to change by 1948 when an established vaudeville and nightclub comic moved into the new medium and became "Mr. Television." Milton Berle, who had been playing to live audiences since he was a little boy, had used an aggressive, wise-guy image, visual clowning, and ad-libbing to become a top stage comedian and master of ceremonies. But he had found only limited success in films and on radio. He lacked the power to shape movie scripts to his flamboyant, ad-libbing, insulting style which was, in any case, most effective in short bursts. On radio he was more successful warming up studio audiences before shows, when he could ad-lib and clown, than during broadcasts when he was tied to a script and could not use his physical humor. When television began to develop commercially in 1947 and most established stars were unwilling to risk their careers in the fledgling entertainment medium, Berle, who was starring in the *Texaco Star Theatre* on radio, leapt at the chance to do a show on television, which he realized "could give a visual entertainer the exposure he could never get from radio."[22]

From the first, Berle made an astute adjustment to the new medium. Even if he did not fully understand all the implications of what he did, he realized that the live audience had trouble seeing the show because they had to look past cameras and cameramen. As Ed Wynn complained of early television, "You just can't get laughs out of cameramen's asses." "I learned quickly," Berle recalled, "that I couldn't do anything small, because the studio audience couldn't see it."[23] So, he dressed flamboyantly, mugged unashamedly, and staged one outrageous slapstick stunt after another. This bigger than life style could not have been better for the audience at home watching the show on small, fuzzy screens no bigger than ten inches. At the time, few people realized that this adjustment to television's technological limitation was a big part of Berle's appeal. But in 1949, when stage and film comedians Olsen and Johnson brought their large-scale slapstick skits to the new medium, television writer Max Wilk recalled that "all those hordes of O. & J. comics and midgets and stooges careening on and offstage, up and down the aisles and here and there, appeared on the home TV to resemble nothing more than some very busy drunken ants."[24]

But not Berle. He looked like a giant, not an ant. "He came out of that machine like the Jolly Green Giant on stilts," writer Tedd Thomey recalled of the first time he watched Berle on a neighbor's ten-inch set in 1949. "When the show was over, I gazed in bewilderment and considerable pain around Pete and Jessie's tiny living room, expecting to see the walls bent outward by the concussion from Milton's guffaws."[25] Berle opened his shows outlandishly costumed as eye-catching caricatures ranging from a hulking Little Lord Fauntleroy to a campy Carmen

Miranda eating a banana from his towering headdress. Then he verbally assaulted the studio audience. "Say, mister," he taunted, "would you mind moving? Your head is shining in my eyes." When the laughter died down, he shot back: "For a minute I thought you were sitting upside down." Berle "is the bad-boy extrovert, the wise-cracking, punning, iconoclastic clown, who in my opinion," comedian Steve Allen observed, "can make *any* audience laugh, whether they want to or not."[26] The effect of Berle's antics and ad-libs, including things that went wrong, was enormous because audiences knew that the shows were broadcast live and that anything could happen.

In the early years of television, America on Wednesday mornings buzzed with talk of the stunts Berle had pulled on Tuesday nights. Two months after his television show premiered, it got a Hooper rating of 80.7 when the number two show received a 28.9. Two years later, in 1950, Berle had a Nielsen rating of 79.9, compared with 55.2 for *Arthur Godfrey and His Friends,* which ran a distant second. During the years that television established itself with the public, an incredible eight out of every ten televisions in use in the country were tuned to NBC on Tuesday at 8:00 p.m. to watch Milton Berle, who deserved the title "Mr. Television."

With Berle's comedy-variety show dominating Tuesday nights and Sid Caesar and Imogene Coca's comedy revue *Your Show of Shows* doing the same on Saturday nights for NBC, CBS countered with situation comedy, including established radio situation comedies. *Burns and Allen, Amos 'n' Andy,* and *The Jack Benny Program* moved to television between 1951 and 1953 with relatively few changes. Lucille Ball, who was co-starring with Richard Denning in *My Favorite Husband* on CBS radio, was one of the performers the network asked to move to television. Although not a top star, she refused unless her real husband, Desi Arnaz, played her husband in the show. CBS felt the public would not accept a Cuban bandleader with a heavy Spanish accent and a redheaded ex-Goldwyn Girl as a happily married couple. But after Arnaz and Ball mounted a stage show and took it on a highly successful tour, CBS accepted the team. When shows were still broadcast live in the East and sent to the rest of the country on poor quality kinescopes, the network insisted that they do the show in New York. Instead, Arnaz and Ball stayed in Hollywood, borrowed money, set up Desilu Productions, filmed their shows before live audiences, provided them to the network for broadcast, and retained rights to the films, which could be sold and reshown any number of times. Before a single episode of the show had been broadcast, Arnaz and Ball had made major breakthroughs in television by making Southern California a production area, controlling their own show, and recording it on film, which had the added aesthetic advantage of making editing a possibility for television programming.

Arnaz and Ball planned their show as carefully as they handled their business affairs. For the pilot Arnaz played Ricky Ricardo, a struggling Latin bandleader, and Ball played Lucy, a housewife who wanted to be in show business but had no talent. "The man would be the master of the house," Ball explained of her original concept for the show, "and she would be a scatterbrain—but wily enough to get her own way, in a comedic sort of fashion."[27] In the second show they added Vivian Vance and William Frawley playing normal neighbors Ethel and Fred Mertz, who provided a contrast to the highly emotional Ricardos and gave Lucy an ally in the battle of the sexes. In the best situation-comedy tradition, both couples were believable and likeable, so that no matter how crazy the action got, it started with credible characters and well-established situations. "Our type of comedy did get pretty wild at times," Arnaz explained. "That is why setting up the reasons for getting to those antics had to be fundamentally solid. There is a very thin line between the honest and believable physical comedy routines and the 'just trying to be funny' routines."[28]

What made *I Love Lucy* so distinctive was that it brought some of the visual humor of silent movies to the situation-comedy format developed on radio. On May 26, 1952, *Time* magazine put Lucille Ball on its cover and observed that "what televiewers see on their screens is the sort of cheerful rowdiness that has been rare in the U.S. since the days of the silent movies' Keystone Comedies." *I Love Lucy* was a highly visual show because of Ball's expressive body and face and her great talent as a physical clown. "I think she is a great comedienne by any standard and at any time," Harold Lloyd observed of Ball. "I don't believe that we have had a comedienne that surpassed her for sheer comic understanding, timing, ability to handle comic slapstick in the traditional manner." There was no need for Lloyd's sexual categorization of Ball's talent. She was simply a great comic. In one famous episode, Lucy had hidden eggs under her blouse, and then Desi insisted they rehearse a tango, which smashed the eggs. After looking sheepishly at Ricky and at the audience, "She then looked squirmishly at her bosom," Arnaz later wrote of her masterful mugging, "and daintily pulled her blouse away from it, shook her torso and her waist a little bit, letting the audience know the broken eggs were finding their way down her body." When the laughter began to fade, "she shook her left leg and foot, which told them the eggs had completed their downward tour."[29] The audience roared.

America loved Lucy. In its first season, 1951-52, only two shows had higher ratings, and that was the worst *I Love Lucy* ever did. In its six-year run, it finished first four times and second once. More people watched the January 19, 1953, episode in which Lucy gave birth, than had ever seen a commercial television program, more than would watch Dwight Eisenhower sworn in as President of the United States the next day. Though production of *I Love Lucy* stopped in 1957, it has been shown all over the world and has never left the air in the United States.

In the wake of *I Love Lucy*, at least fourteen situation comedies premiered between 1952 and 1954, and many more followed. But the situation comedy was only one of the many types of humor on television. Between 1949 and 1954 on *Your Show of Shows*, Sid Caesar, Imogene Coca, Carl Reiner, and Howard Morris used pantomime, slapstick, parody, and comic acting to create weekly, live, ninety-minute revues with some of television's most innovative comedy. In 1952 Bob Hope began to quip and shoot out his one-liners on television. Starting in 1950, Groucho Marx ad-libbed and wisecracked in a quiz format for over a decade. Through the 1950s and most of the 1960s Jackie Gleason, supported by Art Carney and others, used his considerable acting and physical comedy talents in sketches about characters ranging from playboy Reggie Van Gleason III to busdriver Ralph Cramden. From 1948 to 1956 Dean Martin and Jerry Lewis played out the antics of two-man buffoonery, contrasting a handsome, debonair singer-straight-man and a totally uninhibited clown who would do anything for a laugh. Between 1948 and 1971 Ed Sullivan's variety show spotlighted all sorts of comedy, from vaudeville and night-club veterans to promising newcomers. Starting in 1951 and running until 1970 Red Skelton mimed and clowned through his many characters, from the Mean Widdle Kid to Freddie the Freeloader. Since 1954 the *Tonight Show* has brought comedy of all sorts to late-night television in a ninety-minute comedy-variety-interview show that changed tones as it changed stars from Steve Allen's wacky, fast-paced gags and skits (1954-57), through Jack Paar's explosive emotionalism and witty repartee (1957-62), to Johnny Carson's topical monologues and masterful comic timing and double takes (1961-). This list, including only *some* of television's longest running, most popular, and most distinctive comedy vehicles, helps explain why television was taking the family audience away from movies.

As rich and varied as television comedy was in the 1950s and early 1960s, it did not bring all kinds of comedy into American homes. As they had with radio, the sponsors who paid the bills for television did not want to offend anyone, which meant eliminating even mild cursing, almost any sexual innuendo, and any biting social or political commentary. But such humor thrived in nightclubs where comedians such as Lenny Bruce and Mort Sahl used their sharp wit and piercing commentary to continue the tradition of social, political, and ethical criticism through laughter. This humor reached into American homes when recordings became a major comedy medium in the 1950s after the development of the long-playing record. Comedy recordings were certainly nothing new. In fact, some of the first popular records in the 1890s had been humorous, and throughout the decades a wide range of comedy records—from Mack and Moran, "The Two Black Crows," to Spike Jones—sold well. But the three-minute playing time of 78-rpm records could hold only small bits of full fifteen- to twenty-minute comedy routines, which meant that recordings played a minor role in comedy. Records basically carried either comic songs—an adjunct to the music business—or short parts of established comedians' material. Unknown comics were unlikely to make their marks with short singles.

Long-playing records, which ran fifteen to twenty-five minutes per side, provided an excellent medium for the self-contained routine that a comedian honed, refined, and perfected before live audiences. By recording the routine, the comedians could, in effect, use it over and over by having it distributed all over the country. In this way recordings indirectly gave comedians such as Shelley Berman, Dick Gregory, Bill Cosby, Bob Newhart, and Flip Wilson opportunities to learn their craft while playing to small, live audiences and still make decent money through the sales of records, which also could provide the national exposure that might project the comedians into high-paying television jobs.

Once performers appeared on television, though, there was no margin for error, no time to learn, and no way to generate enough new material for repeated appearances. Television's insatiable appetite for new material presented an unsolvable problem for many comedians who earned a spot on television by developing distinctive, *personal* material and styles in nightclubs and recordings and then quickly exhausted their original routines and had to rely on writers who hardly knew them or their styles for additional material. Few comedians could survive long on television doing original monologues, as the experience of Bob Newhart demonstrated. The success of his comedy LP, *The Button-down Mind of Bob Newhart*, a collection of carefully crafted monologues using the inventive device of Newhart talking on the telephone, often to historical figures, with the audience hearing only his side of the conversation, made the relatively unknown nightclub comedian a star. In 1961-62 it earned him his own television variety-comedy show, which opened every week with one of his telephone routines. His material and the show lasted one season. He also lasted only one season as a rotating comedy host on *The Entertainers* in 1964-65, before finding lasting television success in a situation-comedy format that took advantage of his comedy timing and delivery without relying on his original material. Between his own television shows, he performed live, did guest shots on other people's shows, and made record albums. But as important as comedy recordings could be to a comedian's development and income, they were a secondary, supplemental comedy medium for the general public.

Television remained the nation's major source of comedy in the 1960s, with the formats, styles, and content of the 1950s remaining dominant throughout the decade. But in 1968 viewers of a new NBC comedy show saw something fundamentally different—*Rowan and Martin's Laugh-In,* which began as a one-time special in Fall 1967 but was so popular that it was made a series in early 1968 and soon became the top-rated show on television. Though the nominal stars were comedians Dan Rowan and Dick Martin, in reality the stars were the editors of the kaleidoscopic, collage-like show that flipped from one-liners to blackouts, bits of scenes, sight gags, puns, celebrities, film clips, and all sorts of other things with no continuity and at a pace faster than any other show in any medium had ever run. Inexpensive videotape and tape technology, with their capacities for instant replay and editing, made it feasible to record everything from costumed productions shot on location to cameo appearances of famous people, to cut up the tape, to put the snippets together, and to rework the result as many times as necessary. *Laugh-In* executive producer George

Schlatter explained in 1978 that each show averaged "1100 tape edits, 300 film edits, and 300 sound effects."[30] The show simply could not have been done live and would have been very costly to do entirely on film. In form and style it was *television* comedy. Its content was unusually irreverent and sexy, at least for television. It attacked the Vietnam War, the Reverend Billy Graham, and President Richard Nixon; it took liberal stances on social issues; and it made frequent use of suggestive double-entendre humor. Co-star Dick Martin played a lecherous bachelor; mini-skirted Judy Carne commanded "Sock it to me!" and was drenched with water; and cameras took closeups of words painted on the skin of a bikini-clad actress who writhed to pulsating music as the lens zoomed in and out to the same sensual rhythm.

The show rose quickly to the top of the ratings and stayed there for two years, making stars of newcomers such as Goldie Hawn, Artie Johnson, and Lily Tomlin. But it dropped to thirteenth in 1970-71, twenty-second in 1971-72, and left the air in 1973. Its rapid decline may have resulted from many of the talented newcomers it introduced leaving to pursue their careers elsewhere. But it may also have been because the show's greatest appeals were its form, style, and shock value. At first it was something totally different, daring, and exciting. But when it was no longer novel, when the unpredictable had become predictable, the show faded, much like individual comedians when they had used up their best material and were overexposed. It may have fallen victim to its greatest appeal—its frenetic pace, lack of continuity, and lack of characterization, in short, its form. The comedy show that took its place at the top of the ratings used an old format but infused it with new content.

After failing as a pilot for ABC, *All in the Family* first went on the air in 1971 as a winter, mid-season replacement on CBS. At first it did poorly in the ratings, but it caught on during summer reruns. In its first full year the program became the most popular show on television, a position it held for five years. Produced by Norman Lear, based on a successful British working-class comedy, *All in the Family* was something strikingly new in America. Its format of well-drawn characters in a quarreling, working family was familiar enough. But its content was not. Archie Bunker, the main character, was an outspoken, prejudiced warehouse worker married to Edith, a plain, loving housewife. Their daughter Gloria lived at home with her husband, Mike, a liberal college student of Polish descent who was supported by Gloria and the

Bunkers. Mike continually clashed with Archie over his diatribes against kikes, wops, spics, polacks, fags, jigs, radicals, protesters, and almost anyone who was not a conservative, old-fashioned, patriotic White Anglo-Saxon Protestant. Mike's kneejerk liberalism was as stereotyped and predictable as Archie's bigoted conservatism, but both were also believable human beings, as were Edith and Gloria.

All in the Family was totally unprecedented in dealing with deeply disturbing issues, including bigotry, rape, impotence, unemployment, homosexuality, menopause, war, cancer, and a host of other problems that modern people had to face. While using humor throughout, the show took the issues seriously and made them moving human problems by personalizing them. It was Archie who lost his job, Mike who faced impotence, Edith who went through menopause and was confronted by a rapist, and Gloria who was molested. The fine acting and marvelously expressive faces of the leads, especially Carroll O'Connor as Archie and Jean Stapleton as Edith, which were emphasized by frequent use of closeups and freeze frames, made the audience care about the characters and share their feelings. When Archie learned that a transvestite had been killed saving Gloria from muggers, for instance, the audience shared his shock, pain, and awareness of the humanity and worth of all people. Dramatist Paddy Chayefsky, who wrote *Marty* and many other powerful plays for early television, observed of the 1970s: "Nowadays there's no opportunity for a writer to do small dramas and reach the audience with something intimate. Sometimes I think you can often get closer to reality on a network situation comedy, like *All in the Family*, where Archie Bunker and his family are actually dealing in truthful attitudes, than you can in what passes for television drama."[31]

In the late 1970s, situation comedies dominated television as never before. *All in the Family* spawned many similar shows that used laughter as a way to address such serious issues as women's rights (*Maude*, 1972-78), race (*The Jeffersons*, 1975-), and war (*M*A*S*H*, 1972-). *The Mary Tyler Moore Show* (1970-77), with its well-drawn characters, its focus on a competent working woman, and its concentration on laughs not issues, produced other shows centered on strong women, such as *Rhoda* (1974-79) and *One Day at a Time* (1975-). There was also a rash of situation comedies that reverted to the messageless, escapist humor of the 1950s. *Happy Days* (1974-), *Laverne and Shirley* (1975-), and *Welcome Back Kotter* (1975-79) appealed primarily to the new youth market that ABC made the basis of its rise to becoming the most popular of the networks. In May 1979, nine of the top ten Nielsen shows were reported to be situation comedies. "People now live in a pressure cooker every day," NBC vice-president Joyce Burditt observed in 1979. "When people come home, they want to laugh."[32] And television offered situation comedies of all sorts for people to laugh at.

Motion picture comedy, which had been hurt badly by the growth of television comedy, recovered in the late-1960s, led by such major writer-performers as Mel Brooks and Woody Allen. Brooks's wild, iconoclastic humor burst into films in 1968 with *The Producers*, in which he produced a show highlighted by a production number, "Springtime for Hitler," which lampooned Nazis. Brooks then moved to takeoffs on movie traditions, by putting a black sheriff in the prejudiced Old West in *Blazing Saddles* (1974) and spoofing horror movies with *Young Frankenstein* (1974), early film-making with *Silent Movie* (1976), and Alfred Hitchcock thrillers in *High Anxiety* (1977). Despite all the hilarious moments in Brooks's films, the most significant, popular film comedies of the 1970s were the work of Allen.

Like the great silent movie comedians, Allen created a distinctive comic persona and vision which he translated into reality with a series of pictures centered on essentially the same character. In some ways harkening back to Chaplin, Allen portrayed a frail, funny-looking, insecure little guy who wore heavy-rimmed glasses, longed to be loved, and could not find happiness and fulfillment. But where Chaplin created an ambiguous, universal character in the Little Tramp, Allen created a localized, ethnic character. Part of the difference came from the difference between silent and sound films. In silent pictures, the Little Tramp did not have to speak, but if he had, he would have lost some of his universality by betraying Chaplin's English origin, just as Allen's speech revealed his New York and Jewish background.

At first Allen's films drew heavily on his experience as a standup comic and on his keen eye for wacky sight gags. His movies made viewers laugh *at* them, but the parts were better than the whole. As he subordinated his uninhibited humor to characterization and storytelling, his films took on a greater cohesion, depth, and emotional power which made audiences laugh *with* them and empathize with the character. In *Take the Money and Run* (1969), a parody of documentary biographies and prison and crime pictures, Allen's character is so inept that when he tries to rob a bank, the teller cannot read his holdup note and refuses to give him the money because the message "I have a gub" makes no sense. In *Play It Again, Sam* (1969) he was effective with women only when the ghost of Humphrey Bogart told him what to do. In *Bananas* (1971) he stumbled into being a hero of a Latin American revolution. In *Everything You Always Wanted To Know About Sex But Were Afraid To Ask* (1972) he acted out sexual anxieties and fantasies. In *Sleeper* (1973) he was accidentally frozen and brought back to life in 2173. Through these films, somewhat in the vein of Harold Lloyd's hero, Allen's little guy, despite all the humiliation he had to endure and all the wild, crazy gags he pulled, eventually lived out fantasies many people shared, fantasies of heroism, sexual prowess, and immortality. But he was still more a talented gagster than an accomplished film-maker.

In 1977 Allen created a moving, mature film comedy that took his character through an ultimately unsuccessful love affair. Combining the comic contrast of his New York, Jewish life-style and her Hollywood, WASP life-style with a touching personal story, *Annie Hall* won Academy Awards for best picture, director, writers, and actress. Like Chaplin, Allen's character lost at love and then bounced back. In the last scene of *Annie Hall,* after telling a joke about a family that humored a brother who thought he was a chicken because they needed the eggs, he ended the film by observing that "life is crazy, irrational, and absurd. But we keep going through it because I guess most of us need the eggs."[33] And most of us need the laughs.

In the 1980s Americans will probably have incredibly rich and varied comedy choices because of the rapidly expanding entertainment technology. As always the content of the humor will primarily reflect the shifting moods and concerns of the times. But its form and style will continue to be shaped by the media that deliver it to the public. Besides going out to nightclubs and movies or staying home to enjoy conventional radio, recordings, or television, most people will also watch live stage and theatrical comedy at home on cable television or watch previously recorded humor when they want it, on tape cassettes or video discs. Perhaps the satellite and cable systems that make possible specialized television channels will result in a national station broadcasting comedy twenty-four hours a day. The formats that might evolve in that event are impossible to predict. Whatever the medium or the form, Americans no doubt will keep laughing.

Conclusion

Modern technology unquestionably revolutionized the form, content, and structure of show business. In many ways the most important of the numerous changes was the transformation of the average American home into an amusement palace, a fundamental change that had deep implications for American family life and for American business, which sponsored broadcast entertainment. But as pervasive and profound as the changes in entertainment have been, it is clear in the early 1980s that they are only a prelude to the many far-reaching changes to come.

With scientific and technological breakthroughs occurring at a rapidly accelerating rate, popular entertainment, especially in the home, is bound to change radically as existing satellite broadcasts, cable systems, and video recordings are used more widely and are supplemented by new technology. Individuals at home are already beginning to program their own entertainment. Using video recorders and recordings, people can watch what they want when they want it—including first-run motion pictures. In the early 1980s the established television networks for the first time see their total, combined audience decreasing, a trend that could ultimately restructure broadcast entertainment. Perhaps the individual at home using computer terminals and telephone lines will be able to tap new centralized sources of information and entertainment. The future is, of course, impossible to predict, but it is almost certain that the very latest equipment of the early 1980s will soon seem quaintly old-fashioned. It is also almost certain that no matter how radical the changes in the entertainment media, the American people will continue to enjoy the same basic genres that they have enjoyed throughout the centuries and throughout the modern entertainment revolution.

Bibliographic Essay

This brief, highly selective essay, which includes only some of the books that I found most useful and interesting, is intended primarily to provide curious general readers with some entry points into the extensive literature devoted to modern American show business. Most of the entries, which are organized to reflect the general structure of the book, are broad in their scope and have extensive bibliographies. Some biographies and autobiographies of people discussed in the chapters are also included.

General

The best starting point for the general reader is Marshall McLuhan's *Understanding Media: The Extension of Man,* paperback 2nd edition (New York, 1964), the provocative, theoretical book that reshaped thinking about the importance of the media. Gerald Emanuel Stearn (ed.), *McLuhan: Hot and Cool* (New York, 1967) offers a wide range of reactions to McLuhan's ideas. More conventional surveys of American entertainment are Foster Rhea Dulles, *A History of Recreation: America Learns To Play,* 2nd ed. (New York, 1965), an informative, entertaining study of Americans' use of their leisure time; Russell Nye, *The Unembarrassed Muse* (New York, 1970), a broad survey of popular culture; Abel Green and Joe Laurie, Jr., *Show Biz: From Vaude to Video* (New York, 1951), a wide ranging book packed with information; Joseph Csirda and June Bundy Csirda, *American Entertainment: A Unique History of Popular Show Business* (New York, 1978), articles from the entertainment journal *Billboard,* with narrative overviews of the periods.

Introduction

For an interpretive discussion of the development of live show business that includes an extensive bibliography see Robert C. Toll, *On with the Show:*

245

The First Century of Show Business in America (New York, 1976). Gilbert
Seldes deserves to be singled out because he pioneered the serious study of
popular entertainment and because his *Seven Lively Arts,* paperback edition
(New York, 1962), first published in 1924, remains a brilliant starting point
for any inquiries into the popular arts.

The Entertainment Machine in the Theater

The body of writing about film is so vast that it is the subject of several
book-length bibliographies, such as Richard Dyer MacCann and Edward S.
Perry, *The New Film Index* (New York, 1975) and George Rehrauer,
Cinema Booklist (Metuchen, N.J., 1972), which describes the content of
each book it includes.

The best general history of silent films is William K. Everson, *American
Silent Film* (New York, 1978). Supplementing it in various ways are: Walter
Kerr, *The Silent Clowns* (New York, 1975), a study of silent-film comedy
that also illuminates and evokes the experience of silent pictures in general;
Kevin Brownlow, *The Parade's Gone By* (New York, 1978), a fine volume of
film pioneers' recollections of all phases of early moviemaking; George C. Pratt,
*Spellbound in Darkness: Readings in the History and Criticism of the Silent
Era* (Rochester, N.Y., 1966), a valuable collection of contemporary reviews
and articles about early films; Edward Wagenknecht, *The Movies in the Age of
Innocence* (Norman, Okl., 1962), a personal history of silent film especially
valuable for the preface which recounts Wagenknecht's perceptions as an early
movie fan; Terry Ramsaye, *A Million and One Nights,* 2 vols. (New York,
1926), a readable, first-hand account rich in anecdotes; and Geoffrey Bell, *The
Golden Gate and the Silver Screen* (East Brunswick, N.J., forthcoming), a
thorough study of film-making in the San Francisco Bay Area during the silent
movie era.

The broad history of film can be approached through Arthur Knight, *The
Liveliest Art,* paperback edition (New York, 1968), a readable, insightful
survey that has been the basis for many other histories; and Lewis Jacobs,
The Rise of the American Film: A Critical History, paperback edition (New
York, 1968), an important, pioneering general history first published in
1939. The range of approaches to film is suggested by Robert Sklar, *Movie-
Made America: A Cultural History of American Movies,* paperback edition
(New York, 1976), an excellent cultural interpretation of movies; Garth
Jowett, *Film: The Democratic Art* (Boston, 1976), a social interpretation of
films; Tino Balio (ed.), *The American Film Industry* (Madison, Wis., 1976),
a fine collection of articles on the business history of the medium; Alexander
Walker, *Stardom* (New York, 1970), an examination of the qualities of
movie stars; Andrew Bergman, *We're in the Money: Depression America
and Its Films,* paperback edition (New York, 1972), a provocative interpretation of films in one time period; and James Monaco, *American Film Now:
The People, the Power, the Money, the Movies* (New York, 1979), a discussion integrating cinematic, cultural, social, and economic analyses of modern

film-making. Cobbett Steinberg, *Reel Facts: The Movie Book of Records* (New York, 1978) is a handy source of statistics on many phases of the movie business.

Among the most useful autobiographies and biographies of major figures discussed in the chapter are: Mary Pickford, *Sunshine and Shadow* (New York, 1955); Lillian Gish with Ann Pinchot, *The Movies, Mr. Griffith, and Me* (Englewood Cliffs, N.J., 1969); Robert M. Henderson, *D. W. Griffith, His Life and Work* (New York, 1972); Colleen Moore, *Silent Star* (New York, 1968); Jesse Lasky with Don Weldon, *I Blow My Own Horn* (New York, 1959); Adolph Zukor with Dale Kramer, *The Public Is Never Wrong* (New York, 1953); Donald Hayne (ed.), *The Autobiography of Cecil B. De Mille* (Englewood Cliffs, N.J., 1959); Jack Warner with Dean Jennings, *My First Hundred Years in Hollywood* (New York, 1965); Bosley Crowther, *Hollywood Rajah: The Life and Times of Louis B. Mayer* (New York, 1960); Samuel Marx, *Mayer and Thalberg: The Make Believe Saints* (New York, 1975); Bob Thomas, *Thalberg: Life and Legend* (New York, 1969).

The Entertainment Machine in the Home

Roland Gelatt, *The Fabulous Phonograph,* 2nd revised edition (New York, 1977) surveys the evolution of phonographs, records, and tapes. Cynthia A. Hoover, *Music Machines—American Style* (Washington, D.C., 1971), a fine catalog from The National Museum of History and Technology, graphically traces the history of music machines. The starting point for the history of radio and television is the fine work of Erik Barnouw, especially *A History of Broadcasting in the United States,* 3 vols. (New York, 1966, 1968, 1970), an authoritative work particularly strong on institutional developments; *Tube of Plenty: The Evolution of American Television,* paperback edition (New York, 1977), a condensation and updating of his three-volume history; and *The Sponsor: Notes on a Modern Potentate* (New York, 1978), an examination of the power of advertisers in the broadcast media and over the public.

Mary Jane Higby, *Tune In Tomorrow,* paperback edition (New York, 1968) is a superb autobiography combining wit, keen observations about twenty years of acting experience in radio, and a thorough understanding of the medium. Other useful books on radio include J. Fred MacDonald, *Don't Touch That Dial: Radio Programming in American Life from 1920-1960,* paperback edition (Chicago, 1979), which surveys the history of broadcasting and then concentrates on major genres; John Dunning, *Tune In Yesterday: The Ultimate Encyclopedia of Old-Time Radio, 1925-1976,* paperback edition (Englewood Cliffs, N.J., 1976), a valuable reference with good detail on the shows; Arthur Frank Wertheim, *Radio Comedy* (New York, 1979), a fine study of one genre at which radio excelled; Jim Harmon, *The Great Radio Heroes,* paperback edition (New York, 1967), a blend of the fans' enthusiasm with information on shows; Ben Gross, *I Looked and Listened: Informal Recollections Of Radio and TV* (New York, 1954), a good memoir rich in anecdotes by a critic; and John J. Floherty, *Behind the Microphone* (New York, 1941), a journalist's behind-the-scenes account of the way radio worked.

Suggesting the diverse body of writing about television are Horace Newcomb, *TV: The Most Popular Art,* paperback edition (New York, 1974), an examination of the medium as a popular art concentrating on its basic program types; Max Wilk, *The Golden Age of Television: Notes from the Survivors,* paperback edition (New York, 1977), a fine source of the recollections and observations of a wide range of television pioneers; Robert Sklar, *Prime-Time America: Life on and behind the Television Screen* (New York, 1980), a collection of stimulating essays and reviews by a cultural historian; Judy Fireman (ed.), *TV Book: The Ultimate Television Book,* paperback edition (New York, 1977), an anthology of 150 short, uneven articles and a pictorial chronology of television history; Jay S. Harris (ed.), *TV Guide: The First 25 Years* (New York, 1978), a good sample of articles from the nation's largest circulation magazine; Tedd Thomey, *The Glorious Decade,* paperback edition (New York, 1971), especially useful for the personal introduction recalling the initial impact of television on the public; Les Brown, *Television: The Business behind the Box* (New York, 1971), an in-depth look at network decision-making for the 1970-71 season; and Terry Galoney, *Down the Tube, or Making Television Commercials Is Such a Dog-Eat-Dog Business It's No Wonder They're Called Spots* (Chicago, 1970), an insider's witty view of the business of making television commercials. Information about specific television shows and performers is in Tim Brooks and Erle Marsh, *The Complete Directory to Prime Time Network TV Shows 1946–Present,* paperback edition (New York, 1979); Vincent Terrace, *The Complete Encyclopedia of Television Programs, 1947-1979,* 2nd edition, 2 vols. (New York, 1979); and Les Brown, *The New York Times Encyclopedia of Television* (New York, 1977).

Westerns

The best general introductions to the western are George N. Fenin and William K. Everson, *The Western: From Silents to Cinerama* (New York, 1962), a detailed examination of movie westerns with a preference for realistic portrayals of the West; and Jon Tuska, *The Filming of the West* (New York, 1976), written with a love for western movies and considerable detail. The genre receives more analytical treatment in John Cawelti, *The Six Gun Mystique* (Bowling Green, Ohio, 1970), a long essay ranging over all media in search of basic western formulas; Will Wright, *Six Guns and Society: A Structural Study* (Berkeley, 1975), an examination of the different types of westerns and why they appealed to Americans at different times; and Donna and Ralph Brauer, *The Horse, the Gun, and the Piece of Property* (Bowling Green, Ohio, 1975), tracing the evolution of the television western.

Diana Serra Cary, *The Hollywood Posse: The Story of a Gallant Band of*

Horsemen Who Made Movie History (Boston, 1975) tells the fascinating story of her father and other former cowboys who preserved their traditional way of life after the open range closed by becoming extras and stunt men in movies. James Horwitz, *They Went Thataway*, paperback edition (New York, 1976) in a breezy "hip" style surveys the history of western movies before getting to the interesting story of his search for and interviews with western action stars of the past. Andrew Sinclair, *John Ford* (New York, 1979) offers a readable, reliable introduction to the work of the greatest western director. The best biography of John Wayne is Maurice Zolotow, *Shooting Star: A Biography of John Wayne* (New York, 1964).

Popular Music

Two books on American popular music stand out for their excellence and depth. Charles Hamm, *Yesterdays: Popular Song in America* (New York, 1979) examines the melodies and structure of popular songs to discuss the trends and changes in popular music as it evolved. Alec Wilder, *American Popular Song: The Great Innovators, 1900-1950* (New York, 1972) focuses more narrowly on composers who were major melodic innovators in popular music. Among the general introductions to American popular music are Ian Whitcomb, *After the Ball: Pop Music from Rag to Rock,* paperback edition (Baltimore, 1974), a readable survey with perceptive commentary; David Ewen, *All the Years of American Popular Music* (Englewood Cliffs, N.J., 1977), covering all facets of American music with good detail considering the breadth; Edward B. Marks as told to Abbott J. Liebling, *They All Sang: From Tony Pastor to Rudy Vallee* (New York, 1934), an enjoyable, informative, insightful book by an insider; Isaac Goldberg, *Tin Pan Alley* (New York, 1930), a very perceptive, early book, strong on the roles of black musicians; Gilbert Chase, *America's Music: From the Pilgrims to the Present* (New York, 1955), a survey with real depth; John Rublowsky, *Popular Music* (New York, 1967), a brief book most useful for its short summaries of the changing music media and the processes of arranging and cutting a record; Hazel Meyer, *The Gold in Tin Pan Alley* (Philadelphia, 1958), very useful for the business and institutional aspects of music from the 1930s to the 1950s.

Marshall and Jean Stearns, *Jazz Dance: The Story of American Vernacular Dance* (New York, 1968) is an excellent, readable book on a neglected subject.

The rock music revolution can be approached through Carl Belz, *The Story of Rock,* revised paperback edition (New York, 1973), a perceptive survey ranging from 1954 to 1971; and Steve Chapple, *Rock 'n' Roll Is Here To Pay: History and Politics of the Music Industry* (Chicago, 1977), an excellent book on rock music, especially the business side of the industry.

For introductions to the creative musical sub-cultures only peripherally discussed in this book, see Bill C. Malone, *Country Music U.S.A.: A Fifty-*

Year History (Austin, Texas, 1968), a fine history of commercial country and western music that began in the 1920s; John Storm Roberts, *The Latin Tinge: The Impact of Latin American Music on the United States* (New York, 1979), the first survey of the influence of Latin music; Eileen Southern, *The Music of Black Americans: A History* (New York, 1971), a broad survey of black music; and Marshall Stearns, *The Story of Jazz*, paperback edition (New York, 1958), a fine, brief introduction to the history of jazz.

Musicals

In a class by itself is Gerald Bordman's *American Musical Theatre* (New York, 1978), an extraordinary book that manages to be both a comprehensive, authoritative reference work and a readable, interesting history of stage musicals. Other particularly useful, general works on stage musicals are Cecil Smith, *Musical Comedy in America* (New York, 1950), a fine, chronological survey; Stanley Green, *The World of Musical Comedy*, rev. ed. (New York, 1968), the story of the musical stage told through its major composers and lyricists; David Ewen, *New Complete Book of the American Musical Theater* (New York, 1970), a reference work with listings for shows and for writers; Lehman Engel, *The American Musical Theater* (New York, 1967), an analysis of the elements in successful post-1940 musicals.

Film musicals have received far less attention than stage musicals. By far the best broad book is Hugh Fordin, *The World of Entertainment*, paperback edition (New York, 1976), a fine study of the film musicals made at MGM by the production unit run by Arthur Freed. John Kobal, *Gotta Sing, Gotta Dance, A Pictorial History of Film Musicals* (New York, 1971) includes abundant quotes from personal interviews with participants and offers explanations for why things were popular when they were; John Russell Taylor and Arthur Jackson, *The Hollywood Musical* (New York, 1971) begins with Taylor's personal essay on movie musicals and concludes with reference sections of films and people. Among the major books on film musicals that were published after work on this book was completed are Stanley Green, *Encyclopedia of the Musical Film* (New York, 1981) and Clive Hirschhorn, *The Hollywood Musical* (San Diego, 1981).

Major individuals discussed in the chapter are covered in Richard Moody, *Ned Harrigan: From Corlear's Hook to Herald Square* (Chicago, 1980), a study of Edward Harrigan's long career; John McCabe, *George M. Cohan: The Man Who Owned Broadway* (New York, 1973); Gerald Bordman, *Jerome Kern: His Life and Music* (New York, 1980), a comprehensive study of this major composer; Richard Rodgers, *Musical Stages: An Autobiography* (New York, 1975), rich in details of his illustrious career; Arlene Croce, *The Fred Astaire and Ginger Rogers Book* (New York, 1972), a brilliant examination of America's most beloved screen dancing team; Stanley Green and Burt Goldblatt, *Starring Fred Astaire* (New York, 1973), a perceptive discussion of Astaire's entire career; and Clive Hirschhorn, *Gene Kelly: A*

Biography (Chicago, 1974), a fine biography of one of America's great dancers.

Crime

Crime, the most recent major entertainment genre to emerge, has received little serious, book-length attention. The best introductions to facets of the genre are Eugene Rosow, *Born To Lose: The Gangster Film in America* (New York, 1978), combining social and cinematic analysis; John Cawelti, *Adventure, Mystery, and Romance: Formula Stories as Art and Popular Culture* (Chicago, 1976), an examination of the genre in a broad context and conceptual framework; William K. Everson, *The Detective in Film*, paperback edition (Secaucus, N.J., 1974), a survey; Jon Tuska, *The Detective in Hollywood* (New York, 1978), a detailed discussion of the translations of fictional detectives into movies. Richard Meyers, *TV Detectives*, paperback edition (San Diego, 1981), a promising looking survey, appeared too late to be used in this book. Two major crime movie stars have told their own stories: James Cagney, *Cagney by Cagney*, paperback edition (New York, 1977) and Edward G. Robinson with Leonard Spigelgass, *All My Yesterdays*, paperback edition (New York, 1975), neither of which devotes much attention to its author's work in crime plays or movies.

Sexuality

For general introductions to sexuality in movies see Alexander Walker, *Sex in the Movies*, paperback edition (Baltimore, 1968), a book with good detail and interpretations; and Jeremy Pascall and Clyde Jeavons, *A Pictorial History of Sex in the Movies* (New York, 1975), with substantial text, often following Walker. Portrayals of women are examined in Marjorie Rosen, *Popcorn Venus: Women, Movies, and the American Dream*, paperback edition (New York, 1974), a blending of rich textual material with sensitive interpretations; Molly Haskell, *From Reverence to Rape: The Treatment of Women in the Movies*, paperback edition (New York, 1974), a more heavy-handed survey than Rosen's, but useful; Norman Zierrold, *Sex Goddesses of the Silent Screen* (Chicago, 1973), with extensive quotes from the period; Gaye Tuchman, Arlene Kaplan Daniels, and James Benét (eds.), *Hearth and Home: Images of Women in the Mass Media* (New York, 1978), a wide range of articles by many authors. Portrayals of men are examined in Joan Mellon, *Big Bad Wolves: Masculinity in the American Film* (New York, 1977), a wide-ranging treatment of images of dominant males; and Donald Spoto, *Camerado: Hollywood and the American Man*, paperback edition (New York, 1978), covering the full range of male screen characters. Madeleine Edmondson and David Rounds, *From Mary Noble to Mary Hartman: The Complete Soap Opera Book*, paperback edition (New York, 1977) briefly surveys the history of soap operas and then concentrates on topical discussion of living, loving, and working in the soaps.

Censorship of movies is discussed in Jack Vizzard, *See No Evil: Life Inside a Hollywood Censor* (New York, 1970), rich in anecdotes of the enforcement and collapse of the code; and Murray Schumach, *The Face on the Cutting Room Floor: The Story of Movie and Television Censorship* (New York, 1964), surveying the entire history. Censorship of stage shows is covered in Abe Laufe, *The Wicked Stage: A History of Theater Censorship and Harassment in the United States* (New York, 1978).

Among the most useful and readable biographies of major figures discussed at length in the chapter are Charles Higham, *Ziegfeld* (Chicago, 1972); Irving Shulman, *Valentino,* paperback edition (New York, 1967); Booton Herndon, *Mary Pickford and Douglas Fairbanks: The Most Popular Couple the World Has Ever Known* (New York, 1977); Irving Shulman, *Harlow: An Intimate Biography,* paperback edition (New York, 1964); Lyn Tornabene, *Long Live the King: A Biography of Clark Gable* (New York, 1976); Lee Guthrie, *The Life and Loves of Cary Grant* (New York, 1977); Charles Higham, *Kate: The Life of Katharine Hepburn,* paperback edition (New York, 1976); Fred Lawrence Guiles, *Norma Jean: The Life of Marilyn Monroe* (New York, 1969); and Charles Hamblett, *Paul Newman* (Chicago, 1975).

Comedy

Many areas of American comedy are badly in need of serious study. A brilliant exception is the finest book on silent film comedy, Walter Kerr, *The Silent Clowns* (New York, 1975). Gerald Mast, *The Comic Mind* (Indianapolis, 1973) and Raymond Durgnat, *The Crazy Mirror: Hollywood Comedy and the American Image,* paperback edition (New York, 1972) offer broad coverage of movie comedy. Ted Sennett, *Lunatics and Lovers* (New York, 1973) examines movie "screwball" comedy of the 1930s and 1940s. General introductions to comedy in broadcast media are Arthur Frank Wertheim, *Radio Comedy* (New York, 1979), another of the few fine, broad books on American comedy; and Steve Allen's *The Funny Men,* with perceptive observations on sixteen television comedians.

The writing on comedy is dominated by biographies and autobiographies. Among the most useful are Charles Chaplin, *My Autobiography* (New York, 1964); Harold Lloyd and Wesley W. Stout, *An American Comedy* (New York, 1928); Buster Keaton with Charles Samuels, *My Wonderful World of Slapstick* (New York, 1960); Rudi Blesh, *Keaton* (New York, 1966); Allen Eyles, *The Marx Brothers: Their World of Comedy* (London, 1966); Mae West, *Goodness Had Nothing To Do with It,* revised edition (New York, 1970); Robert Lewis Taylor, *W.C. Fields: His Follies and Fortunes,* paperback edition (New York, 1968); Irving A. Fein, *Jack Benny, An Intimate Biography,* paperback edition (New York, 1977); Mary Livingston Benny and Hilliard Marks with Marcia Borie, *Jack Benny* (New York, 1978); Milton Berle with Haskel Frankel, *Milton Berle,* paperback edition (New York, 1975); and Desi Arnaz, *A Book,* paperback edition (New York, 1976). Though he is only mentioned here, Fred Allen wrote two perceptive autobiographies that offer unique insights into American comedy in the first half of the century. *Much Ado About Me* (Boston, 1956) covers his career in vaudeville, and *Treadmill to Oblivion* (Boston, 1954) covers his radio career.

Notes

Introduction

1. Gilbert Seldes, *The Seven Lively Arts*, paperback edition (New York, 1962), pp. 177-78; Eddie Cantor quoted in Michael Freedland, *Jolson*, paperback edition (New York, 1973), p. 110.
2. New York *Mirror*, March 9, 1833, quoted in Francis Hodge, *Yankee Theatre: The Image of America on the Stage, 1825-1850* (Austin, 1964), p. 18; *Boston Weekly Magazine*, November 27, 1824, quoted in David Grimsted, *Melodrama Unveiled: American Theater and Culture, 1800-1850* (Chicago, 1968), pp. 67-68. For a full discussion of the development of live show business, see Robert C. Toll, *On with the Show: The First Century of Show Business in America* (New York, 1976).
3. Haverly Mastodon Minstrel Program, May 31, 1880, quoted in Robert C. Toll, *Blacking Up: The Minstrel Show in Nineteenth-Century America* (New York, 1974), p. 25.
4. Seldes, p. 223.
5. Al Jolson, "If I Don't Get Laughs and Don't Get Applause—the Mirror Will Show Me Who Is To Blame," *American Magazine*, 87 (April 1919), pp. 18-19, 154-58.

Chapter 1

1. *New York Times*, April 24, 1896, quoted in Lewis Jacobs, *The Rise of the American Film*, paperback edition (New York, 1968), pp. 3-4; *New York Dramatic Mirror*, May 2, 1896, quoted in John L. Fell, *A History of Films*, paperback edition (New York, 1979), p. 14; Henry Tyrrell, "Some Music-Hall Moralities," *The Illustrated American*, July 11, 1896, quoted in George C. Pratt, *Spellbound in Darkness: Readings in the History and Criticism of the Silent Era* (Rochester, 1966), p. 16.
2. Edward Wagenknecht, *The Movies in the Age of Innocence*, paperback edition (Norman, Oklahoma, 1962), p. 20.

3. F. H. Richardson, *Motion Picture Handbook* (1910), quoted in Robert Sklar, *Movie-Made America: A Cultural History of American Movies,* paperback edition (New York, 1976), p. 16.

4. *The Billboard,* Oct. 13, 1906, quoted in Pratt, p. 43.

5. Pratt, p. 41.

6. Donald Hayne (ed.), *The Autobiography of Cecil B. DeMille* (Englewood Cliffs, N.J., 1959), p. 68.

7. D. J. Wenden, *The Birth of the Movies,* paperback edition (New York, 1975), p. 87.

8. *New York Herald,* Dec. 3, 1899, quoted in A. Nicholas Vardac, *Stage to Screen* (Cambridge, Mass., 1949), p. 80.

9. W. P. Eaton, "The Canned Drama," *American Magazine,* 68 (Sept. 1909), quoted in Vardac, p. 66.

10. Wagenknecht, p. 89.

11. Robert E. Welsh, "David W. Griffith Speaks," *New York Dramatic Mirror,* Jan. 14, 1914, quoted in Pratt, p. 111; Hayne, p. 111.

12. Lillian Gish with Ann Pinchot, *The Movies, Mr. Griffith, and Me* (Englewood Cliffs, N.J., 1969), p. 173.

13. Griffith quoted on Dickens in Jacobs, p. 103; Griffith quoted on switchbacks in Pratt, p. 111; Biograph quoted in Jacobs, p. 103; *The Moving Picture World,* July 24, 1909, quoted in Pratt, p. 96.

14. *New York Times,* June 6, 1915, quoted in Jacobs, pp. 185-86.

15. William K. Everson, *American Silent Film* (New York, 1978), p. 87.

16. Jesse L. Lasky and Don Weldon, *I Blow My Own Horn* (New York, 1957), pp. 94-95.

17. Colleen Moore, *Silent Star* (New York, 1968), pp. 152-53.

18. *New York Dramatic Mirror,* July 16, 1910, quoted in Pratt, p. 85.

19. Mary Pickford, *Sunshine and Shadow* (New York, 1955), pp. 64-65.

20. Pickford, pp. 75, 97.

21. Pickford, p. 153.

22. Wenden, p. 100.

23. Lasky, p. 129.

24. *New York Times,* April 14, 1919, quoted in Pratt, p. 278.

25. Lasky, p. 129.

26. Jack Warner with Dean Jennings, *My First Hundred Years in Hollywood* (New York, 1965), pp. 167-68.

27. Frank Capra, *The Name Above the Title* (New York, 1971), pp. 101-2.

28. *Photoplay,* March 1929, quoted in Kevin Brownlow, *The Parade's Gone By* (New York, 1968), p. 574.

29. John Kobal, *Gotta Sing, Gotta Dance: A Pictorial History of Film Musicals* (New York, 1971), p. 39.

30. Whitney Stine with Bette Davis, *Mother Goddam: The Story of the Career of Bette Davis* (New York, 1974), pp. 25, 28.

31. Samuel Goldwyn, "Hollywood in the Television Age," *Hollywood Quarterly,* 4 (Winter 1949), quoted in Sklar, p. 276.

32. Stine, p. 259.

Chapter 2

1. Roland Gelatt, *The Fabulous Phonograph*, 2nd revised edition (New York, 1977), pp. 69-70.
2. Erik Barnouw, *A Tower in Babel: A History of Broadcasting in the United States*, Volume I—to 1933 (New York, 1966), p. 101.
3. Ben Gross, *I Looked and Listened: Informal Recollections of Radio and TV* (New York, 1954), p. 64.
4. Barnouw, p. 106.
5. Gross, pp. 66-67.
6. Mary Jane Higby, *Tune in Tomorrow*, paperback edition (New York, 1968), p. 151.
7. Paul F. Lazarsfeld, *The People Look at Radio* (Chapel Hill, N.C., 1946), p. 110.
8. Arthur Frank Wertheim, *Radio Comedy* (New York, 1979), pp. 48-49.
9. Gilbert Seldes, *The Public Arts*, paperback edition (New York, 1956), p. 63; Freeman Gosden quoted in Gross, p. 154.
10. Mary Margaret McBride, *Out of the Air* (New York, 1960), pp. 26-27.
11. Joseph Julian, *This Was Radio: A Personal Memoir* (New York, 1975), p. 47; Higby, p. 12.
12. Higby, p. 36.
13. John J. Floherty, *Behind the Microphone* (New York, 1944), p. 60; Fred Allen quoted in Wertheim, p. 162.
14. Gelatt, p. 268.
15. Max Wilk, *The Golden Age of Television: Notes from the Survivors*, paperback edition (New York, 1977), pp. 85, 221.
16. Wilk, pp. 168-70, 194.
17. Wilk, pp. 130, 134.
18. Wilk, p. 258.
19. Wilk, pp. 259-61.
20. Wilk, p. 40.
21. Les Brown, *Television: The Business behind the Box* (New York, 1971), pp. 125-26.
22. Terry Galoney, *Down the Tube, Or Making Television Commercials Is Such a Dog-Eat-Dog Business It's No Wonder They're Called Spots* (Chicago, 1970), p. 114.
23. Galoney, p. 3.
24. Gary A. Steiner, *The People Look at Television* (New York, 1963), p. 219.
25. Steiner, pp. 203, 234.
26. Hazel Meyer, *The Gold in Tin Pan Alley* (Philadelphia, 1958), pp. 154-55.
27. Gelatt, p. 332.

Chapter 3

1. Diana Serra Carey, *The Hollywood Posse: The Story of a Gallant Band of Horsemen Who Made Movie History* (Boston, 1975), p. 346.
2. *Spirit of the Times*, December 4, 1886, quoted in Robert C. Toll, *On with the Show: The First Century of Show Business in America* (New York, 1976), p. 167.

3. George N. Fenin and William K. Everson, *The Western: From Silents to Cinerama* (New York, 1962), p. 61.
4. Fenin and Everson, p. 67.
5. William S. Hart, *My Life East and West* (Boston, 1929), pp. 198-99.
6. Fenin and Everson, p. 90.
7. Jon Tuska, *The Filming of the West* (Garden City, N.Y., 1976), p. 392.
8. Jesse L. Lasky and Don Welden, *I Blow My Own Horn* (New York, 1957), p. 8.
9. Paul E. Mix, *Life and Legend of Tom Mix* (New York, 1972), p. 193.
10. Tuska, p. 294.
11. Fenin and Everson, p. 250.
12. Andrew Sinclair, *John Ford* (New York, 1979), p. 130.
13. Sinclair, p. 148.
14. Richard Schickel, *The Men Who Made the Movies* (New York, 1975), p. 121.
15. James Horwitz, *They Went Thataway,* paperback edition (New York, 1976), pp. 141-42.
16. Tedd Thomey, *The Glorious Decade,* paperback edition (New York, 1971), pp. 66-68.
17. Stuart M. Kaminsky, *Clint Eastwood,* paperback edition (New York, 1974), p. 29.
18. Tuska, p. 373.
19. Maurice Zolotow, *Shooting Star: A Biography of John Wayne* (New York, 1974), p. 233.
20. Mike Tomkies, *Duke: The Story of John Wayne,* paperback edition (New York, 1971), p. 129.

Chapter 4

1. Space limitations dictate that the nation's creative musical subcultures be discussed only when they influenced the general popular music that entertained the mass of Americans.
2. Edward B. Marks, as told to Abbott J. Liebling, *They All Sang: From Tony Pastor to Rudy Vallee* (New York, 1934), p. 22.
3. Marks, p. 133.
4. Marks, p. 101.
5. Ian Whitcomb, *After the Ball: Pop Music from Rag to Rock,* paperback edition (Baltimore, 1974), p. 16.
6. Isaac Goldberg, *Tin Pan Alley* (New York, 1930), p. 150.
7. Marks, p. 156.
8. John Storm Roberts, *The Latin Tinge: The Impact of Latin American Music on the United States* (New York, 1979), p. 46.
9. Roland Gelatt, *The Fabulous Phonograph,* 2nd revised edition (New York, 1977), pp. 188-89.
10. Marshall Stearns, *The Story of Jazz,* paperback edition (New York, 1958), pp. 126-29.
11. Stearns, p. 120.
12. Marks, p. 207.
13. Charles Thompson, *Bing: The Authorized Biography* (New York, 1975), frontispiece.
14. Stearns, p. 150.

15. Francis Chase, *Sound and Fury: An Informal History of Broadcasting* (New York, 1942), p. 256.

16. Earl Wilson, *Sinatra: An Unauthorized Biography* (New York, 1976), pp. 27, 40-41.

17. Whitcomb, p. 203.

18. David Ewen, *All the Years of American Popular Music* (Englewood Cliffs, N.J., 1977), p. 458.

19. Red West, Sonny West, and Dave Hebler, as told to Steve Dunleavy, *Elvis: What Happened?*, paperback edition (New York, 1977), p. 99.

20. Ewen, p. 558.

21. Ewen, pp. 617-18.

Chapter 5

1. *New York Tribune*, Sept. 17, 1866, quoted in Barnard Hewitt, *Theatre U.S.A., 1665-1957* (New York, 1959), p. 198; Edward B. Marks, *They All Had Glamour: From the Swedish Nightingale to the Naked Lady* (New York, 1944), p. 12.

2. Isaac Goldberg, *Tin Pan Alley: A Chronicle of the American Popular Music Racket* (New York, 1930), p. 68.

3. Cecil Smith, *Musical Comedy in America* (New York, 1950), pp. 150-51.

4. Unidentified newspaper clipping from the Harvard Theatre Collection quoted in Robert C. Toll, *On with the Show: The First Century of Show Business in America* (New York, 1976), p. 195.

5. Richard Rodgers, Guy Bolten, and Jerome Kern quoted in Stanley Green, *The World of Musical Comedy* (New York, 1960), pp. 62, 68, 71.

6. David Ewen, *Complete Book of the American Musical Theater*, revised edition (New York, 1959), p. 190.

7. Green, p. 77.

8. *Photoplay*, April 1929, quoted in John Kobal, *Gotta Sing, Gotta Dance: A Pictorial History of Film Musicals* (New York, 1971), p. 36.

9. John Baxter, *Hollywood in the Thirties*, paperback edition (New York, 1970), p. 207.

10. Kobal, p. 130.

11. John Russell Taylor and Arthur Jackson, *The Hollywood Musical* (New York, 1971), p. 74.

12. Clive Hirschhorn, *Gene Kelly: A Biography* (Chicago, 1974), p. 139.

13. *Photoplay*, April 1935, quoted in Kobal, p. 149; Stanley Green and Burt Goldblatt, *Starring Fred Astaire* (New York, 1973), p. 4.

14. Richard Rodgers, *Musical Stages, an Autobiography* (New York, 1975), p. 218.

15. Hugh Fordin, *The World of Entertainment: Hollywood's Greatest Musicals*, paperback edition (New York, 1976), p. 94.

16. Fordin, p. 118; Gerald Bordman, *American Musical Theatre: A Chronicle* (New York, 1978), p. 536.

17. Vincente Minnelli with Hector Arce, *I Remember It Well*, paperback edition (New York, 1975), p. 145.

18. The quotes, in order, are from Kobal, p. 220; Fordin, p. 270; Kobal, p. 244; Hirschhorn, p. 187.

19. Hirschhorn, pp. 138-39.

20. Hirschhorn, p. 84.

21. Gene Kelley quoted in Fordin, p. 269; Bob Fosse quoted in Hirschhorn, p. 181.
22. Fordin, p. 331.
23. Green, *World of Musical Comedy*, p. 280.
24. *San Francisco Chronicle*, June 21, 1978, p. 6.

Chapter 6

1. Walter J. Meserve, *An Outline History of American Drama*, paperback edition (Totowa, N.J., 1970), p. 185; Eugene Rosow, *Born To Lose: The Gangster Film in America* (New York, 1978), p. 68.
2. Rosow, p. 124.
3. Lewis Yablonsky, *George Raft*, paperback edition (New York, 1975), p. 53.
4. Rosow, pp. 182, 161.
5. Andrew Bergman, *We're in the Money: Depression America and Its Films*, paperback edition (New York, 1972), p. 85; Rosow, p. 226.
6. Rosow, pp. 225-27; *Time*'s observation on Edward G. Robinson is quoted in Bergman, p. 87.
7. Jon Tuska, *The Detective in Hollywood* (New York, 1978), p. 6.
8. Alan G. Barbour, *Humphrey Bogart: A Pyramid Illustrated History of the Movies*, paperback edition (New York, 1974), p. 82.
9. Jim Harmon, *The Great Radio Heroes*, paperback edition (New York, 1967), p. 36.
10. John Dunning, *Tune in Yesterday: The Ultimate Encyclopedia of Old-Time Radio, 1925-1976*, paperback edition (Englewood Cliffs, N.J., 1976), p. 543; Frank Buxton and Bill Owen, *The Big Broadcast, 1920-1950* (New York, 1973), p. 211.
11. Buxton, p. 231.
12. Dunning, pp. 168-69.
13. Dunning, p. 476.
14. Erik Barnouw, *The Image Empire: A History of Broadcasting in the United States, Volume III—From 1953* (New York, 1970), p. 153.
15. Barnouw, pp. 151-52.
16. Stuart Kaminsky, *Clint Eastwood*, paperback edition (New York, 1974), pp. 108-9.

Chapter 7

1. Charles Higham, *Ziegfeld* (Chicago, 1972), pp. 36-37.
2. Rennold Wolf, "The Highest-Salaried Actress in America," *Green Book Magazine* (Nov. 1912), quoted in Robert C. Toll, *On with the Show: The First Century of Show Business in America* (New York, 1976), p. 280.
3. Marjorie Rosen, *Popcorn Venus*, paperback edition (New York, 1974), p. 22.
4. Lillian Gish with Ann Pinchot, *The Movies, Mr. Griffith, and Me* (Englewood Cliffs, N.J., 1969), p. 102.
5. Gish, p. 106.
6. Maurice Zolotow, *Shooting Star: A Biography of John Wayne* (New York, 1974), p. 32.
7. Booton Herndon, *Mary Pickford and Douglas Fairbanks: The Most Popular Couple the World Has Ever Known* (New York, 1977), p. 110.

8. Norman Zierrold, *Sex Goddesses of the Silent Screen* (Chicago, 1973), p. 14.

9. Zierrold, pp. 41-43.

10. Zierrold, p. 46.

11. Donald Hayne (ed.), *The Autobiography of Cecil B. De Mille* (Englewood Cliffs, N.J., 1959), p. 399.

12. Mae West, *Goodness Had Nothing To Do with It*, revised edition (New York, 1979), pp. 45, 51-52, 72-73, 94.

13. Ashton Stevens quoted in West, p. 125; West's lines are drawn from Alexander Walker, *Sex in the Movies*, paperback edition (Baltimore, 1968), pp. 73-74, and from John Kobal, *Gotta Sing, Gotta Dance: A Pictorial History of Film Musicals* (New York, 1971), p. 183.

14. Irving Shulman, *Valentino*, paperback edition (New York, 1968), p. 132; John Kobal, *Gods and Goddesses of the Movies* (New York, 1973), p. 34.

15. Joan Mellon, *Big Bad Wolves: Masculinity in the American Film* (New York, 1977), p. 53.

16. Colleen Moore, *Silent Star* (New York, 1968), p. 129; Margaret Reid quoted in George Pratt, *Spellbound in Darkness: Readings in the History and Criticism of the Silent Era* (Rochester, 1966), p. 455.

17. Joe Morella and Edward Z. Epstein, *The "It" Girl: The Incredible Story of Clara Bow*, paperback edition (New York, 1977), p. 45.

18. Cecil B. De Mille quoted in Walker, pp. 30-31; Hunt Stromberg quoted in Samuel Marx, *Mayer and Thalberg: The Make-Believe Saints* (New York, 1975), p. 103.

19. Irving Shulman, *Harlow: An Intimate Biography* (New York, 1964), pp. 90-91; Walker, p. 122.

20. Rosen, p. 158; Gavin Lambert, *On Cukor* (New York, 1972), p. 63.

21. Warren B. Harris, *Gable and Lombard* (New York, 1974), p. 36; Joan Blondell quoted in Lyn Tornabene, *Long Live the King: A Biography of Clark Gable* (New York, 1976), pp. 207-8; Chester Williams, *Gable*, paperback edition (New York, 1975), p. 46.

22. Frances Marion quoted in Tornabene, p. 156; Williams, pp. 62-63.

23. Mellon, p. 122.

24. Tornabene, p. 15.

25. Madeleine Edmondson and David Rounds, *From Mary Noble to Mary Hartman: The Complete Soap Opera Book*, revised paperback edition (New York, 1977), p. 89.

26. West, p. 181; Francis Chase, *Sound and Fury: An Informal History of Broadcasting* (New York, 1942), p. 210.

27. West, p. 147; *Variety* quoted in Kobal, 187; Quigley quoted in Jeremy Pascall and Clyde Jeavons, *A Pictorial History of Sex in the Movies* (New York, 1975), p. 60.

28. West, p. 181; the code is reproduced in Murray Schumach, *The Face on the Cutting Room Floor: The Story of Movie and Television Censorship* (New York, 1964), pp. 279-92.

29. Pauline Kael, *Kiss Kiss Bang Bang*, paperback edition (New York, 1969), p. 399.

30. Ted Sennett, *Lunatics and Lovers* (New York, 1973), pp. 84-86; Charles Higham, *Kate: The Life of Katharine Hepburn*, paperback edition (New York, 1976), p. 113.

31. Lionel Godfrey, *Paul Newman, Superstar* (New York, 1978), p. 140; Charles Hamblett, *Paul Newman* (Chicago, 1975), p. 149.
32. Pascall, p. 138.
33. Thomas Kiernan, *Jane: An Intimate Biography of Jane Fonda* (New York, 1973), pp. 124, 205.
34. Susan Barrister, "The TV Commercial Audition" in Judy Fireman (ed.), *TV Book: The Ultimate Television Book* (New York, 1977), p. 297.
35. Angie Dickinson quoted in *Us,* May 7, 1978, p. 47; Farrah Fawcett-Majors quoted in Jay S. Harris (ed.), *TV Guide: The First 25 Years* (New York, 1978), p. 263; *Us,* May 7, 1978, p. 46.
36. Paul Klein quoted in *San Francisco Sunday Examiner and Chronicle,* May 5, 1978, Datebook, p. 37; *Us,* May 7, 1978, p. 48.
37. *Newsweek,* Feb. 21, 1978, pp. 55, 57.

Chapter 8

1. Milton Berle with Haskel Frankel, *Milton Berle,* paperback edition (New York, 1975), p. 113.
2. George C. Pratt, *Spellbound in Darkness: Readings in the History and Criticism of the Silent Era* (Rochester, N.Y., 1966), p. 186.
3. Walter Kerr, *The Silent Clowns* (New York, 1975), pp. 26-27. The section on silent movie comedy relies heavily on Kerr's book.
4. *New York Herald Tribune,* April 20, 1915, quoted in Lewis Jacobs, *The Rise of the American Film,* paperback edition (New York, 1968), p. 231.
5. Charles Chaplin, *My Autobiography* (New York, 1964), p. 144.
6. William Cahn, *Harold Lloyd's World of Comedy* (New York, 1964), pp. 101-2.
7. Walt Disney quoted in Richard Schickel, *The Disney Version: The Life, Times, Art and Commerce of Walt Disney* (New York, 1968), p. 112.
8. Andrew Bergman, *We're in the Money: Depression America and Its Films,* paperback edition (New York, 1972), p. 36.
9. Kerr, p. 278.
10. Charles Higham, *Kate: The Life of Katharine Hepburn,* paperback edition (New York, 1976), p. 88.
11. Arthur Frank Wertheim, *Radio Comedy* (New York, 1979), p. 44.
12. Wertheim, p. 91.
13. Irving A. Fein, *Jack Benny, an Intimate Biography,* paperback edition (New York, 1977), pp. 45-46.
14. Wertheim, p. 146.
15. Mary Livingstone Benny and Hilliard Marks with Marcia Borie, *Jack Benny* (Garden City, N.Y., 1978), pp. 89-90.
16. Benny, pp. 65-66.
17. Benny, p. 90.
18. Fein, p. 130.
19. Benny, pp. 64-65.
20. Wertheim, p. 299.
21. Wertheim, p. 302.
22. Berle, p. 286.
23. Ed Wynn quoted in Max Wilk, *The Golden Age of Television: Notes from the Survivors,* paperback edition (New York, 1977), p. 55; Berle, p. 296.
24. Wilk, p. 63.

25. Tedd Thomey, *The Glorious Decade,* paperback edition (New York, 1971), pp. 9-10.
26. Steve Allen, *The Funny Men* (New York, 1956), pp. 79, 83.
27. Wilk, pp. 250-51.
28. Desi Arnaz, *A Book,* paperback edition (New York, 1976), p. 309.
29. *Time,* May 26, 1952, quoted in James Gregory, *The Lucille Ball Story,* paperback edition (New York, 1974), p. 90; Harold Lloyd quoted in Cahn, p. 179; Arnaz, pp. 316-17.

30. *San Francisco Sunday Examiner and Chronicle,* Feb. 12, 1978, Datebook section, p. 33.
31. Wilk, p. 134.
32. *Newsweek,* May 7, 1979, p. 64.
33. James Monaco, *American Film Now: The People, the Power, the Money, the Movies* (New York, 1979), p. 248.

Index